I WANT IT NOW

I WANT IT NOW

NAVIGATING CHILDHOOD IN A MATERIALISTIC WORLD

Donna Bee-Gates

First published in 2006 by
PALGRAVE MACMILLAN™
175 Fifth Avenue, New York, N.Y. 10010 and
Houndmills, Basingstoke, Hampshire, England RG21 6XS.
Companies and representatives throughout the world.

PALGRAVE MACMILLAN is the global academic imprint of the Palgrave Macmillan division of St. Martin's Press, LLC and of Palgrave Macmillan Ltd. Macmillan® is a registered trademark in the United States, United Kingdom and other countries. Palgrave is a registered trademark in the European Union and other countries.

ISBN-13: 978-1-4039-7326-1-9
ISBN-10: 1-4039-7326-1

Library of Congress Cataloging-in-Publication Data is available from the Library of Congress.

Excerpt from *Me Talk Pretty One Day* by David Sedaris appears courtesy of Little, Brown and Company.

A catalogue record of the book is available from the British Library.

Design by Letra Libre, Inc.

First edition: January 2007
10 9 8 7 6 5 4 3 2 1
Printed in the United States of America.

For my husband Dave

CONTENTS

ACKNOWLEDGMENTS

Thank you to my family who has supported me throughout this project. To my wonderful husband, Dave, who has read countless drafts, cooked dinners, run errands and cheered me on, all with endless grace and good humor. To my mother, who provided spiritual guidance and reality checks, my beloved sisters, Michele and Maria, and my father and his partner, Beverly. Thank you to Elizabeth Fishel, my writing mentor, whose expertise and faith in me has kept me inspired. Much gratitude to Arielle Eckstut and her husband, David Sterry, for their invaluable advice. I would not have had the opportunity to write this book without Arielle's belief in this project. Thanks to Sudha Kaul, for reading portions of the manuscript, to my agent Stephanie Rostan, for her guidance and tenacity, to my editor Amanda Johnson, for her expert comments, and Emily Leithauser for her invaluable assistance. Huge thanks to all of the parents who shared their stories with me. I appreciate your wisdom and your valuable time.

INTRODUCTION

On his fourth birthday, my nephew received a pile of gifts. During the party, well-meaning parents told him how lucky he was, and several mothers marveled at what great friends he had. Unimpressed with his windfall, my nephew was more interested in playing monster with his friends than in opening presents. Over a week later, the majority of gifts remained unopened. How to explain such disinterest in new toys? Perhaps, I thought, this child might actually be immune to consumer desire! Just a year later, my nephew had joined in the annual Christmas gift opening frenzy. Like the transformation of the townsfolk in *Invasion of the Body Snatchers*, seemingly overnight youngsters morph from carefree non-materialists to savvy consumers plotting their next acquisition. To those who have witnessed the change: it doesn't have to be this way.

Young children learn to crave the newest and the latest. They're socialized to believe that happiness comes in the form of a superhero or an American Girl doll. How do young ones discover this? We can finger the usual suspects—media, advertising, peers and—you guessed this was coming—parents. Indictment of the media is not new. Many studies document the artful ways that advertising agencies and retailers seduce children into wanting things that they don't need. Peers intensify this need through social comparison (*"Everyone* else is wearing $250 Nikes!"). Parents can unwittingly reinforce this acquisitiveness. Children study up by observing the spending habits of their elders. Maybe they learn the importance of waiting and saving for their objects of desire. Or kids might catch on that one way to soothe hurt feelings is to ask their parents for something new or, for older children, go buy something for themselves.

Parents can preach to their children that money doesn't buy happiness, but the real lessons take place every time children hear their elders talking about the new car, electronic equipment, or bigger home on which they've set their sights. Before parents help youngsters to find their way through the commercial world, it is important that they examine their own relationship to material possessions. How do you deal with disappointments or setbacks? What are your spending habits? How much have you accumulated? *Why* do you buy? Because parents' behaviors serve as a very powerful influence on children, *I Want It Now* focuses both on providing parents with research and analysis on materialism-related issues and on increasing awareness of their own relationship to possessions. In addition, it offers all of us—whether we have children or not—a new way to view our spending habits and attitudes toward material goods.

I have noticed that very few of us completely escape the mashed potatoes and gravy style of consumerism. I experienced my own epiphany while sitting amid a pile of shoe boxes in the middle of a Nordstrom department store. I was using the boots I had picked out as comfort food—they were my mashed potatoes and gravy. Instead of grappling with my overloaded work schedule, I chose to head directly for the mall. Spending to feel good really is like the cure-all tonics of years past. Instead of downing a foul-tasting brew to cure the blues, we cruise to the stores or surf the Internet to buy just the trinket that will make us feel better. Several of the parents interviewed for this book admitted to the spending cure. Lisette, a mother of two young boys, believes materialism affects us all, regardless of what we buy:

> I'm a bargain hunter and I like sales. I'll go to Walgreens and I see buy two and get the third one free, and it's hard to resist, even though I'm bringing home more frickin' Legos. I can't resist getting that free box of Legos . . . . If I see a sale I'm all over it, whether we need it or not. My husband's like this. He comes

home from the Goodwill with all this junk, and he'll say, "Look at all this great stuff, it was only $7.00!" and I'll tell him, "Only $7.00, but look how much space it's going to take." There are different levels of consumerism. There are people who need to have the latest iPod, and people like me are "What's an iPod?" There are people who have to buy "it" before it's even on the market. I'm not like that . . . I'm the type that buys a watch that costs $5.00; I don't need a Rolex. I have a cheap version of materialism . . . My husband has a different version, he likes all the cool, old stuff . . . It's not how much you spend, it's why you're spending it.

Of course material possessions are not inherently bad. Treasured belongings can bring happiness because of what they represent—keepsakes from a special trip or a suit bought for a first professional job. The trick lies in finding a happy medium: the juncture where you value your belongings without depending on them.

During my time as a child therapist, I observed a few parents trying to solve tough family problems using this retail tonic. Like the ancient Aztecs seeking to placate their angry gods with treasures, parents would buy their children things hoping for a miracle: depression soothed, anger quelled, and strained relationships made right. Most parents discovered, however, that over the long haul, spending rarely solves emotional problems. Parents would bring their children to the clinic complaining of misbehavior—picking fights with classmates, talking back to teachers, disregarding household rules. Many of these parents had tried everything they could to address the problems. Some used the lure of new possessions to change their child's behavior—perhaps a trip to the toy store or the ice-cream parlor would do the trick. Typically, these strategies were ineffective. Only after gaining insight into the actual causes of the misbehavior and directly addressing youngsters' emotional distress did parents actually see some improvement in their children's behavior.

Now I teach at a university in northern California. While the population I work with has changed, the big picture remains the same. My college students call spending to feel good "retail ther-apy." Typically when I broach the topic of materialism during class, students smile and nod knowingly. Most can relate in some way to the quick fix. For example, several students received credit cards during their teens. By their early twenties, these young adults have amassed thousands of dollars in debt. According to one young woman, "Whenever I finished a project, or had a bad day or what-ever, I rewarded myself with something new." Countless children, teenagers, and their parents attempt to heal emotional pain through shopping, behavior that can complicate one's life further and lead to more emotional stress.

This is *not* a book about the evils of materialism. The notion that inner happiness comes through renouncing worldly possessions is too simplistic. However, Americans are surrounded by materialism, and we all owe it to our children's emotional well-being, as well as our own, to examine the role that belongings play in our lives. A pair of new boots may seem ridiculously harmless. Research suggests, however, that too much consumerism is hazardous to children's health. Teenagers who over-value expensive clothing and possessions and who put a premium on good looks are more likely than others to behave impulsively; these young people have difficulty making and keeping close friends and depend too much on other people's opin-ions. Compared to less materialistic youth, these youngsters report more insecurity, less happiness, and greater willingness to believe the worse of others.[1] Materialism is not limited to the middle class and the well-to-do. Through media and their fellow classmates, less eco-nomically privileged youngsters find themselves constantly sur-rounded by the wealth of others. In fact, poor youth who are also materialistic are particularly susceptible to unhappiness because they lack the means to satisfy their desires. All families, regardless of eco-nomic circumstances, can benefit from this book.

Ask any parent who has tried to get a child to stop sucking his or her thumb or carrying a well-worn blanket: people will not give something up if they have nothing to replace it with. Banish the blanket and the child will find some other way—constructive or not—to soothe her anxiety. Similarly, *I Want It Now* goes beyond just discussing the hazards of materialism by including advice for parents and educators to help children develop a strong self-concept, which in turn will help them to more cogently negotiate a consumer-oriented, looks-obsessed culture. Much of the information here on materialism is relevant for all ages, from youth to adulthood. Throughout the book I discuss research findings based on inquiry of children and adolescents. In areas where no research on children or teens is available, I report findings based on the responses of college students and occasionally adults.

As part of the research for this book, I interviewed parents about their ideas on materialism. These parents were referred to me from friends and colleagues and represent a range of income levels, ethnicities, and living situations (e.g., single- and two-parent families). Ethnic backgrounds include African American, Caucasian, Indian American, and Latino American. The families live in San Francisco Bay Area and in a metropolitan area in the Midwest. For the most part they are middle income, although two of the parents defined themselves as low income. The majority of views presented by the parents, then, do represent a middle-class perspective. This perspective is balanced by discussion of research on low-income families and their experience of materialism.[2] The parents powerfully reflect on the challenges of raising children in a materialistic culture; they also supply some creative solutions to the problem. One mother, for example, explains how she tackles the very common concern of holidays and present overload:

> We have a tradition now that on Christmas Eve, we read the story about the baby Jesus and talk about why we celebrate Christmas every year. The kids still love opening presents (who are we kidding), but I think they understand that the holiday isn't *just* about gifts.

Another mother discussed how she helped her daughter to appreciate her auspicious life. She found that a trip to India helped to strengthen her daughter's appreciation:

We went to visit India a couple of years back and she saw that
everyone doesn't live like we do. I told my daughter, "You live
the life of a charmed princess." When we returned home, she
seemed to recognize that even here in Silicon Valley there were
people who didn't have a lot and she understood that she is very
lucky.

I Want It Now suggests alternatives to the usual. The book encourages readers to look beyond the traditional benchmarks of success to consider the importance of passion, spirituality, relationships,
and meaningful work in their child's life. Chapters 1 and 2 examine
cultural and historical circumstances that contribute to present-day
materialism. For example, the Industrial Revolution, an increasingly
affluent society, globalism, and conceptions of parenting have all
furthered American's preferences for luxury. Children are no excep-
tion when it comes valuing luxury goods. Among teenagers, for example, owning the "right" brand names can be critical to peer
acceptance. However, for many teens and children, a preoccupation
with brand names and social status can lead to trouble. Chapter 3
describes how the singular pursuit of material possessions, status,
and wealth can be deleterious to children's social and emotional development. Researchers have discovered that a number of conditions—among them, companionship, meaningful hobbies or
interests, and strong critical thinking skills—promote children's
well-being. Owning luxury items and garnering the envy of others,
however, does not make this list. I discuss the outside forces, including peers and media, that conspire against parents' efforts at helping
their children grow toward authentic self-expression. Anecdotes
from parents and children illustrate how others have struggled to
both accommodate the realities of materialism and elevate more important life values.

Children adopt materialistic values for different reasons. Some
youngsters want more things because they're bored. Others crave
"it" items as a way of fitting in or making friends. As one mother
said, "I get concerned because I don't want them to think they re-

ally need this stuff to be socially accepted." In Chapters 4, 5, and 6 I introduce the five forces of materialism, the life circumstances that increase children's vulnerability to materialism. In Chapter 4 I describe the Mimic. This force encourages materialism by persuading children to imitate the consumer-oriented values they see on television, at the movies, or in magazines. Children influenced by the Mimic desire the same clothing, goods, and lifestyles owned by celebrities and other role models. In Chapter 5 I introduce the Comparer and the Lonely One. The Comparer is particularly influential with preteens and teens, during a time when conformity and social comparison are crucial. This force convinces youngsters that the best way to gain acceptance is through material goods and status. Youngsters vulnerable to the Comparer are particularly susceptible to peer directives to buy brand-name goods as a way of fitting in with a desired peer group. The children most vulnerable to the Lonely One have difficulty making or maintaining friendships. The Lonely One tries to convince youngsters that the purchase of material goods, rather than improvement of social skills and confidence, will help them to make friends.

Chapter 6 describes You Complete Me and the Humdrum, Ho-Hum. Children with a poor self-concept or those in the throes of developing an identity can be particularly open to You Complete Me, a force that encourages them to use material goods and appearance as a way of defining who they are. Instead of regarding oneself as an artist, a scientist, or a good friend, You Complete Me champions self-definitions such as "I wear designer clothes" or "I own all the latest video games." Many of us recognize the rush that comes with purchasing something new. The Humdrum, Ho-Hum uses this feeling by inviting children to alleviate boredom through consumerism. The risk of relying on the Humdrum, Ho-Hum is that youngsters can come to rely on retail to cope with boredom rather than developing hobbies and other interests.

Many social scientists believe that a lack of spiritual beliefs lies at the core of our out of control materialism and unhappiness. During these prosperous times, more and more Americans today are actively seeking to integrate meaning and spirit into their lives. Chapter 7 reviews research suggesting that certain spiritual beliefs can fortify children against the omnipresence of commercialism and materialism in the society. For instance, individuals who have a sense of meaning or purpose in life and who value connections to other people and the community are less likely to hold materialistic values. I investigate the ways in which parents define spirituality, and the interpretations are varied and fascinating. For some parents, spirit means cultivating compassion in their children. Others discuss the importance of respecting the earth and appreciating the small, unexpected delights of nature. Still other parents believe strongly in passing on the traditions of their chosen religion. Suggestions for beginning or continuing a spiritual search are included throughout the chapter.

Finally, Chapter 8 presents ways to continue the commitment to a life that deemphasizes material possessions. I discuss strategies for finding and relying on families who also believe in pursuing a simpler more meaningful life. You can also profit from other parents' techniques for handling typically materialistic-steeped events such as birthdays and holidays without feeling like a grinch or compromising your principles.

Henry Adams said "All experience is an arch, to build upon." What I offer here are my experiences—as a counselor, teacher, and most importantly, as a human being who has truly wrestled with these issues. I hope that you might use my experiences to build a well-grounded support for your family.

CHAPTER 1

BELIEVING IN FAIRY TALES

Shoes possess magical properties. Have you heard the story of the orphan girl and her dancing red shoes? The girl came into a beautiful pair of red shoes, just like those the town's princess wore. Being somewhat vain, the girl insisted on wearing her shoes to church, even though she knew that showy footwear was inappropriate for such a sacred space. The shoes, and by proxy the girl, were bewitched by an old soldier, and when she danced with pride at the thought of owning such lovely shoes, she was unable to stop. After ages and ages of dancing over hill and dale, the little girl begged a "kindly" old ax-man to chop off her feet so that she could finally get some rest (apparently the shoes kept on dancing without her). By the end of the tale, our humbled heroine, wearing more respectable wooden clogs, seeks redemption back in church.[1]

In children's folktales, it is not just shoes that are magic. Enchanted beans lead to unimaginable wealth, cloaks lend invisibility, and swords bestow invincibility. Quaint stories, meant to appeal to gullible children? Let's take a look at more modern fairy tales. Stories abound of creams that take off the years, colas that make you cool, and cars that change even the nerdiest among us into sexy, popular hipsters. Historically and across cultures, humans have

chronicled their belief that material objects have the power to transform.[2] But the path to transformation is filled with potholes. Folktales also relate stories of the greedy, the vain, and the wealthy who
all get their comeuppance. The Bible puts it bluntly: A rich man has
a greater chance of getting to heaven than a camel through the eye
of a needle. Both the desirability and the danger of objects are found
throughout literature, politics, religion, parental fiat, and common
wisdom. So what kernel of insight can be culled from these teachings? That it is okay to desire things as long as you don't enjoy them
too much? The cultural rules regarding materialism and its accept-
ability conflict and confuse. Maybe the orphan girl would have kept
her feet if she had not taken so much pleasure in those darn red
shoes.

People define materialism differently. Some individuals place
the label on those who like to shop or who spend large sums on designer items. Katrina, a mother of four children, equates materialism
with the craving to belong:

> It's buying things that you don't really need. Brand names in
> particular. So, if it was a car, it would be materialism if it was a
> name brand like a Lexus. I consider it material items that people
> think they really need to be socially accepted. That's how I think
> of it . . . they have to have the brand names to feel socially ac-
> cepted . . . I know a mother who buys things just to satisfy her
> child, but it's so short term, and it will be something else and
> then something else. It's endless.

Tammy Lynn, a mother of three, agrees that materialism means loving expensive, status items:

> It's really trying to keep up with the Joneses and having to have
> the latest styles . . . There's nothing wrong with rewarding your-
> self now and then. If there's something I want that's popular, I'll
> try to put away for it, but that doesn't happen very often . . . I
> think it's negative when you have to have the latest and the most
> expensive or flashy things. Or putting someone else down be-
> cause they don't have it.

Don describes materialism as "being obsessed with status, wealth, and opportunity rather than the actual value of the things you buy." Because materialism carries many different meanings for people, I offer one definition to guide the discussion throughout this book. In my view, materialists are made, not born. We don't come into this world with a gene that forces us into driving to the mall. Rather, most people learn through various means to value a materialistic lifestyle. The definition of materialism for this book involves a cluster of three attitudes about possessions and wealth. It includes the belief that:

1. Acquisition and consumption should be a *primary* life goal.
2. Possessions bring happiness.
3. Success depends upon the scope and scale of one's belongings.[3]

The first attitude determines one's priorities. Most people have goals for the different areas of their lives—work, academics, family, relationships, community, material, and health, to name a few. A work goal could be pursuing a particular career or getting that promotion. Goals for one's academic life might include learning more about marine biology or pursuing an interest in history. Material goals refer to the acquisition and possession of material goods, wealth, income, and status.[4] In this realm, individuals might aspire to great riches, or they might be satisfied with just getting by. Some people continually strive for "status goods" while others are content with the basics. Status goods can take the form of a high-performance European automobile, Bordeaux wines, or even designer jeans. The term "status" in this context implies that possession of these items imbues the owner with importance or worth in the eyes of others and themselves. Attitude number one maintains that of *all* the life goals one might hold, acquisition and consumption take precedence. A child who subscribes to this first attitude may sacrifice study time by taking on a part-time job to pay for desired possessions. This child could become the adult who pursues a high salary by working long hours at work to the detriment of relationships with family or friends. Or it is the person who purchases unafford-able items, relies on credit, and lives with the anxiety of constantly being in debt.

Attitude number two highlights the belief that money and be-longings lead to happiness. Individuals who claim this belief look to material items as a way to feel good about themselves. Some young-sters may believe that possessions bring happiness through the in-creased regard of peers. This is the child buys designer clothing, for instance, to win acceptance from a particular peer group. Maintain-ing this belief over the long term means that this same child chooses a career not based on interest, but on the social status or income po-tential it brings. This second attitude also manifests as the youngster who buys bags of food to soothe a depressed mood or the teenager who charges $150 athletic shoes on her parents' credit card after a bad day at school. Many of us indulge in a treat now and then to lift our spirits or as a reward for an accomplishment. The behavior be-comes a problem when individuals constantly use material items as an antidote for emotional distress.

Success at life covers a wide swath. For some, success centers on family and raising happy, healthy children. Others define suc-cess based on whether they have contributed to alleviating the suf-fering of others. Those who embrace attitude number three measure accomplishments in terms of material possessions. This calls to mind a friend who visited the town where he was raised after a several-year absence. In that time, he had earned a graduate degree, found a job that he loved, and was happily married. My friend considered himself to be pretty successful. His childhood friends, however, were most interested in whether he owned a home, how much he earned, and the type of car he drove. Their definition of success rested on financial prosperity while my friend's centered on satisfaction with job and relationships. Children who subscribe to this third attitude base their self-worth on what and how much they, or their parents, own.

For the purposes of this book, a belief in one or more of these three attitudes constitutes materialism or a materialistic orientation.

Throughout, references made to "materialists" or "materialistic people" denote those who hold a materialistic orientation. It does not refer to a personality trait or temperament. Further, materialism does not limit itself to a particular economic level. I have noticed that people tend to consider the wealthy to be particularly materialistic, probably because they own more expensive things than other people. However, materialism represents an attitude to which anyone from any income level can embrace. A child from any point on the economic spectrum, from poor to wealthy, can judge others based on what they own or the clothes they wear. Likewise, any child can espouse the belief that a new gadget will be just the thing to make him happy.

As we'll see in subsequent chapters, a number of social conditions can breed materialism. In turn, this materialistic orientation allies with social problems, depression, discontentment, and other emotional difficulties. The goal of this book is to examine how children's materialism manifests. It might be in the way children choose to spend their own money from allowances or part-time jobs. Youngsters can also satisfy materialistic cravings by requesting their parents for goods. Parents, therefore, can explore this issue in two ways. First, they can help to deepen their children's insight into materialistic desire and consumer behavior. Parents can also examine their own beliefs and behaviors related to children and consumption. For example, many of the adults interviewed for this book stated that they frequently give in to children's pleas for new items. The book discusses some of the reasons that parents indulge their children and ways to address this inclination.

Again and again, while writing this book, I heard testimonials to the conflict many Americans feel over materialism. There was the not-in-my-backyard response, which typically included comments such as "My friend/neighbor/coworker (everyone but me) is *really* materialistic. You should talk to them." For some people, admitting to materialistic leanings equals admitting to great weakness. Like the closet alcoholic or the unfaithful spouse, many people loathe admitting to a love of possessions. One striking example of this came from a father I talked with who had just purchased over $2,000 in sports equipment that he "really needed" while simultaneously deriding "materialistic" women who spend money frivolously on shoes and clothing.

I also met with the I'm-so-ashamed response. These parents eagerly confessed to overindulgence; however, very few offered solutions on how to counter overspending. Several interviewees, for example, felt badly about giving in, over and over, to their children's wheedling for treats, toys, and the like. One mother implicated her husband as the hedonistic culprit:

> I get frustrated because I'm not one to buy him things all the time, his dad does. I sometimes give in, his dad *always* gets him something. His dad and I have discussions about this, but it falls on deaf ears.

I believe that the myriad responses come from the same emotional pot. To some degree, Westerners feel shame at desiring and owning many nice things. While I focus here on Americans, this phenomenon of overconsumption describes other affluent, technologically advanced countries as well. Most people learn when they are children—usually from parents or as part of their religious training—that greed is a no-no. Yet garages, closets, playrooms—and that space under the bed—testify that most Americans own more "stuff" than they will ever need. Psychologist David Buss calls it the "hedonic treadmill." He says: "Americans today have more cars, color TVs, computers, and brand-name clothes than they did several decades ago, but Americans are no happier now than they were then . . . people seem to adjust quickly to any gains they experience, creating the hedonic treadmill where apparent increments in rewards fail to produce sustained increments in personal happiness."[5]

Despite the shame, despite the reality that acquiring more does not lead to long-term happiness, people continue to add to their heap of belongings. For many Americans, this paradox leads to uncomfortable, guilty feelings about spending and to an arsenal of familiar justifications: I deserve something special. I've worked hard. I'm depressed. I haven't bought anything for a while. I need this to be accepted at school. There is nothing inherently wrong with these justifications. Most people use them at one time or another. However, the justifications don't usually move people closer to understanding their actions, and they don't help to change unwanted behaviors.

When I begin a discussion in my classes on materialism, I typically present the students with two questions. First I ask them: "How many of you believe that America is a materialistic culture?" Usually everyone raises their hands, many nodding vociferously. Then I ask: "How many of you think that children today are more materialistic than previous generations?" Again almost everyone agrees. Several students give examples of children they know who constantly beg their parents for more stuff. My students' beliefs about modern materialism reflect the opinions of a good number of Americans on this issue. Many contend that materialism in this culture has grown out of hand and that the younger generation is much more materialistic than their predecessors. However, some social scientists suggest that today's propensity toward materialism has more to do with society's economic, social, and political climate than with the burgeoning of a supposedly new self-indulgent generation. One theory on the growth of materialistic values argues that insecurity lays the groundwork for materialism.[6] The term "insecurity" has multiple interpretations. Emotional insecurity, for example, refers to feeling vulnerable or experiencing a lack of confidence or safety. Children of divorcing parents often report feeling insecure and anxious. They also tend to endorse materialistic values more than children from low-conflict, intact homes.[7] Likewise, children who report feeling unloved and unappreciated by their parents also gravitate to material goods for comfort. Possessions provide a sense of security to children who feel they cannot rely on adults to support them emotionally. Further, insecure youngsters who lack confidence in themselves may use belongings to boost self-esteem and garner social acceptance.

The insecurity theory also attempts to explain materialistic attitudes in terms of economic stability. Political scientist Ronald Inglehart asked individuals in the United States and in European countries to identify goals or values most important to them.[8] Based on this work, Inglehart identified what he termed "materialistic goals" and "postmaterialistic goals." Materialistic goals included values like maintaining a high rate of economic growth, job security, and a strong defense. Postmaterialistic goals centered on values such as "making the cities more beautiful" and "move toward a friendlier, less impersonal society." Postmaterialistic values might take the form of campaigns to save old-growth redwoods or endangered toads. Both of these goals illustrate differences in priorities between saving the environment and saving jobs. Essentially, materialistic values focus on factors related to economic and national security, and postmaterialistic values highlight humanistic and environmental concerns. People from poorer nations rate materialistic goals as more important than do those from wealthier nations. As nations' economies grow over time, so does their postmaterialistic orientation. For example, countries such as South Korea and China, which have seen significant economic growth over several decades, show an increase in postmaterialistic orientation.[9]

Over the past twenty-five years, the United States has shown an upward trend in postmaterialistic goals, with fewer people endorsing materialism and more individuals endorsing postmaterialism. This means that perceptions of greater materialism in today's culture may be due to other factors, such as the omnipresence of advertising and the sheer amount of merchandise available to citizens. Younger Americans favor postmaterialism compared to the older generations who came of age during the depression.[10] This doesn't mean that the younger generation is uniformly less materialistic than their elders. It suggests that postmaterialism is growing, especially among the young. Depression-era individuals matured during a time of profound economic insecurity, and because of this many still favor a materialistic orientation, despite the fact that they may now be financially secure. Many of the younger generation in the middle and upper economic levels live in relative affluence and harbor fewer concerns about having enough money to buy basics such as food, clothing, and shelter. It will be interesting to discover how the current climate of instability, with the realities of the Iraq war and the growing national deficit, will influence the trend toward postmaterialism. It may be that greater insecurity will dampen the postmaterialistic inclination. The comments of the parents I interviewed who were raised by Depression-era parents concur with the insecurity theory. Uniformly, the parents described *their* elders as "thrifty," "good money managers," and "frugal." Some parents described their childhoods in this regard as positive, and others found life to be quite challenging. As I discuss later, some of the current parents have followed their elders' lead in terms of spending habits and others have not.

Of course, everyone living in the United States does not enjoy economic security. For some immigrant and ethnic minority populations, poverty and unemployment remain the norm.[11] Consistent with the insecurity theory, these citizens tend to identify most with materialistic goals. For example, inner-city, low-income children report greater desires to be rich compared to youngsters from middle-income backgrounds.[12] Exposure to wealth through the media and through interactions with more affluent peers increases the tension and discontent these children feel about their current situation.

Experiencing hunger as a child is associated with materialistic values. When I was a child, my social worker mother worked with severely abused and neglected children, some of whom had gone hungry for long periods of time. Even after they had been placed in safe homes with plenty to eat, she noticed that many stashed food in their rooms. In the United States, individuals who do not have enough to eat constitute about 10 percent of the population and fall in the low-income range. Research indicates that those who experienced food insecurities during childhood tend to hoard food as adults, even when they are more than capable of providing for themselves.[13] These individuals also score high on materialism scales. Researchers theorize that food scarcity creates anxiety about one's

ability to meet basic needs for survival. This survival insecurity appears to endure into adulthood, regardless of a person's economic
status. Consistent with Inglehart's theory, these insecure adults surround themselves with food or possessions to "ensure that they
never do without."[14] In general, people who hoard report greater
emotional attachment to their possessions and are more likely to
have experienced some kind of physical or emotional trauma as children. For some individuals, however, a job and a paycheck do not
translate into feeling powerful.

The insecurity theory predicts that insecurity, both tangible
(economic conditions) or intangible (psychological distress) can
lead to a materialistic orientation. However, materialism is certainly
not unique to modern society. Some social scientists claim that the
motivation to acquire is a part of being human. Maybe people's tendency to stuff themselves beyond reason does reside in our genetic
makeup; ancestors who gathered more nuts and berries for the win-
ter probably stood a better chance of surviving till the spring than
their less acquisitive neighbors. Or, perhaps it is true, as researchers
like Inglehart claim, that materialism develops in response to life circumstances. Most likely the answer lies somewhere in between.

What social scientists and historians do know is that the notion
of materialism is not an artifact of modern times. Consider the de-
bauchery of ancient Rome, when hedonistic materialism defined the
upper classes. The ancient Pompeiians had their own version of the
miracle mile, with "as many shops and workshops as Fifth Avenue."[15] The Italian Renaissance saw the rise of the merchant class
along with the now-modern belief that all citizens should have the
right to upward mobility and a chance at buying into the good life.
Materialism has always been a part of most cultures. As with our
modern society, economic conditions, political stability, and democracy among other circumstances influenced the rise, or fall, of the
materialistic ethos. In Chapters 3 to 6 I discuss specific conditions
that beget insecurity and materialism in modern youth.

The next section explores the historical circumstances in the
United States that have supported materialism. We can gain per-

spective on the state of the culture today by studying our own history and the ways in which the shift from an agrarian society to the Industrial Revolution and finally to the electronic age have provided greater opportunities for work, leisure, and consumption. The second portion of the chapter explores some of the challenges parents and children face in maintaining a nonmaterialistic stance in today's culture.

A BRIEF HISTORY

From a historical perspective, the desire to improve one's lot in life—to earn more money and improve one's standard of living—drove much of the economic and social growth of the nineteenth century. Imagine life in America before the Industrial Revolution and mass advertising. At that time, the wealth of the nation was concentrated among an even smaller percentage of the population than today. These privileged few owned the beautiful homes, wardrobes, and works of art, and had fleets of hired help to tend the gardens, cook the meals, and care for the children. Unlike the masses, the elite took vacations abroad, threw sumptuous parties, and regularly summered in exclusive enclaves. Odds are, had *you* been born during this time, most of your day would have been spent meeting basic needs for food and shelter. Like the majority of people in the early nineteenth century, you would probably have lived outside the city, perhaps growing crops or raising animals, sewing your own clothes, milking the cows, making bread and butter. Neighbors had to depend on each other for survival during the really tough times. While this scenario may sound like a romantic notion of getting back to basics, the reality for most people involved long, physically grueling days. Mass advertising did not exist; no glossy magazines trumpeting must-buys or profiling celebrity clothing styles. No television offering access to the lifestyles of the wealthy and the famous. No MTV or Home Shopping Network, movies, or Internet. While you might have been aware of how the other "half" lived, you certainly would not have been tempted by an unrelenting parade of material goods that could be yours *if*—the message goes—you work hard enough to earn them. The insecurity theory would predict that the majority of individuals during this time focused primarily on making their lives more economically stable by striving to obtain basics like food and shelter.

Before the Industrial Revolution, stark differences in standards of living carved the boundaries between the privileged and the rest of the nation. Profound advances in mechanization, first in Europe and then in the United States, began, slowly at first, to change the economic fortunes of many in America, particularly those of European descent. Classic inventions—the cotton gin, the steam engine, and the motion picture—made their debut during the late 1800s. A sizable chunk of the population moved from the countryside to the cities, mostly to work in the factories that produced the century's innovative machinery. While jobs were more plentiful in cities than in the country, factory workers certainly suffered exploitation, typically laboring long hours in poor working conditions. In the late 1800s and early 1900s, it was not uncommon, for instance, for fires to break out and destroy factories during this time. The facilities were poorly constructed and hundreds of workers, some locked inside the buildings by tyrannical bosses, lost their lives in the infernos.[16] Over time, however, the revolution did bring relatively greater prosperity and a wider distribution of material goods, particularly for the middle and upper classes. By the beginning of the twentieth century, many citizens could purchase conveniences—washing machines, automobiles, even instant Jell-O and frozen dinners—that made life easier. Over the next half century, many in the United States experienced a better standard of living and an increase in leisure time. At the same time, a burgeoning mass media, in the form of flyers and shop signs, whipped up Americans' consumer desires.

Interestingly, social reformers during this period worried about Americans having too much leisure time.[17] In the Protestant work ethic-infused culture of the time, the image of slacker Americans spending money indiscriminately and lolling about in dance halls, movie theaters, and amusement parks struck the fear of God into community leaders. The solution was ingenious: Nurture the desire to consume while trumpeting the importance of a strong work ethic. Sunday school primers and textbooks emphasized the importance of hard work and the dangers of overindulgence. Surrounded by mass advertising and by heaps of readily available mass-produced products, however, Americans were also primed to buy, buy, buy.

Everybody won. Consumer spending contributed to an economic boom. In order to spend, consumers worked, thus maintaining social order. Throughout the twentieth century, the American Way (in other words, a high standard of living) and free enterprise (e.g., sell and consume) became one and the same thing.[18] During World War II, when patriotism reigned, public schools worked with business interests to promote "consumer education."[19] The curriculum aimed to train students to be good consumers by equating Americanism with consumption. Again, youngsters learned that spending was their right and their responsibility as citizens. Textbooks both during and after the war highlighted the ideal family, typically depicted as Caucasian and middle class. The texts dutifully emphasized the products (washing machines, refrigerators, station wagons) indicative of a happy and contented family. The notion of a secure American family and consumerism were trumpeted as inextricable. Today Americans take it in stride when political leaders exhort them to exercise their democratic rights by shopping. For example, many are familiar with President Bush's contention following 9/11 that continued consumption would show the terrorists that they hadn't killed the American spirit.

The efforts of early twentieth century business and political leaders were a rousing success. In our high-tech, democratized society, how do we love to spend our leisure time? Shopping—American's number-one pastime. It is an obsession. Americans read about it (*Confessions of a Shopaholic, Bergdorf Blondes*), vacation for it (Mall of America is a top tourist destination), pen plays about it (*Shopping! The Musical*), and even have phrases to describe it ("shop till you drop"). The ability to shop defines one's rank in the pecking order. For many teenagers, acceptance or rejection by their peers can rest on owning the right stuff. In high school, I remember a girl, desolate because of a snub by a more popular teen, wondering why she had been rejected. Her well-meaning friend responded that "you're Macy's and she's more Neiman Marcus."

Luxury goods, and the wherewithal to purchase them, illustrate the merging of American democracy and consumption. Luxury goods are the status brands—Gucci, Christian Dior, Mercedes-Benz, and the like—which possess the burnish of privilege and wealth and which imbue the owner of said products with the same glow. Before the Industrial Revolution, only the elite could buy these status goods.[20] However, in the twenty-first century, status has become an "equal opportunity" industry. Today, with lower-priced versions of the originals widely available, middle-class Americans purchase luxury items more than anyone else. Haute couture clothing brands, for example, now offer more affordable lines for the middle-class consumer. Exclusive automobile companies such as Mercedes-Benz and Jaguar produce lower-priced models, increasing accessibility for less wealthy patrons. Luxury goods have become so prevalent that marketers complain that ownership no longer holds the same cachet.[21] According to some, "The movement to extend luxury brands to a wide array of products is diluting the word 'luxury.'"[22] This sentiment is epitomized by a comment I overheard on the street. As he looked over a lower-priced version of a luxury car, a man sniffed, "It's just a wannabe." Apparently, wide accessibility of luxury goods might now actually detract from their reputation.

The notion that you are what you wear has certainly been nurtured by advertising. While Americans were making gains in the manufacture of mass-produced goods, advertising began hitting its stride in early to mid-nineteenth century. Advertising grew from sandwich boards (think back to the old black-and-white movies with men traipsing the city, festooned with wooden billboards announcing hot roast beef sandwiches at the local diner) and posters, to the printed page, to electronic media. Advertising moved from public locations (flyers plastered on buildings) and took up residence in the home—through television, the Internet, even fax machines.

Can you think of a public area today that doesn't have some form of advertising? Just the other day I learned about liposuction and tanning booths in the bathroom stall of the local gym. Apparently no space is sacred. One consequence of mass advertising is that all of us, regardless of ethnicity or economic circumstances, are constantly exposed to material goods. With our basic needs met, those of us with the means can focus more fully on consumption: planning the next purchase, displaying our acquisitions, working harder to afford the successful lifestyles promised in the ads. Focusing on acquisition to the detriment of other goals can leave youngsters vulnerable to meeting developmental milestones—forming an identity, fitting in with peers, coping with setbacks, managing anxiety—through buying things and trying to impress others. As mentioned, for those struggling to meet basic survival needs, constant exposure to goods and a lifestyle that one cannot afford can create frustration and an even greater sense of deprivation.

Poor Americans, many of whom are racial and ethnic minorities, experience the same materialistic cravings as do the middle class and the wealthy. They are subject to the same advertising and the same pressure to consume. However, poor minority families and youth do not have the same means to satisfy these cravings. Perhaps not surprisingly, some poor minority youngsters do not believe that they can reach financial success through the standard cultural channels—education and career advancement.[23] The twist of the knife is that corporations and their advertising henchmen specifically target these neighborhoods, particularly poor, predominantly African American areas, with campaigns for expensive products. One marketing strategy, termed "bro-ing" by one company, involves traveling to impoverished African American communities and assessing youngsters' reactions to expensive sneakers and clothing.[24] Marketers then take this information and, using Black athlete and celebrity endorsements, market their products to young people, including the low-income Black youth who can't afford them in the first place. This strategy is particularly effective for marketers, as middle-class Caucasian, Asian, and Latino youngsters have been shown to imitate the dress styles of Black youngsters, copy-cat behavior that reaps even greater financial rewards for businesses.

The research shows that youngsters use media to help figure out who they are and what they would like to be; the use of respected celebrity role models adds particular appeal to material goods.[25] Developmentally, youngsters are primed for this type of influence. Children tend to emulate individuals of their same race and sex, whether in real life, on television, or in advertising campaigns. The favorite television characters of ethnic minority children, for instance, tend to be actors of their same race.[26] These actors can make a powerful impression on children. For example, the occupational choices of African American youngsters have been shown to be influenced by the jobs of their esteemed television characters. Marketers use this research by recruiting celebrity endorsers to add allure to their products. Children learn to associate particular brands with their beloved celebrities; a famous basketball player may be forever "branded" to a certain athletic shoe. This marketing strategy works. Studies show, for instance, that Black celebrity endorsements influenced Black teenagers' decision to buy athletic shoes.[27] These ads play on young people's desires for peer status, self-esteem, and identity. So what does this mean for youth in their everyday lives? Youngsters seduced by advertisements are more vulnerable to equating status, beauty, power, and success to material possessions. This situation leads to multiple pressures. Parents want to be able to buy their children the goods that more affluent families enjoy and can overextend themselves financially to do so. Youngsters determined to own these expensive items work long hours in after-school jobs, which can detract from academic performance and extracurricular pursuits.[28] In terms of materialism, this situation encourages families to adopt the notion that expensive possessions signify worth.

THE PRESENT DAY: MATERIALISM AND THE ELECTRONIC AGE

When I was a child, my mother called me the can't-wait girl. During the school year, I'd complain that I couldn't wait for the summer to come. During the summer, I'd claim boredom and fret for school to begin. I had the vexing habit of looking forward to the next birthday, holiday, or family outing, probably thinking that whatever was happening in the future would be even better than my regular old life. America can be considered the can't-wait nation. One result of living in an affluent nation is that many people feel they need just a little more to be happy. According to this thinking, happiness lies just ahead in the next promotion or pay raise. In surveys conducted over the last twenty years, Americans consistently say that a little more is better. In one survey, the majority of individuals claimed that an annual income of $90,000 would be required for a comfortable life.[29] Families earning $75,000 to $100,000 per year say that they cannot afford to buy "everything I really need."[30]

Humans are social animals. We compare ourselves not only to our neighbors but to the lifestyles, both real and fictionalized, that bombard us daily on television, in magazines, at the movies, even in the bathroom stalls. And, for the most part, the lifestyles people choose to view on television include people — most often Caucasian and economically secure — in prestigious professions who often spend remarkably little time actually working.[31] Given the unrealistic portrayal of family life in the media, it shouldn't be surprising that Americans expect to live that way as well. At this writing, of adolescents, *Desperate Housewives* is their favorite prime-time television program.[32] Besides the actress who plays a more traditional role of the (very) harried and overworked mother, the women on this program do almost no actual work yet live privileged lifestyles. Perhaps unrealistic portrayals account for the misguided belief of many modern teens' that high-status careers come without a lot of hard work.

History shows that materialism exists, in part, in the context of specific social and economic conditions. What is unique to this time in history is what some social scientists have coined "the instant culture."[33] We now have the means to satisfy work, leisure, social interaction — just about everything — almost in the blink of an eye.

What Is Instant Culture?

Recently I switched from dial-up to a microwave dish Internet service. Now I get e-mail in almost the blink of an eye, and I can't imagine going back to the lumbering pace of a modem. Never mind that not that long ago, I relied on snail-mail and the telephone to communicate with the rest of the world. While not a techno-geek, I appreciate the technological advances of the last decade that have allowed me to dig up research, print hundreds of pages of articles at home, schedule interviews, "talk" with other writers, and even order dinner when I'm so tired I can't fathom slicing a tomato. As far as I'm concerned, the Internet is truly a thing of wonder. Some social observers have coined the term "instant culture" to refer to the new electronic age. Instant cultures are communities in which new technologies enable people to satisfy work, social, leisure, and other needs very quickly. The term also refers to an attitude where old and slow are devalued and fast and cutting edge are revered.

Because of the rapid upgrades in technology, the lives of each generation now seem qualitatively different from the ones before. When I started kindergarten, I remember the thrill of learning to read about Dick and Jane and their dog Spot. Today, learning to read with Dick and Jane is passé. At four, my nephew regularly used computers and learned basic addition, subtraction, and problem-solving skills using educational software. With the Internet, youngsters can browse museum sites throughout the world, contact experts in almost any field, log onto blogs to learn about the experiences of people in Iraq, and frequent chat rooms to "talk" with like-minded peers. Cindy, the mother of a six-year-old boy, told me that her son learned about breast cancer by frequenting an oil company Web site that features toy cars. The site also happened to feature information on breast cancer awareness. As a result of his exposure, Cindy's son wanted to wear a pink ribbon to support the cause. The point here is that new technology has created a different world for today's children compared to the one that many of us experienced.

Clearly technology can enrich lives. But is there a catch to living in this electronic age? Because of its relative newness, research-based knowledge on the potential psychological and emotional effects of this evolving culture on children remains meager. Looking to research based on older technologies, such as television, provides some guidance as to how youngsters might be impacted. For example, we know that television advertising encourages youngsters to want the products they see on the screen. Youngsters who watch commercials promoting sugared cereals, for instance, are likely to request the product from their parents (multiple times). Lisette describes her son's response to television advertising:

> I don't like the craving they get when they watch commercial television, and if it were up to me they wouldn't watch any of it. But my husband doesn't see anything wrong with it. They'll watch this stuff and then come up to me and say, "You know what I want?" They end up getting a lot of plastic junk.

But what about spending hours playing video games, surfing the Internet, visiting Web sites, using e-mail, or frequenting chat rooms? One might expect that advertising on the web influences children similarly to advertising on television. But there is so much more to the Internet than run-of-the-mill advertising. Speed, access to almost unlimited information (much of it unregulated and unscreened), new forms of advertising—all of these features make Internet technology different from the garden-variety television program or magazine. It seems implausible that the development of children growing up in the electronic age would not be impacted in some significant ways both positive and negative.

Much has been written about the values and skills that children need to develop into emotionally healthy, economically productive citizens.[34] While an all-inclusive review is not possible here, I do feel that some capabilities are particularly susceptible to both the influences of new technology and to materialism. The notion of an instant culture with its emphasis on speed, immediacy, and quantity suggests that the development of some abilities, such as reflective thinking and delay of gratification, might be impacted. The ability to delay gratification has particular implications for materialism. We want our children to learn to resist the temptation to respond to every material craving that comes their way. In the following sections I discuss some potential impacts of new technology on self-control and propose ways that parents can support our children's development and lower their vulnerability to materialism.

Look before You Leap

Consider the importance of delayed gratification. Countless children first learn the hard truth about self-restraint at home, in the grocery checkout lane, or at the toy store. For many children, lessons on delayed gratification come dressed in annoyingly familiar phrases like "I'm not made of money"; "You can't have everything you want"; and the ultimate, "Life isn't fair." As children leave the preschool years, delayed gratification becomes crucial for negotiating academic work and social pressure. In primary school, working cooperatively in groups, finishing class projects, and learning new, frustration-inducing skills all require self-control. In the social realm, every parent hopes that their child can resist temptation and bypass the allure of drugs, alcohol, tobacco, or overspending. "Starving" college students endure academic rigor and modest lifestyles for the promise of future career success. Problem-solving, achieving long-term goals, social adjustment, and, at the core, overall life satisfaction all rely, in part, on exercising self-control. Although the definitions do differ slightly, I use the terms "self-control," "delayed gratification," and "impulse control" interchangeably throughout this discussion to refer to behaviors that involve putting off fulfillment of immediate needs in order to obtain a long-term goal. Several of the parents I interviewed wanted their children to learn to delay gratification. Primarily, they wanted their youngsters to learn the value of saving money and waiting for desired possessions. One mother described her frustrations in trying to achieve this with her six-year-old:

[If we keep giving in] he's not going to learn that you sometimes have to wait for things. He'll think that his parents are human ATMs. If he doesn't learn now, when he gets older and you say there's no money for that in the budget right now, they're not going to believe you. I try to address it. If we're in a toy store and he asks for something, I'll say, "I don't understand why you need more when at home you still have ten toys that you haven't played with." Or I'll say, "Christmas is coming, maybe Santa will bring it."

This mother provides a fitting example of how difficult just saying no can be. Fran, a single parent of one son, has tried teaching her son to delay desire through money management:

Part of why I started giving him an allowance was because I didn't know how to deal with all the begging when we'd go shopping. I didn't want to do what my mom did, which was always say no. I thought there had to be something in between giving in all the time and saying no, and at the same time teaching him what it means to have to spend money . . . learning that if you spend the money right away, you may miss what you really want by not waiting. I'm trying to teach him to make how own choices.

Fran learned about the importance of self-control through experience:

I fluctuate from "stick to the budget" to emotional shopping. At one point, I said to myself "Dropping $1,500 in one day on clothes is not a good thing!" After I did that, I learned to bring it down. You know, if you have a bad day, you buy a really nice bar of soap. Some places like [furniture store] are really slippery because I just think, "I want." It's hard when you see this beautiful couch and yours is this tattered old thing. I'm in grad school so I know this isn't forever.

So does this mean that eating dessert before dinner actually can hurt you? Research suggests that the inclination to resist temptation goes hand in hand with stronger social and academic skills. In typical delay of gratification studies, children are asked to choose between immediately receiving a treat (imagine tantalizingly displayed M&Ms) or waiting it out for the promise of something even yummier (perhaps a big cupcake).[35] Those children who wait it out tend to score higher on cognitive ability tests, to be more socially responsible, and to hold loftier academic goals than those who give in to temptation. As teenagers, the holdouts lead their less stalwart peers in social and academic competence. Characteristically focused long-term planners, the holdouts also deal more effectively with frustration and setbacks than do their counterparts.

Developing self-control has always been considered an important developmental task for children. One by-product of an instant culture may be that some children, accustomed to feedback on demand, do not develop a mature ability to delay gratification. The risk increases when a child spends large chunks of time interacting with various new technologies. Most parents already know that television has become a frequent companion to children; it has for a long time now. Youngsters spend more time watching television than they do anything else: learning in the classroom, interacting with family, hanging out with friends (face to face, that is, not on the computer), even listening to music.[36] Internet use by children is quickly gaining, with about half the population of children in the United States logging on at home.

New technologies such as Internet accessibility present modern children with formidable challenges for self-control. For instance, many networks now offer Web sites designed specifically for youngsters that complement their television programming. The sites provide lots of temptations for impulsive young children. Take the example of the program *Blue's Clues* which airs on Nickelodeon Jr. Television. A young visitor to the site will find links to Blue's Clues-themed games and activities as well as a link for parents describing the "goals and teaching philosophy" of the show.[37] The Web site contains ample opportunities to consume; there are advertisements for electronic equipment and fast food as well as links to a Blue's Boutique and a Nick Jr. Shop. The shopping venues carry clothing, videos, stuffed dolls, room decor, and costumes. Even more educational-based channels incorporate consumerism on their sites. The Children's Television Network (CTW), presumably less commercial than other networks and more focused on learning, offers games for children, stories, and art projects on its Web site.[38] Their Web page also includes a link to the Sesame Street store where children (or rather their parents) can purchase toys and other items. This Internet site touts its philanthropic efforts to improve the literacy of children in other countries. The more parents buy, the more poor children benefit; a portion of the proceeds from the sale of toys goes toward the literacy fund.

Child-targeted Web sites give cause for both celebration and concern. Many of the sites offer useful educational material that can help supplement children's learning, and some encourage altruism and community service. Yet these sites are frequently subsidized by advertising, and many incorporate online shopping. As mentioned, even the CTW site promotes some consumerism, albeit for a worthy cause. This poses particular problems for young children. Research shows that youngsters below the age of seven or eight do not understand the persuasive intent of advertising. They are therefore particularly vulnerable to the hazards that await the unwary. Clicking on a link that promises a prize for completing a survey appeals to young ones' desire for instant gratification. However, the Web page might actually be an advertisement for merchandise. Also, many of these sites entice children to complete "fun" surveys and quizzes that can pose as opportunities for businesses to collect information from children so that they can further promote their products.[39] Most notably, advertising-laden sites increase youngsters' desires for material goods. Over 50 percent of children ask their parents for merchandise they have viewed on the Web.[40]

Many children's sites continue the disturbing trend of pairing education and commerce—the joy of learning with the intoxicating narcotic of consumption. The constant intrusion of advertising does not allow children a free space in which to explore their interests and passions. It reinforces the role of the citizen in a free market society as, first and foremost, a consumer. While consumerism plays an important role in supporting the economy, most of us would agree that it should not be the primary focus of efforts to develop children's social, emotional, or cognitive vigor. Consumerism focuses heavily on the promise of satisfaction through extrinsic means. This is the bait—almost anything is possible through acquisition: forming an identity, attaining social and career success, inspiring envy, soothing emotional distress, all based on one's possessions—or the possessions one would like to claim one day. And, as I discuss in Chapter 2, the overuse of extrinsic rewards can actually lay waste to children's intrinsic motivation to learn out of interest and curiosity.

Instant culture has fashioned a paradise of almost unlimited information available for the taking. Professor Stephan Bertman coined the phrase the "power of now" to refer to the power of large amounts of immediately available data to influence one's perspective.[41] The power of now has the potential to saturate the senses, overwhelming our ability to process information with waves of unfiltered facts, advice, opinions, products, and choices. With so much knowledge available, children face the daunting task of critically analyzing a chorus of facts and nonfacts that can lead, according to Bertman, to difficulty prioritizing and making decisions; to skimming over the details and settling for a superficial understanding of complex concepts. The current emphasis on speed, on valuing what is cutting edge over the slightly used also shortchanges the importance of history, reflection, and intuition.

One of the critical tasks of childhood is learning to take the time to reflect, to integrate the freshly acquired with what is already known, to trust one's gut instincts, and to make thoughtful decisions about one's life. Looking to history as well as relying on past personal experience gives children the broad perspective that they need to make good decisions. The power of now has implications for delayed gratification. Youngsters accustomed to getting what they want when they want it in interactions with technology will need opportunities to learn this skill in other ways. Parents should exercise great care in helping children learn to wait for objects of desire.

At this point, only a thimbleful of empirical research examines the impact of new technologies on children's psychosocial growth. Some studies indicate that self-control-related behaviors—such as aggression—are influenced by modern technologies like video games. Trying to make sense of the research and rhetoric on violent media and childhood aggression is akin to watching a vigorous tennis match. On one side, critics of violent media claim that playing brutish video games leads to behavior problems in children. Dissenters claim that more aggressive children tend to prefer more aggressive entertainment and that this explains the association between violent media and children's problem behavior. Research has demonstrated an association between video game play and physical aggression. The more time children spend playing video games, the more physical aggression they show toward their peers.[42] These children also tend to involve themselves more in *relational aggression*—damaging another child's social relationships by spreading rumors and encouraging others to reject the victim. However, these studies can only claim an association between game play and aggressive behavior. They don't tell us what *causes* the behavior problems.

Studies conducted in the laboratory show that exposure to violent video games can lead to increased aggression in children. In these types of studies, researchers assess children's pre-experiment aggression levels through parent and teacher reports. They might also observe children at play to determine their peer interaction style. Next, some of the youngsters play the violent video games while a second group plays a nonviolent game. The children are then observed again in free play. Children in the violent-game condition demonstrate increased aggression in their play. Thus, at least in the short term, these games do impact behavior. Even minimal levels of playtime can lead children not only to play rough, but to think more aggressive thoughts and to misinterpret ambiguous information as hostile. So, for example, when Steve accidentally knocks over Bill's block building, Bill, who enjoys *Mortal Kombat* and *Doom*, pushes Steve, assuming that Steve *meant* to destroy his masterpiece. This bellicose stance has been referred to as the "mean world" perspective. Mean world believers tend to frame the world as violent and unsafe, populated by people who use aggression to solve their problems.[43] These beliefs have been found among youngsters with a diet of violent media: video games, television, movies.

A diet of aggressive media in combination with Internet use and exposure to advertising may prove damaging to children's developing ability to delay gratification and exercise self-control. This combination of factors has implications for a number of areas of children's development. However, in terms of materialism, constant satisfaction of every desire focuses children's attention squarely on the material world. This increases the chances that youngsters will rely on possessions, rather than other resources, as an answer to life's challenges. Given the preponderance of evidence, parents should be concerned and *active*. Some ways to maintain vigilance:

- Be aware of what your children are watching and playing. Research shows that even with an electronic rating system in place, most parents are unfamiliar with even the popular violent video titles. Children, however, claim great familiarity with these games, either through word of mouth or because they play them at home or when visiting friends.[44]
- Explore with youngsters appropriate ways to manage frustration and anger. Discuss the ways that television and video game characters express angry feelings.
- Talk with your children about advertising tactics, about the various ways that companies try to whip up consumer desire. Chapter 4 covers ways to increase your children's media savvy.
- Help your children to differentiate between the real and the imaginary. Just as children need to learn that in real life,

when someone gets punched or kicked, they don't just get up again, they also need to understand that toys don't bring lasting happiness and popularity and sometimes they don't even work they way they're shown in the commercial. They need to make the connection.

Ethics, Materialism and Modern Times

For many students, the temptation to cheat and materialism can go hand in hand. Recall that a component of materialism includes the desire to impress others with one's belongings. For some young people, and their families, this translates into intense academic and career ambition. The pressure to succeed is exceedingly intense in many communities. In some families, concern about academic success and learning begins at birth. In my community, parents have been known to stand in line for hours to gain admission into private, academically rigorous preschools. Some readers may be familiar with the "baby ivy" scandal in New York: Allegedly, a parent was so desperate that his child be admitted to the "right preschool" that he engaged in illegal behavior to ensure acceptance.[45] Even as early as elementary school, some parents are thinking about their children's economic future. One mother says:

> I tie this whole cheating and academic pressure and overscheduling thing together. In ballet class, these kids don't just tumble around and have fun; they're serious. They don't just run on Sunday afternoons for pleasure. They have a coach that meets them and works on their form. The expectation here is perfection. You put these kids where I was at twelve, with a television and a sunny day, and they're bored to death.

For some youngsters, thinking about success instead of learning becomes entrenched by high school. Stanford University lecturer Denise Clark Pope calls it the "who wants to be a millionaire" mentality.[46] Children endure tremendous academic pressure, some of it self-imposed, for the opportunity to attend a prestigious university and ultimately to earn a large paycheck working in a high-status position. An incident at a high school in the Silicon Valley illustrates this "millionaire" mentality. A group of students allegedly pilfered course exams and answer keys through some computer finagling. One of these students was later implicated in stealing chemicals from a school lab that could be used to make a bomb. This particular high school is renowned for superior academic performance, an outstanding faculty, and highly involved parents.[47] Many of the affluent parents at this school consider straight As, admission to a top-notch university, and a high-paying career to be de rigueur for their children. Young people take this pressure from parents as well as their self-imposed high expectations and develop a success-at-any-cost point of view. There is a distinction between a disciplined young person who works hard at his studies out of true interest or passion and one who wants desperately to achieve to satisfy someone else's expectations. Those children who feel tremendous external pressure to achieve, whose goals include more materialistic rewards, are extremely vulnerable to cheating and other forms of academic dishonesty. Schools and parents can either help or hinder children's ethics. In the case of this local high school, teachers and administrators pledged to emphasize integrity over grades. Parents expressed commitment to backing off from exerting pressure on their children for perfection in both grades and performance in extracurricular efforts.

Parents can approach ethical decision making in a number of ways. In the hustle of everyday life, discussion about ethics may get pushed aside in favor of more pressing issues, such as driving the kids to soccer practice or getting dinner on the table. However, giving a bit more attention to ethics with children now may reap substantial benefits later when they are faced with decisions regarding success and achievement. Parents can also emphasize the importance of learning to increase knowledge or to develop interests, not just to build a resume or to earn a good grade. This tact can bring great rewards. Children with an intrinsic motivation to learn — those who relish challenges and who strive to increase their skills and knowledge—truly enjoy school and feel confident about their intellectual abilities. These children also focus much less on material rewards and much more on the joy of learning. In Chapter 6 I discuss more fully the notion of intrinsic motivation and materialism.

SUMMARY

Far from being unique to modern times, materialism has been a part of human cultures since antiquity. Consumerism became particularly prominent in the United States with the emergence of the Industrial Revolution and the more comfortable lifestyle it afforded many Americans. Along with the revolution came a proliferation of advertising and the equation of democracy with the right to consume. Consumerism strengthened materialistic values that place the pursuit of status and goods as paramount. While everyone lives in this consumer-oriented culture, not everybody adopts materialistic values. Insecurity, in part, distinguishes the vulnerable and the less vulnerable. Insecurity, whether for economic or emotional reasons, leaves individuals more likely to hold strongly materialistic values. Our modern, electronic culture presents unique challenges to parents and educators. Youngsters have entered into a world of great abundance—an abundance of resources, information, products, and access to others—which present them with distinct developmental challenges and opportunities. Most notably, children experience constant temptation from advertisements and promotions on the Internet, television, billboards, and more. Developing the ability to delay gratification is sorely tested by the constant barrage of exhortations to spend. Those who care for children can meet these challenges by carefully monitoring their use of media and anticipating the ethical and psychological challenges that accompany life in this culture.

CHAPTER 2

THE PARENTING EVOLUTION

Imagine an era when concepts of preschooler, teenager, and emotional development do not exist. No parenting books crowd store shelves, and exhortations from child development experts to provide children with quality time or age-appropriate play experiences do not inundate anxious parents. In the early twentieth century, the field of child development, as we know it, was just revving up. The terms "teenager" and "preschooler"[1] had not yet been invented, and the field of child psychology began shifting its focus from healthy physical maturation to emotional health. Advice in the 1920s included discouraging mothers from smothering their children with love lest they interfere with healthy psychological development.[2] Instead, moms were encouraged to "get a life" by focusing more on their marriage and less on their children's every move. Ironically, parenting mavens applauded the more emotionally detached style of many fathers during that time as the best mix of distance and encouragement.

Since the beginnings of the modern child development movement, the definition of "good parenting" has changed frequently, sometimes drastically. Keeping up with the latest wisdom can be a real challenge—are time-outs the "right" way to discipline? Is permissive or strict parenting most effective? Should one focus more on

encouraging self-esteem or self-control? The questions seem endless
and so might the variety of advice. Remember the classic scene from
the *I Love Lucy* television series? Lucy and Ethel try in vain to keep
up with a conveyor belt bearing chocolates to be packaged. The two
women end up eating most of the candy and getting upset stomachs
to boot. Years of parenting advice resembles that chocolate; it looks
great, but try to use it all and risk feeling overwhelmed.

Traditionally, guidance on parenting has come from many
sources: family members, research, child development gurus,
physicians, the media. Scientific investigation on infant maturation, for example, has led to significant advances in knowledge
about parent-child attachment, cognitive capacities, and the importance of play. Some advice stems from changes in the culture.
For instance, as gender roles in society have changed, so has expert opinion on the parenting roles of males and females. At other
times, "guidance" springs from businesses and marketers trying to
convince parents that their product is *essential* to children's happiness (e.g., good parents will buy their children the new Tickle Me
Elmo toy (TMX Elmo) for Christmas, thus avoiding disappointment and possible future emotional problems). The cacophony of
advice from parenting magazines, television talk shows, children's
videos, radio call-in programs, advertisements, and more can lead
individuals to feel confused about the "best" way to parent. In this
chapter, I discuss how the notion of "good parenting" has evolved
and the ways that individuals have increasingly come to rely on
material goods in order to reach their parenting ambitions. I hope
that readers use this information to gain perspective on the basis of
their own parenting behavior.

FROM AUTOCRACY TO DEMOCRACY

In one of my first college jobs, I worked at a preschool immersed in
the newest rage among the child care set: Parent Effectiveness
Training (P.E.T. for those in the know).[3] The P.E.T. program promised to improve communication and decrease conflict between adult

and child. Disciplining children by force or by invoking parental privilege was frowned on; according to the program, the do-it-be-cause-I-told-you-so philosophy only served to increase conflict and misunderstanding. Showing children respect and understanding by truly listening and responding to his or her concerns would lead, the program promised, to happier, more responsible youngsters. At my preschool, using P.E.T. translated into more reasoning and less di-recting. So, for example, when Susie threatened to bop Jenny with the foam bat, teachers could be heard saying "I sense that you're angry, Susie" rather than "Put down that bat!"

The popularity of P.E.T. is a perfect example of how parenting advice has evolved over the last century. In this country, parenting style has generally shifted from strict to more permissive, from a focus on obedience to a concern over every aspect of children's emo-tional and social well-being. In the nineteenth century, those in the know viewed children as a bundle of hedonist impulses and "insisted that children's 'will' be broken."[4] The twentieth century introduced a more progressive, child-centered approach to understanding youngsters: "The old adage that children should be seen but not heard cried out for revision in the century of the child, reform-minded Americans in the Progressive Era agreed . . . . The new im-perative was, above all, for adults to use their eyes and ears in ways they had never before bothered to—to cultivate a voracious, almost childlike curiosity about children."[5]

During the early 1900s, the family slowly began its metamor-phosis into a system that now devotes most of its energy, effort, and worry to children. For many families, the bulk of the budget goes toward children: their schooling, after-school activities, cloth-ing, and entertainment. Even family vacations focus squarely on the child. Disney theme parks are the number one vacation desti-nation in the United States.[6] Many of the parents I talked with ad-mitted that when they do succumb to consumer urges, they typically spend on the children. The majority of parents claimed that "I rarely buy things for myself; it's usually for the kids." Lisette describes her friend:

A friend of mine is a total toy junkie, she buys tons of toys and she's a stay-at-home mom . . . the house is full of them. She doesn't buy for herself; she wears sweats and T-shirts, and you will see her in the same thing for I don't know how long. She doesn't shop for herself, but get her in Toys-R-Us and she will walk out with a wagon full. There is nothing that comes out on the market that she's not all over and that she hasn't bought it before it hits the shelf.

Behaviorism was one of the popular child rearing theories and practices in the twentieth century. The theory downplayed punishment and advocated the use of consequences to shape children's behavior. Dr. John B. Watson, behaviorism's creator, admonished parents to exercise rigor in their administration of behavioral consequences. He believed, for example, that toilet training should be a simple matter easily mastered by leaving a child alone on the pot, without parental interaction, until the desired behavior was achieved.[7] No chitchat or dawdling allowed. Early behaviorism rejected the display of too much affection and coddling. According to Watson, parental affection "is built up of (and comes down to) physical, self-centered indulgence."[8] The optimal parental stance resembled the coolly detached demeanor of a white-coated scientist, which ultimately would result in independent, resilient children. While parents did not necessarily buy wholesale into behaviorism (most mothers, even Watson's wife, Rosalie, rejected the edict to withhold affection from their children), some remnants of the theory remain to this day. Specifically, the use of rewards and punishment to elicit desired behaviors, also called behavior modification, have become an integral part of both the education and parenting culture.

REWARDS FOR BEHAVIOR

Star charts, poker chips, behavior management plans, end-of-the-week treats—you name it, and schools, parents, youth camps, prisons, and more have tried it. Today most elementary school classrooms rely on some form of behavior modification to shape students' behavior and motivate academic performance. The system has also made its way into the home and has been used on everything from toilet training to household chores.[9] Many teachers and parents swear by behavior modification techniques, and it's true that many children will change their conduct, at least in the short term, for a desirable treat. Empirical research supports the effectiveness of behavior modification under specific conditions. For example, focusing on one or two problem areas with clear criteria for behavior and using rewards that actually appeal to the child can lead to behavioral change.[10] Behaviorism principles have been used successfully for a potpourri of problems including conduct disorders (e.g., criminal activity and antisocial behaviors), attention deficit hyperactivity disorder (ADHD), and autism.[11]

Behavior modification has its critics. Some observers believe that any plan that metes out rewards and punishments for behaviors (typically determined by a more powerful adult) manipulates children and can result in some hard feelings. To its harshest critics, behaviorism is not very different from rewarding the household dog for sitting or not chewing the carpet. Even without the threat of punishment, some believe that behavior modification can damage children just through the use of rewards. According to writer Alfie Kohn, for example, when a parent promises a child a trip to the zoo for good behavior during the week and, due to some slipups, the child fails to earn to the expected treat, disappointment and resentment loom large.[12] In the worst-case scenario, claims Kohn, relying on rewards to change behavior damages the parent-child relationship, and youngsters grow to mistrust adults and their motives. Children are no different from adults. Think of a time when you felt forced or pressured into doing something. Did you carry out your obligations with a spring in your step, or did you complain every inch of the way? Most of us like feeling as if we have some say over our life; that we are not being controlled or manipulated by others. As a young character from one of my favorite childhood books proclaims, "I'll do it because I want to — not because you tell me to!"

When children experience some control over their lives, they show higher self-esteem and more creativity, interest, and confidence in their work and play. In one self-determination study, for example, researchers probed high-achieving third and fourth graders on their perceptions of academic competence and autonomy.[13] Students who perceived themselves as independent experienced more opportunities to take initiative and to make choices about what or how to study. These "independents" displayed more intellectual curiosity and involvement in their schoolwork compared with those children who felt less control over their academic lives. The "controlled" children endorsed such statements as "I do my homework because I'll get into trouble if I don't." The controlled students give the impression of the prototypical worker drone who punches in at 9:00 A.M. and out at 5:00 P.M., beaten down by the demanding boss and the uninspiring routine of the workday. Indeed, these children express greater boredom and anxiety in their academic pursuits and admit to procrastination and to just getting by in school.

Studies such as this suggest that at least *perceiving* that one has *some* choice (e.g., do you want to wear the blue dress or the green dress? Would you prefer to study math or science?) promotes greater interest and engagement in children. The term psychologists use to describe this type of interest is "intrinsic motivation." Most researchers believe that human beings are inherently curious and motivated to master their environment. An intrinsically motivated individual typically engages in activities out a desire to learn or out of the sheer joy of the pursuit. An intrinsically motivated child shows less concern about, say, doing well in school to please his parents, to get an A, or to earn a prize out of the goodie box and more interest in mastering a subject and feeling proud of his accomplishments. Trudy, a mother of two boys and a girl, notices motivation differences in how her two sons view the external trappings of success:

> Trent could care less, give me a T-shirt and a pair of pants and
> I'm happy. He loves his guitar and his amp; things that he gets

lost in. Jeffrey gets lost in things that are really beautiful . . . he gets lost in all of the superficial crap that you could think of. If he sees an ad for a piece of jewelry that he thinks is really beautiful he'll say gosh, isn't that incredible, and can you believe it has this many carats and this color diamond is the rarest in the world, and comes from wherever . . . it's the wow and then some. Take the Maserati; he knows everything about it, where it was made, how fast it goes, what kind of engine it has. He longs for things, and I worry about that for him.

Trudy worries that Jeffrey will choose a career for its financial rewards rather than out of interest or passion:

He is adamant that he will be able to afford the things he wants in life and that's just how it's going to be. He's not quite sure what he's going to do professionally, but he knows he's going to be successful. And I tell him there's successful financially and there's successful because you love what you do. And, at the end of the day, when you've got to get up and do it again in the morning and you're there long hours . . . if it doesn't feel good you're not going to care how much money you're making, trust me.

In terms of emotional fulfillment, those individuals guided by more intrinsic reasons to achieve report greater life satisfaction. Intrinsic motivation is associated with a whole host of psychological indicators: self-confidence, emotional well-being, persistence, creativity, enhanced performance. *Extrinsic motivation,* on the other hand—achievement based on money, status, grades, threats, orders, imposed goals, and the like—links arm and arm with a greater focus on materialism. This makes intuitive sense. A child who over time performs for the reward or who sets goals based on material gain or social approval may come to view worldly goods as goals in and of themselves and ignore other aspirations, such as personal satisfaction, learning, and contributing to the community. This can also work in reverse. A child who experiences emotional deficits may look to material goods in order to feel better about herself.

Critics of behavior modification charge that the method encourages a materialistic worldview.[14] Think about the behavior modification plans that you may have used or that have been used by your child's teacher. Generally the plans involve material items—not necessarily extravagant goods, usually grab-bag tchotchkes that delight a young child. As children get older, however, a plastic car or beaded necklace no longer serves to encourage new behaviors. One of my college students related a story where she presented a behavior modification plan to a fourth-grade boy she was tutoring in English. The boy refused to do his work and used the tutoring sessions to complain about his boredom with the student and her efforts to motivate him. Exasperated, she devised a plan where he could earn points toward toys for completing assignments. His response was "Those are stupid prizes! I can buy better stuff myself." Back to the drawing board.

Material rewards are a form of extrinsic motivation, and a large body of research has determined that material rewards rob children of their internal drive and their creativity. Take the example of the collage study.[15] One group of school-age children was allowed access to a camera to take photos with the stipulation that they design collages afterward. A second group of children gained access to the cameras but were not told anything about making collages ahead of time. After the camera time, as expected, children in the first group commenced making collages. After using the cameras, the children in the second group were directed by the researchers to create collages. A panel of creativity experts (yes, such a thing does exist) rated the creativity of group 1 as lower than that of group 2. These findings suggest that when children believe that they are participating in an activity for a reward (e.g., use of the camera), their creativity suffers. The children in group 1 believed that their camera time was contingent on the obligation to create a collage. The youngsters in group 2 felt no such constraint. When children perceive that participation in an activity is based on obligation or a promise, they put less of themselves into the endeavor. Think about how this principle applies in the classroom. Teachers frequently promise rewards for "getting through" the tedium of schoolwork—"When you finish your math set, then you get an extra star for good behavior." Or consider the home front. One of my college students said that when she was young, her mother wanted to encourage her children to read and tried all sorts of strategies. The student recalls that when she or her brother misbehaved, her mother would say, "Keep it up and you're going to go read!" While well intended, this mom wielded reading as a punishment rather than a privilege.

Not only creativity suffers when children perform for extrinsic rewards. The promise of a treat can in fact squash intrinsic interest. In a seminal study by Stanford University social psychologist Mark Lepper and his associates, nursery school children participated in an intrinsic motivation experiment.[16] After first observing the youngsters during free play, researchers chose those who showed the most interest in drawing. The investigators placed these children into one of three groups. In the expected-reward condition, the youngsters learned that they would receive a reward for drawing pictures. Children in the unexpected-reward group received a reward after their art activity; however, they were not told of this beforehand. In the third group, the children received no reward.

Following the art activity, researchers observed the youngsters during free play. Those in the expected-reward group engaged in less drawing time than children in the other two groups. Essentially, the offer of a reward destroyed the intrinsic interest that children in the "expected" condition initially demonstrated during free play. Why might rewards dampen children's natural interests? First, an anticipated reward appears to pull children's attention away from the actual activity and focus it on finishing so that they can get that treat. Second, self-determination theories postulate that rewards facilitate the view that the outcomes of events or circumstance lie beyond one's control. Children attribute their behavior to incentives rather than to internal drive. A child with this view might believe, for example, that his or her performance on a test depends on the difficulty of the material, the mood of the teacher when grading the exam, or just plain luck. When parents and teachers resort to rewards to mold behavior, children act based on what they think is expected rather than on what truly moves them to take on a challenge.

Researchers theorize that a rewards-for-behavior method funnels children's focus on getting stuff instead of learning or developing their interests. The method fits right into American culture, which thrives on material rewards. Businesses offer their employees incentives for outstanding performance. Parents pay their children for making good grades. Teachers give out prizes to their pupils for reading books, finishing their assignments, and sitting quietly in their seats. Individuals reward themselves for successfully negotiating various and sundry obstacles—completing a project, finishing the holiday shopping, surviving another day. In fact, advertising encourages us to satisfy desires simply because "We're worth it." In this country, it has become the norm to reward achievements with goods and money, no matter how insignificant the feat. Cindy and her husband use a reward system with her son, but admit to feeling uncomfortable with the strategy:

> We're really terrible because we reward [son] when he eats fruits and vegetables . . . It's a huge issue getting him to eat healthy, and usually he gets a car or a train or something new. It's because we're at our wits' end . . . He'll take a bit and he'll eat it once but he won't eat it again, it's really frustrating. I don't think it's right to reward a child for eating vegetables, but we're so concerned about his health.

Fran also acknowledges that behavior modification is not optimal:

> We'll use the token economy even though I don't like it. I use it sparingly when all else fails. We have a system of checks. We mostly use it to get him out of the house and to school on time. If you get four checks then you get cookies in your lunchbox. I always have to change the rewards because they lose their appeal after a while. Now it's sixteen checks and he gets a gecko . . . I wasn't brought up with the system; my mom used to call it BS Skinner.[17] Parenting shouldn't be about manipu-

lating children, about getting them to do things because you want them to do it. It's about teaching how to treat people, to show respect, and to be responsible. We try to rely more on natural consequences.

Some parents find alternatives to reward systems. Lynette, a former teacher and mother of two, has never used material rewards to motivate her children, relying instead on consequences for expected behaviors:

> We give them choices. We have a pet rat and we say, "You can hold the pet rat as soon as you make your bed." We will use denial of privileges. Doing the things they love, like holding the rat, swim practice, or playdates, is predicated on good behavior. I don't know that the girls are motivated by stuff anyway, and I just don't feel like giving them rewards for chores that are their responsibility. We expect them in the morning to make their beds, brush their hair, that's about it. And it [rewards] lends itself to inflation, to working in "star currency" and to giving them more stuff that we don't really want to give them.

Mandy also depends upon other methods of discipline with her son:

> Oh yes, that shaping stuff. We should use it, I suppose, but we don't. We've done it in the past with things like toilet training. Now we praise him when he is successful doing something. If he's not listening or acting obnoxious then we do the 1–2–3 thing where you give him a series of warnings and when you get to 3 it's an automatic take a break, time-out. I do think there's something to be said for using rewards though. It helps to be able to track success so there's a tangible sign for them of their progress.

These parents illustrate both the drawbacks and the advantages to the use of behavior modification. At its worse, an over-reliance on reward systems has the potential to create materialistic children whose top goals involve gaining wealth and status. Indeed, some

researchers believe that the reliance on extrinsic rewards has contributed to the materialistic value system embraced by so many
children today. When children work *just* for the externals—money,
toys, special outings, even grades—they develop the idea that putting out effort is worth it only when a reward is involved. This
what's-in-it-for-me attitude comes at the expense of children's autonomy and self-expression.[18] Pursuing activities out of interest,
enjoyment, or for the challenge rather than for reward furthers
children's identity, competence, independence, and creativity. Motivation based on rewards sends the message that, in terms of accomplishment, it's the outcome, not the process, that counts.
Cindy's son, for instance, runs the risk of concluding that loving
one's body and keeping it healthy and strong pale in comparison to
getting stuff. He also gets the notion that he doesn't have to do
things that he doesn't like without the promise of a reward. Most
adults know that the ability to persevere through adversity and un-
pleasantness signifies maturity and increases the likelihood of success in life. In the long run, rewards for behavior don't work. In
Cindy's case, her son still won't eat his vegetables.

The what's-in-it-for-me attitude also breeds discontent. For example, researchers asked college students from the United States
and South Korea to describe a recent satisfying event.[19] The description included how the student felt and the importance of money
and luxury to enjoyment of the event. Students for whom money
and luxury held great importance reported fewer positive and more
negative emotions during the event. This survey represents one of a
handful that imply that when individuals focus more on external reward and less on intrinsic interest, they experience less fulfillment.

The material presented so far may sound a lot like behavior
modification bashing. Although a large body of research does show
that material rewards kill intrinsic interest, I am not suggesting that
they be completely swept from the table. Studies on motivation and
academic achievement suggest that some types of extrinsic motivators dampen drive less than others. For example, the criterion one
uses for rewarding behavior significantly affects children's perform-

ance. Motivation suffers most when youngsters receive rewards for just showing up. Researchers call this form of criteria *performance independent*.[20] In real life, such a reward would be giving the child a cookie simply for working on her homework, regardless of the effort or quality of the work. A second strategy rewards youngsters for completing their work. Here, a child might be rewarded for finishing a certain number of books on a reading list, regardless of his or her comprehension of the material. This *completion-dependent*, technique encourages children to choose books based on their length or ease of reading instead of their interests. Under both of these reward systems, children receive no useful feedback on their performance. They don't learn about their strengths or how to go about reinforcing skills that need improvement. This drawback reflects the concerns of parents like Fran, who see her role as teaching new skills rather than manipulating behavior.

A third motivation system, *quality dependent*, involves awarding children based on some preestablished criteria. For example, youngsters understand that if they read three books from the reading list and write a book report for each that demonstrates their understanding of plot, style, and content, then they receive a treat or a privilege. In the parenting realm, a child could receive a treat if he is in bed, with his pajamas on, with no whining by a designated hour. While quality-dependent rewards do not address all of the criticisms leveled against behavior modification, they do go further to ensure that youngsters receive more useful information about the quality of their work or behavior. This technique also does more than other methods to foster appreciation of effort and the process of the work, not just the outcome.

Some researchers have determined that only certain types of rewards hurt intrinsic motivation.[21] When children expect compensation before they even begin a task, their motivation suffers. For example, when children hear, "If you finish your book you get extra dessert," they're less likely to linger over and enjoy the reading than if they receive a surprise on completion. Research also finds that nonmaterial rewards, such as praise, are less damaging than material goods. In terms of praise, the more specific and informative the better. My students frequently complain about getting writing assignments returned from their professors with a good grade and comments like "nice job" or "good work." While the students are gratified about the high score, they say they've learned nothing about what the teacher liked or what could have been improved on. Similarly, children need to know what behaviors parents consider unacceptable. Less general and more informative praise—such as "You included a glass and napkin and all the utensils when you set the table. Nice work" rather than "Oh what a good girl you are!"— gives children something they can work with. Youngsters also require feedback on how to clean up their act and improve their behavior while at the same time meeting their emotional needs. A child who hits her brother may need more direction on other ways to expression frustration. Or, she may be asking indirectly for more time with a parent.

If you do decide to use a reward system, think small. Little acknowledgments have a less damaging impact on intrinsic motivation than do big awards. For example, in studies where children have been promised either a small or a large monetary reward for completing a task, those anticipating a smaller reward showed more creativity and intrinsic interest in their efforts.[22] A small amount of money proves less distracting to youngsters than a big payoff. These results suggest that children's performance on *some* tasks may benefit from a small token. Specifically, educators and researchers propose that effort on boring, uninspiring work may benefit from an incentive or two. Some school tasks or subjects will probably never stimulate children's intrinsic interest. In my adult life, that task is paperwork; no matter how it's packaged, I will never enjoy it. In this case, I use external rewards to slog through the reports: One more hour and I can do the crossword puzzle.

Used appropriately, rewards can enrich children's lives. Instead of a trip to the toy store for finishing a book report, try recognizing a child's accomplishment with a new book. The reward is relevant to the task and gets closer to acknowledging that reading and writing are valuable pursuits in their own right. Also, when using a reward system, be sure that the child understands the criteria for success and that you reward real effort, not "going through the motions." Use the smallest incentive possible (less is more) and, most importantly, be certain that the child has the capability of achieving the behavior. For example, most nine-month-olds won't potty train no matter how many stickers they earn. Similarly, a treat does not solve the problem of a child who becomes aggressive at school because of problems at home. Essentially, parents need to assess each situation carefully. At the core, behavior modification is not appropriate for every childhood behavior or situation.

PARENTING BY MEDIA

Many forces influence individuals' views on parenting. Clearly child-rearing "authorities" such as Watson in the 1930s held some sway over parenting behavior. Advertising also became an increasingly powerful factor in teaching people how to parent in the twentieth century. Through print media—magazines, newspaper ads, city posters, and the like—advertising instructed parents on how to raise a child successfully. And how did media define success? According to historian Gary Cross, advertising provided tutelage on how to nurture the wonder of childhood, the natural delight that children take in nature and in the world around them.[23] Presumably, the drudgeries of the adult world destroy children's natural wonder. Rational thought, real-life responsibility, restraint—all of these align against more desirable characteristics: spontaneity, delight, and indulgence. Advertisers in the early 1900s warned of the dangers of not purchasing the right products: "Commercial messages in women's magazines promised brighter, happier futures for children whose mother endowed them with modern products and warned parents of the dangers of disease, financial ruin and lost opportunities if they did not purchase the right soap, life insurance or education toy or book for their offspring."[24] This doesn't sound so much different from advertising pressures today does it? Then as now, mothers were exhorted to scour their homes with pine cleaner and feed their children puffed cereals in order to ensure healthy development. In this case, good parenting amounted to making smart purchasing decisions. Pressure to preserve the innocence of childhood extended to gift giving as well. Surprising children with a gift will kindle delight in your children promised the advertisers. Children's utter delight in receiving gifts brought joy both to adults and their offspring.[25]

Beginning in the mid-1900s, gift giving became much more central to Christmas and other holidays. Today, very few people would deny that not only has Christmas become about the exchange of material goods but also about good parenting; the pressure to fulfill their children's desires is huge. Trudy describes how she responds to her teenager's requests for expensive Christmas gifts:

> Jeffrey really wanted an X-Box for Christmas, and these things, if you buy all the extras, are at least $200! And they already have a system that plays all the games anyway. I tried to explain to him that the extra bells and whistles on this thing, he wouldn't be using anyway. I told him, you really want this to play games, so why not make a list of some new games that you'd really love instead? I try to give the kids some perspective when they get caught up in wanting the latest thing. And Jeffery was fine with that, he got it.

Of course, most of us don't make decisions based simply on what advertisers dictate, and pampering one's child arises from a complexity of motives. According to one mother, providing for one's children gives people an opportunity to relive their childhood:

> There's a certain amount of self-pleasure when you're buying something for a child. There's a feeling of "Oh, she's going to love it." When I bought this princess dress for a friend's daughter, I was reliving my childhood. *I* wanted a princess dress. I think people who didn't get a lot when they were children, when they go into the toy store and see all these gizmos and toys, they're thinking, "I didn't have this when I was a kid!" With my

husband, he bought my oldest son [six years old] an electric gui-
tar with an amplifier! And an electronic organ, which is in the
middle of my living room. He said he bought it because the children need to be exposed to music. Well, the only person who
plays it is him [laughs]. At a young age he wanted to experience
music but he couldn't. Now, if the kids show the slightest interest in music, well, it feels really good to be able to provide that.
A lot of this buying has to do with our own satisfaction. When
you buy your child a bike and you're putting it together and putting on the stickers, you're reliving your childhood, and those
good feelings come back.

Thus, delighting children with material goods allows the parent to
reexperience the unfettered joy of childhood (or at least our version
of it). According to Cross, by the time we reach adulthood, we have
become jaded consumers who need much more than a pleasing trinket to send us over the moon. Gifting children also gives parents an
opportunity to rewrite their youth, this time with a more pleasing
ending. The longing to indulge children with treats and the desire to
protect them from too much advertising and consumption creates an
ongoing conflict for many of us.

As advertising beat the message that good parents seek to satisfy their children's desires through consumerism, the advice of
the parenting experts began to adopt a more permissive edge. The
counsel had softened considerably from Watson's cries not to
overindulge oneself or one's children. By the late 1940s, Dr. Ben-
jamin Spock had arrived on the scene. Instead of requiring strict
adherence to a schedule of rewards and consequences, Spock told
parents, "Trust yourself. You know more than you think you
do."[26] Spock championed intuitive parenting. To be in tune with
the needs and temperament of the child and to anticipate and respond appropriately to his needs would create the environment
necessary for each child to reach his full, unique potential. To encourage optimal growth in this new child-centered culture, experts encouraged parents to make good use of children's free time.
"Good use" translated into providing entertaining, educationally

useful opportunities for play and learning; much of this could be met through consumer products.

The prevailing theme of both child-rearing experts and the media in the twentieth century, while certainly not identical, highlighted children as the center of the family and called for parents to anticipate their needs and to facilitate healthy emotional development. Doing this might mean allowing children to express themselves more fully through less parent control or by preserving their natural wonder (thus ensuring good emotional growth) through purchasing material goods. Easy, right? Without the benefit of training, the job of parenting demands the expertise of a child psychologist, the nurturing attention of June Cleaver, the investigative skills of a Ralph Nader, and the bank account of Oprah Winfrey. It is no wonder that so many parents today feel such anxiety about making the right decisions: choosing just the right stroller, educational toys, clothing, computer software, college prep course, university education, graduate degree program, after-school program. . . . Theresa describes the anxiety that goes with making parenting decisions:

> There's a whole thing with the schools too, it's a whole consumerism thing. Even at the preschools, people are camping out, in some cases two nights! It comes from the parents, they get competitive about who's going to get there first . . . you totally get sucked into it, even if you think you're not going to do it . . . then you start thinking, "I'm not doing it and they are." The root of it is "Am I being a good parent? Am I not valuing his education? Will it affect his school career?"

Many parents feel the pressure of high expectations and can lose perspective on what's responsible parenting and what's over the line. I discuss this dilemma further in the next section.

CULTURE AND PARENTING

Gender roles have certainly changed over the last few generations. The other night, my husband and I watched the 1950s movie *How to*

Marry a Millionaire. When asked about her plans for marriage, the character played by Marilyn Monroe (who just happens to be a sexy, not-so-bright model) responds, "Of course, it's the ultimate goal for a woman." Marilyn Monroe's character aspired, along with her two roommates, to snag a rich husband so that she could avoid the humiliation of working for a living. Clearly attitudes about women in the workplace have undergone an enormous shift since the 1950s when Monroe and her colleagues set out to fulfill their womanly destinies. For one thing, the majority of women today work outside the home. This shift in work patterns represents a change primarily for middle- and upper-class women. For ethnic minority women and those struggling economically, work outside of the home has been commonplace for some time. For these women, work in the early days was less career development and personal enhancement and more survival. In the 1930s, for example, scores of African American women were employed primarily as domestics and earned 38 percent of a white woman's earnings; this—despite the fact that many more African American than white women worked.[27]

For the middle class, beginning around the 1950s, employment was re-conceptualized as an opportunity and an integral part of women's civil rights, the notion being that women's "work" goes beyond parenting and should include the choice to pursue gratifying careers. Since that time, married women's employment has doubled and two-parent working families are now the norm.[28]

As with all profound cultural shifts, changes in family work patterns bring both good news and bad news. Now women have more opportunities than ever to fulfill their desires for challenging, financially rewarding work. While they still earn less than men and are more likely to occupy less prestigious positions, women continue to make impressive gains. When I was a child, if someone mentioned a doctor or dentist, most people assumed that person was a male. To live at a time when female astronauts, fighter pilots, mechanics, coal miners, and secretaries of state inhabit a work world along with male nurses and stay-at-home dads represents a monumental transformation in notions of sex roles. Contemporary young women and men truly have a much broader range of role models from which to emulate.

Inevitably, complications accompany the richer, more satisfying work opportunities available today. Remember the Enjoli perfume ads of the 1970s? To paraphrase: "I can bring home the bacon. Fry it up in a pan. And never, ever let you forget you're a man." Call it what you will—a balancing act, the superwoman syndrome, having it all—cultural expectations for women loom high. In this culture, the challenge of finding balance typically falls to women. And the injunction to foster a successful career, to maintain a home, and to care for the husband and children can be crushing. The pressures and opportunities are not just on the women. Whereas previously the culture dictated that men just "bring home the bacon," now they are also expected to be sensitive caregivers more fully involved in the rearing of their children.

The evolution of work and parenting roles has influenced consumer behavior in modern families. Because parents simply don't have the time to take care of every household need, some responsibilities fall to the children. Today youngsters have great pull over shopping decisions, with some actually bearing the responsibility for doing the family shopping. Children's spending power tripled in the 1990s, through their influence over the family budget as well as over their own money.[29] This trend has implications for youngsters' physical and psychological health. In terms of physical health, commercial advertising has particular sway over children's desires for fast food and candy and can affect eating habits. This fact is quite concerning given the burgeoning problem of childhood obesity in the United States.[30] In terms of psychological development, unmonitored shopping by children can contribute to a materialistic orientation. Children who shop independently are less likely to learn from their parents about the importance of making good purchasing decisions and of not giving in to impulse or emotional spending. Finally, many overworked, overcommitted parents confess that they buy their children more treats. For some, exhaustion decreases their resistance to children's persistent requests for products. Other parents, feeling badly about spending less time with their youngsters, buy treats out of guilt.

Parenting by Guilt

One result of trying to squeeze career, parenting, marital, and personal responsibilities into one life is something that clinical psychologist Diane Ehrensaft calls "parenting by guilt."[31] In her book, *Spoiling Childhood*, Ehrensaft examined the experiences of predominantly middle-class families working in professional careers. According to Ehrensaft, hardworking parents who put in many hours on the job growing successful careers feel tremendous guilt about work obligations detracting from time spent with children. The notion of parenting by guilt probably feels familiar to most readers. To some extent, the guilt comes as a result of the huge increase in dual-earner families and the "culture of occupations."[32] Silicon Valley, for example, illustrates an intense work culture that encourages employees to virtually live where they work and equates success with burning the midnight oil. During the dot-com boom, when companies were flush with capital, some actually provided meals and nap rooms for employees who were expected to work through the night regularly.

Guilty parenting, then, results in part from the intense conflict between pursuing a successful career with its seemingly endless demands and the desire to devote more time, energy, and focus on one's children. Add to this mix the challenge of providing for a family economically in a culture that values consumption and material displays of success. Many individuals feel that in order to maintain a desired standard of living, both mom and dad must work. Recall the survey discussed in Chapter 1—even those earning $100,000 per year feel they cannot afford everything that they really "need." Americans' desired standard of living goes way beyond the basics. The financial pressures faced by so many families stems from both the high costs of living in this modern economy and a very generous interpretation of "necessity."

The notion of "quality time"—the idea that what matters for children's psychological well-being isn't so much the amount of time one spends with one's children but the quality of that time, even if it is discouragingly small—grew from the dual-career family dilemma. The creation of quality time helped to assuage the guilt many parents felt about shorting their children on family time. However, many modern, well-meaning, ambitious parents have interpreted quality time to mean make-the-most-of-every-second time. Families feel the pressure to fill children's spare hours with productive *and* fun activities. The pressure springs from several sources: themselves, the perceived judgments of other parents as well as cultural expectations to be an über-parent. Failure to live up to the edict of quality time again leads to defeat and feelings of inadequacy.

Parents, urged to make the most of time with their children, try to fill every moment with "meaningful" activities—no hanging about the house or playing outside in the street (which doesn't happen much anymore anyway). Under the doctrine of quality time, preferably organized educational or sports activities—trips to the museum or competitive play on the soccer team—are the more appropriate way to go.[33] Parenting magazines often feed the insecurity. Browsing some of the popular magazines for young parents, I notice ads for designer furniture, designer clothing for children (swimming suit $77; matching cover-up, $72), and "the activities"—music, dance, science, academic and gymnastics camps; art, swimming and ice-skating lessons; sports institutes, and more. Birthday parties have taken on a life of their own. The über-parent doesn't invite children over just to feed them cake and ice cream. Try throwing a theme party—clown and circus parties, magic shows, or the "wildlife experience." Organize a gala at the gymnastics studio, pony farm, or the pizza parlor/game center. Rent a jumping booth or materials to throw a carnival. Some parents believe that ever more elaborate parties encourage materialism:

> I don't like to have birthday parties because I don't want to have all of this new stuff coming into my house. So sometimes I'll tell

them you can have your friends over but we don't call it a birthday party because then they'll bring all this stuff. . . . My husband comes from a huge family of twelve kids so they didn't have birthday parties. And I grew up with five kids, but we just had the parties when we were little. I remember when I was in high school and all the materialism so I think too that's part of why I do this. We do things for the kids, we're not depriving them.

Theresa comments on the zeitgeist of activities:

The activities, that is, a whole consumer, materialistic thing. They cost a lot of money, as much as buying all the toys and all the stuff. . . . Everybody's got their kid in all these things, and you feel like if your kid is only in school, he's missing out, because his friends are taking this and his friends are doing that . . . . What I've decided to do is the kids can do two things a year, that way it's manageable. As a parent you want to give your kids every opportunity, but it's like, how many things can you fit into a week? And the expense! I feel more pressure about the activities than about buying too much stuff. And I feel bad because I worry I'm not spending enough time doing things for them.

Mandy reflects on the conflict that many experience between allowing children free time and providing them with enrichment opportunities:

We worry, should he be taking this lesson or is he getting enough of that? So-and-so is taking twelve different things. Are we giving him enough, are we taking him to enough museums, and so-and-so is doing all of that with her kid. It's that kind of keeping up that's difficult. Then you realize that you can't do everything. I realize that it's an internal pressure that I put on myself . . . his day is so organized; I would like to see him just have some downtime where he can come home and play on his own and he can figure out for himself what to do. It's a real push-pull.

Again, the directive to immerse children in enrichment experiences affects most parents. Those with the financial means can purchase these experiences, though they may feel the anxiety of not doing "enough" or the resentment of feeling pressured into keeping up with other families. Those without the means may feel as if they're failing their kids. As with other materialism-infused endeavors, practitioners come to believe that enough is never enough. Probably because of the stress of organizing meaningful time and taxiing kids to their various activities, many mothers do not rate family leisure time as particularly relaxing.[34] In addition, children today complain more and more, of being overloaded with both school and extracurricular activities. So, the quality of life for parent and child alike suffers from high expectations.

Many social scientists contend that the legacy of quality time has begotten overindulged, materialistic children. Parents feeling remorse over spending so much time away from their children and fueled by the desire for their children to feel loved and cared for indulge them with "guilt gifts." These parents make fewer demands on their youngsters; the least a parent can do for an overscheduled child who doesn't see her parents much is to ease up on asking her to wash the dishes, vacuum, or even keep her room clean, so the reasoning goes. Advertisers take full advantage of this guilt by hawking products guaranteed to improve one's parenting and create happy children to boot. Instead of letting their children sit with frustration, discontent, and anger, some overcommitted parents soothe their child's discomfort with a little something new. It's the mashed-potatoes-and-gravy approach to mental health. Parents also use material goods to maintain a presence in their child's life. One full-time career mom says:

> While I was at work I would buy these plastic toys on my lunch break. And I would give some to my mom (who cares for the children during the day) and I would take some home so I would feel as though I was still part of their child rearing. It was my way of micromanaging, like I'm still at home.

As this mother demonstrates, parenting, like other esteemed institutions, is interwoven with consumerism and materialism. Similar to the way that democracy equates with the power to buy, good parenting has become tied up with money, purchasing, and competition. And also, like democracy, the haves and the have-nots distinguish themselves through spending power: the power to purchase educational, social, and cultural enrichment and, most notably, to secure the promised good life in America.

Love and Money

My parents divorced when I was young, so for my sisters and me, precious time with Dad took on added excitement as it meant a trip to our favorite fast food restaurant for tacos and milk shakes. What a marvelous treat! I have delightful memories of making the ritual trek to Jack-in-the-Box with my father and sisters and then moving on to something fun like peewee golf or the park. Excursions to Jack-in-the-Box didn't happen every day; my father treated us to our beloved junk food only now and then. Regularly relying on material goods and treats to demonstrate love to a child, however, can have negative repercussions. Studies suggest that adults who say they were overindulged as children are more likely to feel entitled, to be self-absorbed, and to suffer from anxiety and depression.[35] Too much permissive parenting (overindulgence, not setting reasonable limits for children) increases the risk of raising youngsters who have difficulty delaying gratification, who never develop the value of working hard for what they want and feeling the satisfaction of a job well done.

Overindulgence can lead children to equate love with gifts.[36] Children can come to measure their worth by the pound; more toys means more loved. Fighting the love-equals-money credo is truly a formidable task. Messages abound, particularly in the media, confirming the idea that when someone truly loves us, they aren't shy with the gifts. Recently I saw a newspaper advertisement that read "Wife Insurance" accompanied by a photo of a big, fat diamond ring.[37] Apparently gifting one's spouse with pricey items helps to insure a long and loving marriage. Children also learn that love equals money from many sources: advertising, movies and television, and when parents lavish them with treats and gifts. I know I have created a potential guilt moment here. Don't use this information to add to your guilt pot; use it to heighten your awareness of why and how often you might treat your children to special things. Are the gifts intended to compensate for perceived deficiencies—time with you or the stress of an overloaded life? Or is a little something special just that—special?

Having It All? The Wealthy

Research on affluent families shows that material wealth coupled with parental absence can lead to discontent among children. Wealthy youth are only now beginning to receive attention from researchers, in part because many people presume that rich kids do not, or should not, have any "real" problems. This assumption taps into a core belief to which many ascribe, whether implicitly or explicitly: Money leads to greater happiness. The research presents an alternate view of wealth and happiness. In some studies, when compared with children from low socioeconomic situations, affluent children report greater stress, anxiety, depression, and substance use.[38] How can this be?

It seems that the same circumstances that provide affluent children with advantages can also make life a pressure cooker. Many of these children feel isolated in their own families, partly because of a full slate of extracurricular activities, parents' demanding career obligations, and the belief by some elders that time on one's own breeds self-reliance in young people.[39] The few studies conducted so far reveal the complexity of privileged children's lives. Many of these adolescent youngsters are unsupervised by any adult during after-school hours yet yearn for a closer relationship with their parents.[40] This finding is particularly troubling as closeness with parents—both physical and psychological—is associated with emotional well-being among children and adolescents.[41] New research also finds that closeness with parents relates *inversely* to income; that is, more wealth equals a less intimate relationship with Mom and Dad. This fact helps to explain, in part, why affluent adolescents left unsupervised experience more anxiety and depression and engage in more delinquent behavior and substance abuse than those children who spend more time with their parents. Children need the security of a close relationship with their parents to help them to make good decisions.

Many affluent children grow up in a subculture of high expectations. These children hold very high standards for their academic achievement and future career goals and feel pressure from their parents and from themselves for superior performance. The culture of the wealthy can be highly competitive; parents expect only the best from their children. One researcher writes that: "faced with unrelenting pressures to excel (to be average is tantamount to having failed), many children develop stress-related symptoms such as insomnia, stomachaches, headaches, anxiety, and depression . . . some youngsters come to exaggerate the slightest of health problems to attain 'acceptable' routes out of competing with others."[42]

What does academic pressure look like? For a high school student, it means enrolling in the most challenging courses and being satisfied only with perfection; focusing on grades and other accolades at the expense of actual learning; aiming for admittance into only the most prestigious colleges—anything less is unacceptable; cramming one's schedule with extracurricular activities in the hopes of improving one's chances of college admission. Please note that I am not condemning high standards or lofty goals. High standards become a problem for youngsters when only perfection suffices and when goals exist solely to gain status and the approval of others. Under these conditions, children risk emotional, social, and physical difficulties. Youngsters yearn for parental pride and acceptance regardless of the grades they bring home or the accolades they receive for outperforming others. They long to be loved and accepted for who they are, not for their accomplishments. Too much money is not the culprit here; rather it is the ethos of a culture (or at least some of those in the culture) that overvalues status and money.

Readers of all income levels can benefit from the research on affluence and children's well-being. The story so far suggests that when parents, acting out of guilt over less time spent than they'd like with their children, are more permissive in terms of setting and following through on limits, children suffer in the long run. Most relevant to this discussion are when money, material goods, or other treats get used to assuage guilt and calm children's distress. Under this scenario, children run the risk of not learning to value working for and saving money, for delaying gratification and developing self-discipline. They also may come to confuse love with money. The next quote from a local high school paper characterizes the dilemma of wealth and responsibility: "Some teenagers do not comprehend what it means to work for one's money. They become accustomed to lifestyles in which the parents do not set any expectations for their children to be fiscally aware or responsible. . . . Whether it is CDs, clothing, gas, food or a new iPod, there is a gap between necessity and frivolity that is bridged by some [city] teenagers who have neither past recollections nor future concerns of being financially unstable."[43]

Extraordinarily wealthy children face a particularly intense challenge of building character and identity. Jamie Johnson, an heir to the Johnson & Johnson pharmaceutical empire, produced and directed a documentary film on the unique predicament of the super rich.[44] Johnson interviewed several wealthy scions, one of whom was Josiah Hornblower, heir to the Vanderbilt/Whitney fortune. Hornblower says that too much money can overwhelm children: "I remember when I was a little kid my mom let me spend the day with my Uncle and he took me to Grand Central Station and he said this is yours [laughing]. I mean, it's just the worst thing. And he just took me all around New York saying 'yes we own this.' It's the dumbest thing in the world to do to a kid." According to Hornblower, the best, most satisfying time in his life came from work where he learned that "working hard makes me feel good."

Some evidence indicates that the relationship between academic pressure and isolation from parents and emotional problems manifests itself postpuberty. In one of the few studies examining this issue, Suniya Luthar and Chris Sexton at Columbia University found that the emotional and behavioral difficulties of affluent sixth graders were within the normal range.[45] By seventh grade however, youngsters began to report such problems as alcohol abuse (7 percent of seventh grade boys, for example, admitted drinking enough alcohol to become intoxicated), declines in grades, aggressive behavior and depression (for girls, twice the national norm). This research suggests that the optimal period for parents to really attend to the amount and type of time spent with their children and the level of expectations set for them is before puberty sets in and problems start to arise.

A note on the research presented here on affluence and child development. For the most part, these investigations have focused on Caucasian children. Very little information is available on middle class and wealthy ethnic minority youngsters. While one might expect that ethnic minority youth experience similar circumstances as Caucasian youth, other unique factors must also apply. For example, in well-to-do communities, ethnic minority youth typically represent a very small fraction of the student population. Research has shown that issues of acceptance and fitting in and cultural identity influence their self-esteem and school performance.[46]

SUMMARY

The definition of "good parenting" has evolved over time to encompass a more permissive stance and a greater reliance on material goods. The embrace of behavior modification as a parenting tool has increased the use of products as a way of influencing children's behavior. However, overuse of this method can have deleterious effects. Research shows that an overdependence on material goods to shape behavior can decrease intrinsic motivation and foster materialism in children. The cultivation of materialism is further stimulated by media messages that good parenting can be achieved through the purchase of consumer goods.

The increase of affluence in this country has implications for many two-parent working families. When two parents work to achieve both a comfortable life and personal fulfillment, they run the risk of sacrificing time with their children, which leads to guilt, which might lead to overindulgence and permissive limit setting. If this isn't enough, the guilt dilemma resides in a culture where success and regard equate with "the externals"—wealth, belongings, good schools, high-powered careers. Like their parents, children also feel the burden of cultural expectations; some translate these expectations into perfectionist expectations for academic and extracurricular performance.

Embracing quality time for some parents translates into frenzied time—trying to make every moment count by filling family free time with quality activities. What suffers here are mellow moments spent chatting over dinner or tossing a ball after work. June, a single working mother of three, works hard to find downtime with her two daughters:

> No matter how busy we are, we have tea time everyday. We talk about what happened during our day; this is how I've been able to teach my daughters not to be passive, to speak up, to be honest, to respect others, and to share the earth.

Whether you find space in your week for teatime, Sunday brunch, or sharing Gatorade and shooting some hoops, the investment is well worth the time. It may be that cookies and tea reaps greater rewards than adding another activity to the resume.

CHAPTER 3

WHY DO WE DO IT?

Part of doing research for this book involved me going "undercover" to get the real life stories. In my capacity as an undercover snoop, I eavesdropped on conversations in department store dressing rooms, restaurants, shops, museum exhibitions, on the streets and at the malls. What did I hear? Gaggles of teenage girls discussing the sweatpants and the really cute peasant top that they just *have* to buy. Sophisticated, upwardly mobile professionals sharing tales of their latest real estate acquisition, remodeled bathroom, or trip to Europe. Too-cool young boys describing their footwear as "off the hook." I learned that practically everybody, regardless of economic circumstances, thinks about, talks about, dreams about stuff—the stuff they have and the stuff they hope to own in the future.

It seems that everyone has caught the materialism bug. This chapter explores two themes related to "the bug." First, I examine the origins of materialistic desire. Like many life values, materialism springs from both family and cultural influences. Of course, culture covers a lot of ground; it can include one's ethnic and racial membership, gender, neighborhood, school, media, and more. Among many things, culture informs individuals' values and priorities. It is manifested in how we spend our time and money (and in what we talk about on the streets and in department store dressing rooms). Here

I concentrate on the contributions of family and ethnicity to materialistic attitudes. I discuss contributions from the media in Chapter 4.

Second, I consider how the materialistic orientation impacts the emotional well-being of both individuals and communities. Many people believe to some degree that material comforts and contentment go hand in hand. For instance, consider our society's idolatry of wealth and fame. Many youngsters manifest this idolatry by emulating the clothing and lifestyles of their favorite celebrities. For some, this behavior stems from the belief that expensive clothing and accoutrements will create positive self-esteem, garner the admiration and acceptance of others, and ultimately bring happiness. But does money truly bring happiness, or is there a catch? For some youngsters, certain life circumstances can increase their reliance on materialism as an antidote to unhappiness. I refer to the circumstances that can increase children's vulnerability to materialism as the "forces of materialism." At the end of the chapter, I introduce the five forces that will be the focus of Chapters 4, 5, and 6.

THE ORIGINS OF DESIRE

Whether one characterizes materialism as evil or an asset depends partly on one's family and larger cultural background. An individual's culture can serve as either a breeding ground or a respite from consumerism. How much you spend, what you buy, who you shop with—people's buying habits are strongly influenced by culture. And not just American culture or ethnic background, but the more intimate, palpable culture of childhood. Early experiences stay with us and, with or without our knowledge, shape our views on acquisition. How did you learn to shop? Were your parents practical shoppers, planning ahead before making a purchase, getting in and out of the store with only the budgeted items in hand? Or was a day at the mall a chance to spend treasured time with Mom or Dad, and maybe an opportunity to splurge? Shopping behavior, in part, reflects lessons learned from parents.[1] The parents whom I interviewed cited their own parents as significantly shaping their views on acquisition. Lisette learned about shopping from her mother:

> I came from an immigrant family. My mom came from —, where she grew up in a village on a hill, country people, in a one-room shack. If you wanted to go to the bathroom, you had to go to the outhouse. They had one telephone for the village. And when she came to the United States she was overwhelmed by all the wealth! She got a job at sixteen years old and was able to buy things, and she's always been very good with money . . . . My father was raised in a poor family in the South. I grew up in San Francisco, and my parents tried to provide everything for the kids. My dad was always looking for age-appropriate toys and educational toys. When we wanted something, they went out of their way to get it for us, but they were always reasonable, they'd also say no a lot. I notice now that I spend money on the kids by buying all of the educational enrichment stuff . . . and sometimes I go a little overboard with it. But it feels okay because it's helping them to learn.

Observing the way her mother approached money management influenced Lisette's spending priorities with her children. Trudy learned about frugality from her immigrant parents:

> I grew up in a lower-middle-class family. My parents were immigrants from Italy, my father was a gardener. We had what we needed and pretty much nothing beyond that. You worked as soon as you could. There were very few extras that my father could afford. If you wanted to go to college, you paid the tuition, you got yourself a job. There was no going off to Cal and having the collegiate experience. I worked full time and I went to school at night. If I earned enough money I handed some of it over. There were no privileges beyond the basics. Having come from that kind of an upbringing and marrying into wealth, I have seen both sides of the fence. I like nice things and I will spend money on them. But I'll spend money on something classic that will last a long time. This purse I've had for years. I'm not one to go out and just shop and spend lots of money.

Research confirms that parents' attitudes toward and behaviors regarding acquisition can take root in their offspring. Materialistic parents tend to raise materialistic children.[2] In one study, investigators found that materialistic-oriented children agreed with such statements as, "I'd rather spend time buying things, than doing almost anything else," "I have fun just thinking of all the things I own," and "I'd rather not share my snacks with others if it means I'll have less for myself."[3] These children loved to shop, and their parents considered them experts on brand names and on the best products to buy. The materialistic-oriented youngsters also expected their parents to pony up; these children looked forward to receiving high-priced items from their parents for their birthday or for Christmas. As with their youngsters, the parents of these acquisitive children also scored high on the materialism scale, agreeing with such statements as "I would be much happier if I had more money to buy more things for myself" and "I would put up with a job that was less interesting if I was paid more money." Other studies have also identified parent attitudes as contributors to children's beliefs about wealth and consumption. For instance, mothers who value financial success raise children with similar values.[4] The overall picture suggests that children learn more than just shopping habits from their parents. They learn about the complicated relationships between owning things and self-worth and identity. The lessons culled from materialistic parents have implications for career, relationships, emotional well-being, and more. Children can learn that expressions of love come in the form of goods and services. They can acquire the belief that dressing well or owning expensive things smooths the way to greater happiness and the esteem of society. They can develop the belief that the purpose of work is not to foster interest or to demonstrate talent but to make money.

The attitude that status and luxury hold the key to happiness can shape the goals children set for themselves, the activities they pursue, and the friends whom they seek out. When asked about their hopes for the future, consumption-focused youngsters consider financial success to be more important than independence and control of their lives, over time spent with friends and family, and over efforts to improve the community.[5] This financially driven youngster might be the adult who works eighty hours a week at a job he hates in order to support an expensive lifestyle. Experiencing a lack of control over one's life translates into unhappiness. Parents who value financial success for their children *over* goals such as self-esteem, autonomy, and a fulfilling family life are more likely to raise children who might be financially successful but emotionally bereft.[6]

In addition to parent attitudes, parenting styles also contribute to children's materialistic values. Parents who display warmth and acceptance toward their children, who have high expectations for their behavior, and who set and follow through on limits rear less materialistic children. The term "authoritative parenting" refers to a style of raising children that emphasizes both warmth and control. In a host of studies, children of authoritative parents report superior social and academic competence and greater feelings of independence relative to children subjected to other parenting styles.[7] For instance, children of authoritative parents tend to steer clear of drugs and exhibit fewer behavior problems. In contrast, parenting styles that emphasize strict adherence to authority without warmth (*authoritarian*) or that accentuate warmth and acceptance without rules or limits (*permissive*) tend to result in less positive outcomes for youngsters. Children of authoritarian parents display less adeptness at independent decision making, show greater conformity to social expectations, and experience greater anxiety and depression. Permissive parenting can result in a child with poor self-control, disappointing academic performance, and greater involvement in drugs and other problem behaviors. These parenting typologies apply most closely to middle-class Caucasian families.[8] Effective parenting styles vary based on culture and/or life circumstance. For example, in some Asian American families, a parenting style based on Confucian principles that emphasizes "the importance of hard work, self-discipline, and obedience" has been shown to facilitate academic success in young people.[9] For families living in dangerous, high-crime areas, it might be inappropriate to foster curiosity, independence, and friendliness in one's children. A more adaptive stance would be to inculcate obedience and self-protection.

How does parenting style relate to materialism? Authoritative parents interact with and communicate more with their children. Part of this increased interaction includes more discussions on consumerism. Greater dialogue, along with limit setting and monitoring, give children a more prudent perspective on consumption. These parents talk with their children about the goals and tactics of advertisers. They monitor their youngsters' television consumption. They shop with their children and solicit their opinions on purchasing decisions.[10] Of course parents do not have to adopt an authoritative approach in order to raise consumer-smart children. All parents, regardless of their preferred style, can protect their youngsters by involving themselves in their children's lives: monitoring their activities, modeling rational shopping behaviors, and discussing issues related to acquisition. Lynette describes how she confronts consumerism:

> When we watch cartoons on Saturday morning and a commercial comes on the girls will say, "Oh, look, they're trying to make us buy that." When we used to watch *Barney* and *Sesame Street* when they were young, I'd talk with them about how commercials are trying to get you to buy things. Now they're pretty good at it. I can't think of a time now when they ask for things they've seen on TV.

Through the interviews and discussions with colleagues and friends, I have noticed that dialogue about consumerism and materialism is not the norm in some families. Few of the individuals I interviewed, for example, actually initiated conversations about materialistic desire or impulse buying. Some parents hoped to teach their children about these issues by modeling responsible consumer behavior. Others evidenced a reactive rather than a proactive stance. For instance, one mother I talked with said that her son learns that "he can't have everything he wants when we're shopping and I tell him no." Several parents practice "pre-shopping warning" systems, where they inform their children before they go to the market that "we're buying for other people today, not ourselves." All of these methods can help youngsters to learn responsible consumerism and perhaps even about managing materialistic desire. However, as the research suggests, a more direct approach is most effective.

Beyond the culture of the family, an individual's race and ethnicity can influence beliefs about acquisition and ownership. In the United States, people from many ethnic backgrounds hold a variety of beliefs about consumption. While all of us, in general, see the same media and the same materialistic messages, the culture to which we belong filters and interprets the information differently. Take the message, for example, that a treat is an appropriate way to mark a mood—perhaps a pretty sweater to compensate for a really bad day or new shoes to celebrate finishing a project. Media celebrates the impulse buy—unplanned purchases made based on one's mood, an enticing advertisement, or even because a peer brought a desirable item to school one day. Impulse buying generates an estimated $4.2 billion a year in revenue.[11] Clearly an important source of income for businesses, advertisers pull out all the stops in an attempt to get people to buy on impulse. Take a look at teen magazines. Headlines that trumpet "Get the season's must haves now!" clearly try to goad youngsters into rushing out to buy the latest.

Whether one indulges in an impulse purchase depends, in part, on one's cultural membership. The degree to which a culture is *collectivist* or *individualistic* can shape one's beliefs about spur-of-the-moment purchases. Collectivism emphasizes preserving harmony among group members, putting the needs of the group before individual concerns, and maintaining loyalty to one's kin. Maintaining harmony extends to emotional displays. Children, for example, might be encouraged to control negative emotions in order to preserve goodwill in relationships. A person's life goals and values in these societies center more on benefits to family and community rather than individual éclat. Cultures with a stronger focus on loyalty and group welfare include communities from Mexico, China, and India.[12]

Individualistic cultures stress the importance of personal rights and the prerogative to make choices based on a person's own needs over group concerns.[13] People living in individualistic cultures usually feel less loyalty to any one group; they are also more likely to describe feelings of alienation. This is manifested when Americans, for example, complain of a lack of community feeling in their neighborhoods. Western countries such as the United States and Britain accentuate individualistic values. In these countries, one is likely to see competition and personal achievement rewarded. Of course, the United States is a multicultural nation and not all Americans harbor individualistic values. Families living in the United States whose cultural heritage descends from collectivist groups may still preserve values of group loyalty. The 2002 film *Real Women Have Curves* provides a fitting example of the conflict that can ensue when collectivist culture and individual needs clash. In the film, the teenage heroine, a Mexican American youngster, wants to leave home to attend college. The needs of her family, however, dictate that she stay home to work in the family business. The girl goes through tremendous emotional conflict and suffers her mother's rejection before deciding to attend college. The film illustrates that people maintain elements of both individualism and collectivism. Various cultures highlight some values more than others.

Research demonstrates that people from highly collectivist groups give in less frequently to impulse buys compared to those from individualistic societies. One reason might be that collectivist individuals consider more seriously how an extra expenditure might impact the family. An American youngster might be shopping with friends, for instance, and decide to blow the paycheck from her part-time job on CDs and clothing. She's not likely to consider how the purchase might affect the financial circumstances of her family. Indeed, research on American adolescents and work confirms that most youngsters, particularly those from the middle class, spend money from after school jobs on themselves.[14]

Collectivist values are associated with less impulsive spending. Researchers asked college students from the United States, Australia, Singapore, Malaysia, and Hong Kong about their impulsive buying behavior.[15] The United States and Australia represented individualistic societies, and Singapore, Malaysia and Hong Kong represented collectivist groups. The students completed a survey on attitudes about shopping. An individual identified as an impulsive shopper would agree with statements such as "When I see something that really interests me, I buy it without considering the consequences" as opposed to "I avoid buying things that are not on my shopping list."[16] The students from individualistic cultures admitted to more impulse buying than those from collectivist cultures. Even students from Hong Kong, a collectivist culture, showed less impulse purchasing, despite living in an area replete with shopping opportunities. Although they are surrounded by commerce, these young people show less inclination to give into their spur-of-the-moment acquisitive urges.

Studies on culture and consumption suggest that ethnicity and family have a tremendous impact on consumer behaviors such as spending patterns and attitudes about money management. This fact implies that despite the strong presence of materialism in the society, parents can still have a significant impact on children's behaviors and attitudes about spending. However, while inculcating collectivist values might keep individuals from impulse buying, it does not prevent them from harboring materialistic values. Teens from some collectivist cultures enjoy shopping just as American youth do. Teens in Japan and China, primarily collectivist cultures, spend millions of dollars per year on material goods.[17] Cultural norms appear to influence the *reasons* that young people crave belongings. For example, one hypothesis contends that purchases in collectivist societies reflect desires for group membership rather than individual identity. Specifically, social conformity drives the acquisitive desires of some collectivist youngsters, while expression of one's individuality drives the purchases of individualistic youth. A collectivist-oriented teen might buy bright purple socks because all her friends own them. An individualistic adolescent might buy the socks to reflect his own unique personality.

To test the notion that culture influences the meanings ascribed to material goods, investigators examined beliefs about wealth and materialism among Japanese, Chinese, and American teenagers.[18] Asian youth more readily agreed that owning the "right" things is crucial. According to the study's authors, the notion of owning the right things stems from Confucian societal beliefs that stress the importance of social harmony and common goals: "The young teen is intensely focused on being appropriate, and she negotiates the path by testing on friends what's leaned in the media—discovering who she is by what her friends like—to wear, to hear and to buy."[19] American youth purchased items as a means of self-expression. These youth overwhelming agreed that one's possessions reflect identity. A fitting example of the study findings comes from three preteens I observed shopping in a department store. One girl held up a multicolored sweatshirt jacket and exclaimed that, "Oh my god, this is sooo cute!" Her friend responded, by "It's funny looking. It's just not me." I was surprised by this girl's willingness to disagree with her friend. Clearly conformity, at least as applied to velour sweatsuits, was not required for group acceptance. The phrase "It's just not me" also implies that clothing for this young woman served to reflect how she viewed herself. It is important to keep in mind that research points out general differences in culture. Clearly, American teens are influenced by peer opinions. Likewise, American youngsters from families with collectivist values still care about forging an identity and about personal success. However, issues of personality and self-expression through material goods appear to play a bigger role for individualistic teens than they do for collectivist youth. This individualistic perspective on ownership and identity calls to mind an advertisement that provides a less than definitive answer to the question of "Who am I?": "It's not your handbag. It's not your neighborhood. It's not your boyfriend. It's your watch that tells most about who you are."

Thus, children learn about shopping and absorb attitudes about materialism from multiple sources. Parents' attitudes about financial success, their shopping behaviors, and their child-rearing styles all communicate messages to youngsters about how to regard the material world. In addition, aspects of ethnic background can impact both shopping behaviors and the meanings that material goods have for children. Parents can make use of this information by increasing self-awareness of their own consumer behaviors. Do you spend time discussing consumption-related issues? How do you define success and achievement with your youngsters? What consumer behaviors do you model for your children? Consider these questions to start exploring this issue for yourself:

- What kind of shopper are you? Do you emphasize the importance of saving, the joys of shopping, or do you fall somewhere in between?
- Are you an involved parent? Do you know who your children shop with or hang out with? Do you have rules for your children's behavior, and do you follow through on them? Children with warm, involved parents score lower on materialism scales than those with uninvolved parents.
- How often do you discuss issues related to money management, shopping, and materialistic desires with your child? Even young children can benefit from these types of conversations. Consider informal or formal discussions about the importance of responsible shopping. What are the consequences for irresponsible spending? Explore with children the feelings and circumstances associated with materialistic desire. Children need to understand, for example, that when they don't give in to the impulse purchase, they do survive, and the feeling eventually passes.
- Do you and your children know the people in your neighborhood? Do you involve yourself in efforts to help those in need? Research on collectivism suggests that living by the

mantra "Do what's best for you" might encourage reckless spending and self absorption.

WHERE'S THE HARM?

I recently read a newspaper article arguing that materialism keeps our nation economically productive. Without people constantly buying things, the author reasoned, businesses would fail and the economy would stall. The economy does depend on consumerism. Companies and advertisers know that stock values rest on the ability to generate huge demands for brand-name products[20]. And social and political observers argue that the means to purchase helps to frame this country as a democracy. Armed with a willingness to work hard, anyone—theoretically—can take advantage of the opportunity to achieve financial success and buy in to the good life. Perhaps the call to simplify our lives and to rid ourselves of excess belongings is shortsighted and overly simplistic. Beyond a benefit to the economy, can materialistic predilections actually enhance one's life?

Child development studies indicate that material goods *can* help children to express their burgeoning identities. Merchandise such as posters, music, and clothing serve to publicize youngsters' likes and dislikes and their membership in particular peer groups. At any school, the groups have names like the jocks, the brains, and the populars. However, a *materialistic orientation* is associated with negative consequences for children's social and emotional well-being. Remember, a materialistic orientation refers to making consumption central to one's life and equating possessions with worth.

Youngsters who admire such characteristics as owning costly possessions and wearing expensive clothes report more anxiety, low self-worth, insecurity, and social problems.[21] Some of these emotional difficulties may arise from family factors. Children with divorced parents and those from homes with high amounts of conflict report greater materialism than children from calmer, two-parent families.[22] In addition, children who perceive their mothers to be cold, uncaring, and controlling endorse materialistic values more than those who perceive their homes as warm and loving.[23] This line of research findings reveal a pattern of adverse circumstances leading to greater materialism. One explanation for this finding is that when children do not form secure attachments to their parents, they look for other ways to obtain security and self-esteem. One problem, however, with relying on money and material possessions for self-esteem and contentment is that it simply doesn't work.

Adopting materialistic goals for one's life impacts the potential for personal growth in addition to emotional health. For example, in one study, college students reported on their sense of personal well-being and on their aspirations for financial success.[24] Several factors comprised the personal well-being measure. *Self-actualization*—the drive to optimize personal growth and self awareness, to be fully authentic, and to resist conformity—has long been considered one of the key steps towards enlightenment (and, as part of the package, true bliss). Researchers measured the drive toward enlightenment through questionnaire items such as "It is better to be yourself than to be popular." They next assessed the students' vitality—what the French call joie de vivre. A vital person wakes up loving life, eager to face a new day. Most of us don't feel fully vital every waking moment (at least not those we care to spend time with), but hopefully people feel that joie de vivre some of the time. Students also described the importance of relationships in their lives and their feelings of responsibility to their communities. Finally, participants reported on their levels of anxiety and depression. Researchers also measured financial aspirations—the importance young people place on career status and wealth.

The study's primary finding speaks to the importance of nonmaterial goals in shaping an emotionally satisfying life. Those students who considered the pursuit of financial success to be the most important aim in their life suffered from more depression and anxiety and realized less self-actualization than those with more humanistic aspirations. Apparently, the lust for money ultimately brings fewer rewards than a love of family, community, and personal growth.

This is not an isolated finding. A host of studies have linked materialism to less happiness, life satisfaction, and self-actualization, to more antisocial behaviors and to greater envy, narcissism, and low self-esteem.[25] Siddhartha, the main character in the Herman Hesse novel explains, that the single-minded pursuit of one goal causes people to miss out on life:

> "When someone is seeking," said Siddhartha, "it happens quite easily that he only sees the thing that he is seeking; that he is unable to find anything, unable to absorb anything, because he is only thinking of the thing he is seeking, because he has a goal, because he is obsessed with his goal. Seeking means: to have a goal; but finding means: to be free, to be receptive, to have no goal."[26]

Individuals so concerned with financial success may be ignoring the very things that could bring them greater happiness.

In addition to individual well-being and personal growth, materialism has negative implications for community and environment. From a community perspective, overconsumption devastates our ecology. The discarded computers, television sets, once-coveted toys, and rejected furniture clog landfills; the proliferation of more and more automobiles and the dependence on oil to run them compromise wildlife sanctuaries and muddy the air. Mihaly Csikszentmihalyi, who has written widely on consumption and motivation, says: "Recent calculations suggest that if the rest of the world's population was to develop a lifestyle approaching that of the United States or of Western Europe, at least two additional planets such as ours would have to be harnessed to provide the required energy and materials . . . since at this time we have no access to two spare planets to exploit, we should look more closely at what leads us to consume."[27] Raising children's awareness of community and environment will reap benefits beyond protecting the earth. Some research suggests that individuals scoring high on materialism scales are more self-centered and less concerned about the welfare of others, their communities, and the earth. In a series of studies, college students imagined that they had $20,000.[28] They could spend the money in six ways: buy things for themselves, donate to a charity, give or lend money to loved ones, travel, pay off debts, save the money, or use it for some other reason. Researchers also measured students' materialistic attitudes. High materialists were those who considered possessions to be critical to their happiness and who valued financial security over values such as warm relationships. Compared with those low in materialism, high materialists spent more of the fantasy cash on themselves and much less on conservation efforts, charity, or friends. This study implies that nurturing children's concern for community and the environment might encourage them to "get outside of themselves" by showing them that life extends beyond their own concerns. As adults, these children might show more willingness to contribute toward preserving the planet.

The picture presented so far indicates that a materialistic orientation reaps few long-term benefits to children's social and emotional well-being. Many youngsters (and adults) cling to the belief that happiness depends on what and how much they own. This tenacity can lead to an endless spiral of buying. An individual makes a new purchase and experiences the momentary good feeling that comes with a new possession. Their insecurity, depression, or anxiety begins to creep its way back into the person's life, and another buy becomes necessary in order to feel good. Individuals continue this buying spiral in part because they haven't discovered the things that do make them secure and happy. If dogged pursuit of wealth does not bring lasting contentment, what does? Lucky for us, many paths lead to happiness. For some it's the "minor ecstasies" that can bring joy: "gardening, hiking in the wilderness, holding an infant, watching a sunrise or sunset, cooking a terrific meal, coming home to the companionship of family, listening to favorite music . . . having tea and cookies with an elderly grandma. . . ."[29]

In addition, to the minor ecstasies, research shows that particular life circumstances link with greater happiness. It seems that the seven dwarfs did get it right when they sang "whistle while we work." Challenging, absorbing work does point the way toward a more satisfying life. Fulfilling work does not necessarily depend on income or status. Individuals engaged in pursuits as varied as manning the assembly line, teaching, performing surgery, or learning in school all report great satisfaction on the job compared with those employed in unsatisfying work. Inspiring a love of work in children and adolescents is more important now than ever. Many teenagers who work in after-school or summer jobs report a "relatively unenjoyable and unhappy experience."[30] The feelings may be due, in part, to the types of jobs teenagers tend to hold. Typically these positions include babysitting, working at fast food restaurants or retail establishments, and doing lawn work and manual labor.[31] In many of these positions, youngsters have few opportunities to interact with adults or to learn challenging new skills. Adolescents "are developing rather negative images of work. Even though everyone agrees that work is important to one's future, it is still, by and large, felt to be depressing and dull."[32] Chapter 6 discusses in more depth the importance of fulfilling work and play to positive emotional health.

Quality relationships also contribute to happiness and well-being. Diverse literatures have found that close friendships and intimate relationships enhance the joy of living and protect people from illness and emotional ennui. Child development experts have long known that children with close friends fare much better emotionally and socially than more isolated children. Studies chronicling children's lives from early youth through adolescence and adulthood attest to the power of friendships in youngsters' lives. In one study, investigators examined the friendships of fifth graders.[33] As young adults, those individuals who enjoyed close friendships in the fifth grade described themselves as more socially competent than their friendless counterparts. Enjoying childhood friendships produced adults with greater self-worth and feelings of competence in both work and social life and higher aspirations for future career success. In addition, befriended youth suffered from less depression and psychopathology than their socially challenged cohorts. Quality friendships also have implications for materialism. Youngsters who value and put effort into maintaining relationships rely less on materialistic values to provide support and meaning in their lives.

The ability to maintain positive relationships can actually distinguish between happy and unhappy people. In another study, investigators identified what they called "very happy people" by asking college students to nominate likely suspects.[34] These very happy people did not necessarily leap joyously through life; they experienced down days just like everyone else. However, they rarely reported strong negative emotions, such as profound sadness or anxiety. Happy students spent little time alone, enjoyed highly satisfying social relationships, and tended to be outgoing. Unhappy youth, however, reported poor, unsatisfying relationships. Friendships provide the support that individuals need tolerate negative experiences and emotions without sinking into depression or turning to material goods to soothe distress.

It is not just the quantity of friendships that facilitates well-being. The quality of one's relationships can bear on both well-being and materialistic attitudes. The psychologist Tim Kasser found that college students who scored high on a materialism scale maintained short-lived relationships.[35] These young people competed more intensely with their friends and believed in resolving grievances through aggression or revenge. Other studies on materialism have discovered the same thing: Children with materialist values report feeling more alienated and disconnected from their peers than children low in materialistic values.[36] Do lonely, less socially confident children turn to material goods in an attempt to bolster their self-esteem and make themselves more attractive to their peers? Or do some children succumb to the false promises of materialism and direct their efforts toward consumption rather than making and sustaining friendships? Researchers do not know, at this point, which comes first, materialism or relationship woes. However, for concerned parents, the important aspect of this research is the idea that attention to children's relationships can help attenuate the influence of materialism.

Other life circumstances, such as civil rights, freedom from poverty, and religious faith, also go arm and arm with psychological well-being. Intuitively, one might expect that life in a country that tolerates diverse political and social views makes for a more pleasant existence than life in an oppressive society, and the research confirms this. Freedom from poverty also contributes to emotional well-being. For example, people living in very poor, undeveloped countries report less happiness than those from more affluent countries.[37] Within the United States, poor people are slightly less happy than the wealthy.[38]

The freedom to practice one's religion is a particularly important element to happiness. A religious practice and spiritual beliefs facilitate well-being. In my family, all the children attended religious schooling every Saturday and church on Sundays. I suppose my mother, a single parent of three spirited girls, was on to something when she dragged her whining daughters to weekly services. Youngsters who undertake some form of religious worship several times a week report greater happiness and endorse fewer materialistic attitudes than those who attend services infrequently.[39] The advantages of spiritual involvement go beyond participation in an organized religion. Spirituality, or holding the belief that a force greater than oneself exists, brings social and emotional rewards. Teenagers who experience spiritual well-being benefit from higher self-esteem and a lower incidence of mental illness compared with those who report low levels of spiritual well-being. I discuss spirituality and materialism in Chapter 7.

In sum, a number of life circumstances contribute to happiness and emotional well-being in children. Meaningful work, relationships, freedom from poverty, civil rights, and spiritual beliefs all have the potential to buffer youngsters from the powerful influence of materialism. Youngsters need these buffers; in this society, materialism represents a constant and potent force to vulnerable youngsters grappling with social, emotional, and physical changes. In the next section, I describe the five forces of materialism that have particular relevance for children and adolescents.

THE FORCES OF MATERIALISM

The forces of materialism represent specific circumstances that increase young people's vulnerability to developing a materialistic orientation. Force number one, the Mimic, uses humans' natural tendency to imitate other people to create materialistic desire. The force directs youngster's attention toward consumer-oriented images in the media or materialistic models in their communities, trumpeting the message that "everybody does it and so should you." Imagine for instance, a child watching her favorite television program. The Mimic might encourage the child to emulate the actors' expensive clothing and lifestyle. It tries to convince children that mimicking materialistic images will ensure popularity, success, happiness, self-esteem, and more. The Mimic is described in Chapter 4.

The second force, the Comparer, exerts particular influence on preteens and teens at a stage in life when conformity and social comparison become paramount. In their efforts to forge feelings of competence and a positive self-concept, these youngsters evaluate themselves relative to their friends and to other children in an effort to gain peer acceptance. Youngsters use social comparison to answer questions such as "How do I stack up compared to other kids?" "Am I am as pretty, smart, or as talented as other people?" Social comparison helps youngsters to establish their place in the culture and provides goals to strive for and role models to emulate. However, children who lack confidence are particularly susceptible to the influences of peers and other role models. The Comparer encourages these children to ignore their own interests and talents and to rely on the opinions of others, leaving them susceptible to materialistic messages to consume as a way of fitting in and gaining acceptance. This force is discussed in Chapter 5.

Friendships are essential to children's healthy emotional development. Children who have difficulty making friends or who lack social confidence are particularly vulnerable to force number three, the Lonely One. This force tries to convince lonely children that material goods will provide them with a way out of their isolation. The

Lonely One might persuade a youngster that owning the latest video game will get children to like him. Or it may tell a child, "Who needs friends when you own such nice things?" This force is discussed in Chapter 5.

Children with poor self-esteem and identity are susceptible to the fourth force, You Complete Me. The idea behind this force is that children use material goods as a primary way of defining who they are. For these young people, self-concept hinges strongly on brand name products and on the admiration of others. You Complete Me leads youngsters to base identity on extrinsic sources, such as material goods, status, and outside approval rather than intrinsic motivators, such as talents and personal satisfaction. You Complete Me is described in Chapter 6.

Finally, force number five, the Humdrum, Ho-Hum exploits youngsters' inclination toward boredom. Clearly, boredom is part of the human experience. To grow into an engaged and contented adult, children must learn how to make constructive use of their time. The Humdrum, Ho-Hum works by enticing youngsters to turn to external sources to alleviate boredom. The danger here is that the use of shopping and merchandise to cope with boredom can foster impulsive spending and a reliance on goods to assuage negative emotions. In Chapter 6, I discuss the Humdrum, Ho-Hum.

The five forces discussed in this book do not represent every possible motivation for reliance on materialism. However, these forces are particularly relevant to children's social and emotional development. Chapters 4, 5, and 6 will help parents to determine where their child might be most vulnerable to developing materialistic values. Each chapter also includes discussion questions that families can use to help them to begin exploring issues related to materialism.

CHAPTER 4

THE MIMIC

I learned to drive a manual transmission in college. My roommate taught me to wrangle with a four-speed on the straight, gravelly back roads of the college town in which we lived. The experience proved humbling. Eventually, however, I acquired such proficiency with the clutch that I didn't even think about shifting gears as I was driving. Many years later I made the move to the automatic transmission. Even after three years of driving "clutchless," my right hand still occasionally reaches out to shift gears. Through years and years of practice, many actions can become second nature, and changing established behavior can prove challenging. Most people must exert a great deal of conscious effort to change deeply rooted patterns.

Making the decision to shed materialistic attitudes and behaviors presents greater challenges than giving up the clutch. For one thing, invitations to consume invade the senses from morning to night. Even the most resilient among us have difficulty now and then resisting the call to spend. To complicate things further, most people don't even think consciously about their patterns of consumption or the ways in which they are subtly nudged into viewing life through consumer-tinted lenses. The consumerism bug can even find the mediaphobes who avoid television, magazines, or the radio.

It stares out from billboards, wends down the supermarket aisles, and infiltrates the comments of friends, neighbors, and family. It camps out on Web sites and in chat rooms. One mother told me how her six-year-old son learned to navigate the iTunes Web site and bought the song "YMCA" nine times (apparently each version was slightly different). In this electronic age, even young children need media smarts. The solution to unlearning materialism is not to isolate oneself from temptation—that's impossible—but to increase awareness of consumerism's influence and to discover why some lures look more attractive than others.

The last chapter made the case that materialistic values and behaviors negatively impact children's emotional well-being. It presented the five forces that can encourage children to adopt these values. In this chapter I describe the first force, the Mimic. This force works on children by persuading them to imitate materialistic behaviors and attitudes observed in their everyday lives: at home, on television, in the movies, on the radio, and magazines. Children of all ages can be influenced by the Mimic, and sometimes this influence is quite apparent. One of my students told me that shortly after watching a *Sports Illustrated* swimwear special on television, her seven-year-old daughter pranced into the living room modeling her swimsuit, the bottom firmly pulled up her behind to simulate a thong. The girl announced that she needed a bikini "so I can be pretty like the girls on TV." The Mimic can also work in less obvious ways, by influencing youngsters' beliefs about their appearance and self-worth.

The chapter begins by discussing the ways in which various media foment materialistic desire. Advertisements, television programs, and the Internet all have the potential to nurture materialism in children and adolescents. Fortunately, parents can counter these materialistic aspects by increasing their youngsters' ability to understand how advertising and programming can manipulate their emotions and behavior. Youngsters high in this media literacy can enjoy media without experiencing the constant cravings for the latest promotions.

The second section of the chapter examines a special aspect of media, the teen magazine. Many adolescents, particularly girls, use these magazines for information on body image, shopping, dressing, dating, and friendship. Often these publications promise their readers happiness through beauty—which in this case means being thin, well dressed, and perfectly made up. Beauty is achieved through merchandise—clothing, cosmetics, jewelry, and so on. For teenagers eager to fit in with peers and hungry for ways to forge an identity separate from their parents, teen magazines can represent a significant influence on their attitudes about consumption.

The final section provides ideas on how to counter the Mimic. Here parents share strategies for teaching their children to negotiate media and materialism. In addition, discussion questions are provided to help families think about and begin examining their beliefs related to this force. Parents can use these questions to increase knowledge of their own attitudes and to stimulate conversation with their youngsters.

MEDIA AND THE MIMIC

Some longtime family friends decided to move to the country to get back to basics and escape from what they perceived to be the dangers of urban life—crime, crowds, consumerism, the lack of community spirit. The couple and their two young children moved to a rustic farmhouse, raised animals, and grew vegetables. During their free time, the youngsters built "secret" forts, produced dramatic theater, and read books. There was no television: no Saturday morning cartoons, no *Barney* or *Sesame Street* or *Dora the Explorer.* One Christmas a relative sent the children some videos. Unbeknownst to the parents, the videos contained promotions for toys and games. For the first time in their young lives, the girls began begging their parents to buy them toys.

This story illustrates two basic truths. Number one: Advertising begets begging. Research shows that television, particularly commercial television, has the power to create little consumers. The quantity of television viewing significantly influences children's acquisitive desires. The more programming children view, the more they will plead with their parents for products when out shopping.[1] Vulnerability to advertising tactics occurs among children from all over the globe. Young viewers in England and Japan, for example, also fall prey to the temptations of commercial programming.[2] This fact suggests that something beyond American culture must explain youngsters' reactions to advertising. I discuss this in more detail later in the chapter.

Truth number two: Begging begets results. Researchers working undercover at shops and toy stores have observed that, most of the time, parents give in to their children's requests for material goods.[3] When asked, parents themselves admit to eventually caving in to their youngsters' pleas. Cindy describes her reasoning strategy, which is a typical response to her son's requests for more toys:

> I tell him that he has more toys than anybody should be allowed to have. He literally has hundreds of trains and hundreds of cars. And he's always asking for a train or a car. He'll say, "My friends [meaning his cars], my friends would really like him!" I sometimes give in.

Lisette has observed the link between commercials and craving over and over:

> When they're watching cartoons on commercial TV, there's a zillion commercials for plastic toy crap. The shows are packed full of commercials that say "You've got to have it *right now.*" It's shoved down their throats. . . . My younger son gets totally consumed. He'll come up to me and say, "You know what I want for my next birthday? I want the Bionicles because it does this and it flies like that!" I always say, "No I'm not going to buy that for you." I make no promises. Because if they don't get it, they'll think, "My mom lies to me." My husband tells them, "I'll put it on my list," I think hoping they'll forget about it. . . . If they go to Toys-R-Us, they want their Bionicles. I say "No, we're not getting those," but my husband will buy the stuff every time. He

says it's good for their fine motor skills. If they weren't watching TV, they probably wouldn't even care about Bionicles. If it were just up to me, I wouldn't have them watch all the commercial TV.

Katrina is one of those parents who rarely caves in to her children's campaigns for "must-haves":

> My three-year-old, we were at The Gap and she wanted everything. She was marching through the store *chanting* "I need more clothes!" I just pulled her out of the store. I didn't pay a lot of attention to it. I think the more attention you spend, the more they'll keep going. I used to be really analytical and explain to them the whole thing, and I think the more talking I did the worse it got, it just turns into a drama. I've learned that for me, less talking is best; keep it short, simple, and direct. Of course, I may feel that way because I have four children.

These quotes from three parents of young children illustrate how store displays and television advertising can whip up youngsters' desires for new products. While all children respond to advertising, preschoolers are particularly vulnerable to merchandising tactics due to their lack of media savvy and their immature cognitive capacities. "Child-targeted" advertising aims directly at the young, unsophisticated viewer. These ads typically promote toys, junk food, and the "free" doodads that come in cereal boxes. Research has shown that preschoolers have great difficulty differentiating between actual programming and commercials. In one study, researchers showed kindergarteners and first graders videotapes of children's programs.[4] The investigators stopped the programs periodically and asked the children whether what they were viewing was "part of the show" or a commercial. Only about half of the children correctly identified the commercials, about the same rate as chance.

Even children who can correctly pick out a commercial do not qualify as media savvy. The ability to identify an image as a "commercial" does not necessarily indicate true comprehension. Most preschool children, for instance, do not understood that commercials are not a part of the television programs' storyline.[5] Young ones have a very rudimentary understanding of the commercial concept, and this understanding is based primarily on superficial elements. Children might describe commercials as "more funny than programs" or may say that "commercials are short and programs are long."[6] The child of a mother I talked with characterized commercials as "those short movies." Just like teenagers and adults, children identify with and admire the characters in their favorite shows. Unlike their elders, however, young ones are more likely believe that their beloved characters actually use the advertised products themselves because of the blurry line between programming and commercials. If their favorite character carries a backpack, they want it too. In part then, the Mimic acts by exploiting children's immature cognitive development. Youngsters imitate by desiring the same toys, clothing, and food that their media "friends" use. They can be like the superhero they admire through purchase of a mask and laser sword. They can experience the same joy as the television kids by securing the rocket launcher.

Advertising strategies also work because young children don't realize that what you see is not always what you get. It takes some time for youngsters to fathom the hard truth: The really cool rocket that does loop-de-loops on television and comes "free" with purchase in the cereal box is really just an unimpressive, cheap plastic toy. After a number of disappointments, children do develop some skepticism about advertisers' promises and realize that commercials can mislead. However, young children's skepticism tends to apply only to products with which they have experience.[7] They may understand that the disappointing rocket is a rip-off, but they can still be seduced into wanting the new motorized car. The more experience youngsters accumulate with commercials and with products, the more likely they come to doubt advertiser claims. Parents can use this knowledge to lessen the impact of the Mimic. Reminding children of past disappointments with advertised products and teaching them that merchandise in an ad does not represent reality can facilitate their consumer awareness.

Not until about seven or eight years of age do children comprehend the true purpose of commercials: to persuade. Older children and adults understand that a commercial is designed to sell products. They understand that advertisers will do whatever they legally can to make that product attractive enough to get a consumer to open his or her wallet. Imagine all the ads you come across during any given day—ads suggesting that wearing certain clothes or makeup will increase attractiveness to the opposite sex. That driving a particular car denotes class and taste, or that owning an advertised toy will lead to fun and friendship. Most people know that these claims contain some element of exaggeration. We might roll our eyes or harrumph "yeah, right" when listening to some of the ridiculous assertions. Not so with young children. They simply have less experience with media and have not learned yet about media tactics. For example, older children understand that different types of commercials have different goals. Consider two television pitches—an infomercial and a soft drink commercial. In the former, the ad seeks to inform the viewer on the multiple uses of the product (e.g., "Not only does this amazing knife cut food, but you can also use it to prune your foliage!") The soft drink commercial, which may contain a popular celebrity singing, dancing, and drinking soda, hopes to capture the viewer's attention and perhaps associate the sugared drink with hip glamour. When queried, adolescents have much more sophistication at differentiating between advertiser intentions than do school-age and preadolescent youth.[8]

Parents tend to overestimate children's understanding of television programming and advertisements.[9] Preschoolers, however, have not developed the cognitive ability to understand differences in perspective—that people have varied points of view and experiences and behave based on those experiences. The ability to take on another perspective doesn't develop until youngsters begin kindergarten or first grade.[10] Before this time, children have difficulty understanding that their thoughts and the thoughts of the person next to them (or on the television screen) differ. Imagine, for example, that I show your friend a box filled with chocolates. Your friend leaves the room and I dump out the chocolates and replace them with pencils. I then ask you, "When your friend returns, will she think there are chocolates or pencils in the box?" Obviously as a highly skilled adult, you would say "Chocolates." However, preschoolers are more likely to say "Pencils," because that is what *they* know.[11] A preschooler doesn't understand that differences in experience influence knowledge and expertise. Because of these developmental limitations, young ones have difficulty understanding that the goals of an advertiser (to sell stuff) might be different from the interests of the child (to be entertained or delighted with a new product). A youngster won't consider that the advertisers want to sell their products regardless of whether those products meet the child's expectations.

Children clearly need help making sense of advertisements, and this is another way that adults can combat the Mimic. However, parents generally do not watch commercials with their children.[12] One mother I talked with diligently limited her son's television viewing and knew about every show that her six-year-old watched. However, when I asked her whether the shows contained commercials, she hesitated and admitted that she wasn't really sure. Although she knew the names and the general content of the programs, she didn't actually watch them. Other parents, in an effort to protect their young from the cult of commercialization, restrict their children to noncommercial programming or ban television use completely. Mandy, for example, restricts her six-year-old to programming on PBS or to movies on video.

Whatever the television rules might be, parents or other adults really do need to both monitor and help interpret the content in both TV programs and commercials in order to build youngsters' knowledge about advertising tactics. The final section, Defeating the Mimic, provides ideas on how to help children learn more about media and advertising. However, remember that persuasions to buy don't just occur in commercials; marketers can get their message across in a dozen subtle ways. Take product placement, for example. Youngsters who admire the fashions and belongings of their favorite TV characters can go search for products on Web sites like www.asseenin.com.[13] On a recent visit to this site, I discovered how to purchase the kitchen timer and pink dish gloves used by a character on the television program *Desperate Housewives*. If I so desired, I also could buy jewelry and accessories worn by characters on the program.

By the time they reach their teens, youngsters have developed a healthy skepticism of advertising. In some ways, one might consider teenagers to be experienced media connoisseurs. At around twelve years old, the average child has viewed close to 500,000 television commercials, not to mention ads from other sources: radio, magazines, the Internet, and others.[14] Children learn by watching and buying. In fact, watching television *can* actually make children smarter, more knowledgeable consumers.[15] Youngsters can learn that advertising may be misleading; that advertisers and viewers have different interests; that some skepticism is necessary to avoid manipulation; and, most importantly, that the goal of advertising isn't to entertain or to help the viewer find the most reliable and desirable product at the best price. After a few years of buying advertised items, youngsters come to recognize that products do not always deliver on their promises.

Developmental changes in cognitive ability also facilitate children's understanding of advertising tactics. At around the age of eleven or twelve, abstract thinking takes root. Preteens and teens begin to think in relative terms. At this stage, for example, youngsters more frequently question the veracity of information presented as "fact." Thinking becomes more flexible, as young people come to recognize that the notion of "acceptable behavior" depends on the context. As parents of teenagers know, these youngsters tend to question everything: household rules, social mores (e.g., sex, drugs, relationships), the whole gamut. These cognitive changes can mean bad news for the Mimic. Youngsters are less likely to believe everything they see on television and in the movies. They can understand, for example, that a television program featuring wealthy teenagers with unlimited funds and exciting love lives does not represent reality. This skepticism can extend to advertising. With adequate training, teens can ignore dubious promises of popularity, attractiveness, and happiness that will come with the purchase of the right product.

Teenagers, however, need more than skepticism. "Experienced" youngsters with low self-esteem are still quite vulnerable to ad manipulation and the Mimic. Some investigators have found that children "who are low in self-esteem lack the self-confidence to rely on their own beliefs and judgment and therefore fall back on the judgment of others."[16] These "others" include the marketers. For example, youngsters who strive to increase their social status by buying material goods are particularly susceptible to the influences of advertising, despite their years of experience with media.[17] This circumstance reminds me of a product I once came across called "Hope in a Bottle." The name of the product, a facial moisturizer, pokes fun at the fact that most people know that some lotion won't make them look ten years younger, but they buy it anyway, hoping that this product might be different from the rest. Like the wishful clients of Hope in a Bottle, vulnerable youngsters might understand rationally that material goods can't change their lives, but they still go for it.

While children do eventually learn to see through the advertising hoopla, parents should not just wait for this awareness to happen. Years of unmonitored media exposure can reap deleterious consequences. Exposure to television, for example, increases materialistic values.[18] Here again, the Mimic plays a significant role. This force directs children's attention to advertising that arouses their desires for new products and implies that happiness is best achieved through merchandise. Further, the Mimic affects youngsters' relationships with their parents. Children's persistent requests for products coupled with parents' refusals to buy create can tension in the relationship.[19] Without parental intervention, young consumers in the making can develop positive, uncritical attitudes toward advertising. Remember that adolescents' mistrust of advertising relates more to disbelief about product claims. This mistrust does not necessarily increase their awareness of how commercials activate emotional insecurities. Without this awareness, youngsters may come to consider commercials as a viable source of information.

Youngsters who watch large amounts of television can also develop a skewed perspective about the prevalence of wealth. They can come to believe that luxury items and affluence are commonplace.[20] The Mimic convinces them that most people live "the good life" and that this life comes with minimal effort. These youngsters more frequently buy in to the idea that "work is about status, power, and money but does not require any difficult labor."[21] These attitudes call to mind young children's unformed notions of future career options. A young girl once proudly informed me that "I want to be a ballet dancer and a doctor when I grow up." She figured that she could be a doctor during the day and dance at night. While not this simplistic, the perspectives of older children, shaped by media's biased worldview, can embody a skewed, inaccurate view of wealth, success, and happiness.

TEEN MAGAZINES AND THE MIMIC

The Mimic exerts tremendous influence through teen magazines. These publications have significant impact not only on children's materialism, but on their self-esteem, body image, identity, and notions of intimate relationships. Magazines possess particular relevance for girls, with over 75 percent of young women perusing them.[22] For many young women, teen magazines symbolize entry into adolescence. The magazines that they read as children are quite different from the teen publications. While both genres extol celebrities and contain plenty of advertising, magazines for the younger set offer lots of games, comics, and profiles of popular cartoons and movies. Teen magazines read like an ode to the mantra "Happiness through beauty"; the bulk of articles and advertisements devote themselves to cosmetics, skin products, fashion, and boys (and how to attract them through the use of aforementioned beauty products and fashion).

Teen magazines offer guidance to young women at a time of profound physical, social, and emotional change. During puberty, girls undergo a rapid increase in body fat, and the growth of breasts and body hair. Researchers believe that increases in weight lead young women to feel dissatisfied with their bodies and to begin dieting. Girls who develop early experience even greater pressures. Early maturers experience lower self-esteem, poorer self-image, and higher rates of depression, anxiety, and eating disorders compared to others of similar age.[23] How to explain these differences? Early-maturing girls weigh more than their peers in a society that values the thin, lanky look of preadolescence. To complicate things, these girls undergo greater pressure to date and to have sex than their later-maturing counterparts. Most likely because of these stresses, girls who develop early use drugs and alcohol, engage in sexual activity, and experience academic problems more than other girls, and they are particularly susceptible to the influence of the Mimic. Recall that poor self-esteem and a lack of self-confidence leaves youngsters wide open to this force.

Adolescence is fraught with peril for many females. In point of fact, a large body of research shows that the rate of depression for girls increases precipitously during puberty.[24] Social scientist Jean Kilbourne explains this increase in depression as the result of loss.[25] She maintains that girls undergo a series of losses as they enter adolescence: loss of self-confidence, self-esteem, academic and career ambition, and assertiveness. Females purportedly go from active, confident, adventurous beings, to passive objects concerned primarily about their appearance and, for heterosexual youngsters, attracting boys. Media exploit this situation with messages encouraging female adolescents to spend money impulsively and to forgo delaying gratification. For example, a scan of teen magazines yields buzzwords such as "must-haves," "essentials," and "treat yourself." Clearly this barrage encourages a greater focus on materialistic pursuits. For girls who are already feeling insecure about their bodies and their minds, these magazines can provide a convenient road map for how to be female. With a focus on externals, magazines also provide ample opportunity for the Mimic to influence girls to take on materialistic values. For youngsters who do experience depression, the Mimic can persuade them that possessions will lift their mood.

For some adolescents, mainly girls, the greater societal pressure to be thin and attractive can contribute to the development of eating disorders. Not surprisingly, some eating disorders, such as anorexia nervosa, emerge during early adolescence.[26] Regular reading of teen magazines, particularly those centered on fashion, can increase youngsters' desires to be model thin. For some youngsters, this push for a slender body moves into disordered eating. Both eating disorders and thinner media images of women have increased over the past twenty to thirty years. One study surveyed the body types of models depicted in fashion magazines over the last forty years.[27] It found that the models featured on the covers of these publications have become progressively thinner. In addition, the modern magazines are more likely to show full-body shots and fewer face shots on the covers, thus exposing readers to many representations of thinner bodies. The results of this study complement other research indicating that depictions of women in the media have become thinner, and to a greater degree, unrealistic. Again, the edict to maintain a svelte, attractive form plays right into the hands of the Mimic. For some youngsters, this edict can lead to dangerous eating patterns.[28] While many youngsters read these magazines, most do not develop eating disorders. Likely a combination of societal pressures, culture, biology, and family circumstance best explains why some youngsters succumb to eating disorders or to the edict to be skinny.

Along with the pressure to be attractive and slender, girls are expected to be "nice" and to refrain from overt expressions of anger and aggression considered by the culture to be "unfeminine." This thesis calls to mind a *20/20* special titled "The differences between boys and girls".[29] The commentator, John Stossel, presents school-age children with an undesirable "gift" (pencils and socks). The boys in this pseudoexperiment typically reacted with comments like "Aw man, what do I need with these for?" and "What a rip-off!"

Many of the girls in the survey politely responded by saying "Thank you, they're just what I needed!" When Stossel pushes them, the girls admitted that the items really weren't just what they've been waiting for.

The informal experiment illustrates something that many parents have observed themselves: in terms of emotional expression, boys and girls are socialized differently from an early age. Girls receive the message to be agreeable and nurturing. Boys have greater latitude to express anger and disagreement yet much less freedom to show their sadness, hurt, or fear. Not all of the girls interviewed lied to spare Stossel's feelings. Those who spoke their minds tended to come from homes where the parents encouraged them to make choices and assert themselves rather than just be nice. This point is crucial. Not all girls lose themselves once they enter adolescence. However, adults must apply concerted effort for them to maintain their spirited nature. Helping girls to maintain a healthy self-concept will also increase their resistance to the Mimic. Youngsters who feel confident and good about themselves are less likely to be persuaded that the best way to express oneself is through appearance and material goods.

Teen magazines, and by proxy the Mimic, play a crucial role during puberty. For girls, the magazines offer a particular brand of female identity. First and foremost, fashion magazines project a standard of beauty. Magazines do not necessarily create this standard, but they certainly reinforce and further the notion that much of female identity rests on an appearance that can be enhanced through purchase of the right products. As we've seen through research on body weight, this standard of beauty has become more and more difficult to attain.

The publications can also guide girls' ideas about relationships. The topic of boys, boys, boys permeates most of the teen magazines for girls. Given the spin, even boys become a product. Publications package boys by presenting them as either undesirable (e.g., the superficial, highly sexual, emotionally unavailable type) or desirable (e.g., the romantic types who don't shy away from real intimacy).[30]

The magazines encourage girls to attract the desired type by working on their presentation (hair, makeup, clothes, weight management) with the understanding that once they snag the guy, they will
still be responsible for the emotional life of the relationship. Note the
headline: "Make Your Boyfriend Open Up 2 U." Girls learn
through the magazines that "it's a competitive market so they better
have the right understanding of boys, as well as the right body and
outfit to go with it."[31] Teen magazines provide the Mimic with lots to
work with. Girls' tasks are to be attractive, thin, and nice. Magazines implicitly promise that by imitating the models and the offered
advice, girls will get the guy.

Boys are not immune to the effects of magazines and other
media images, but much less research has been conducted on media
and body image in males. The scanty research available suggests
societal expectations for strong, muscular male bodies. Men's magazines over the last thirty years shows that articles on building mus-
cle have increased.[32] Further, slim or overweight males are
underrepresented in magazines and television programs. Some evidence suggests that magazines do influence young men's expectations about female bodies and attractiveness. For example, when
males are exposed to images of beautiful, slender models and ac-
tresses, they tend to hold similar expectations for their real-life
mates.[33] In terms of teen magazines, the Mimic likely affects adolescent boys most in terms of consumption of fitness and sports products. This means having the latest skateboard, athletic shoe, ski
equipment, or snowboard.

The Mimic can foster unhappiness among both boys and girls.
In a study on body image and mass media, investigators asked the
teens to indicate their ideal body type and to describe the magazines
they read and the celebrities they emulate.[34] Not surprisingly, the
males in the study preferred a muscular physique over a slender
frame for themselves. Consistent with their veneration of the muscular, the boys exercised and took steroids more than the girls. The
majority of girls selected a very thin figure. The adolescent girls also
read teen magazines more than the boys. One factor that increases

unhappiness is when a large gap exists between an individual's ultimate goals (e.g., their ideal) and their current situation (e.g., reality). In this study, females were twice as likely as males to perceive themselves as heavier than their admired celebrities and models. The girls also indicated that they wanted to look like their celebrity role models and, not surprisingly, had lower self-esteem than the boys.

Teen magazines present a standard of beauty which includes a very slender female body and beautiful features and a muscular male physique comparable to those of an actor or model. Even though for most people, this standard is unattainable, the publications encourage the effort to meet it through consumption. Both boys and girls who rely on these magazines for beauty, fashion, and body image guidance more frequently report dissatisfaction with their appearance.

Before I sound like a total killjoy, I do believe that teen magazines have their useful side. Youngsters enjoy reading them and can learn quite a bit about pop culture and the rules of acceptance for their social group. They provide bonding for young people; I'm sure many readers can remember poring over *Seventeen* or *Glamour* with girlfriends, discussing the latest styles. However, as with other forms of media, children need adults to help interpret the information they are presented with. Parents might talk about the real goals of these magazines (e.g., to sell products and promote movies and television programming through celebrity profiles) and the strategies they use to achieve these objectives. Teen magazines aim to provide their advertisers with young clients primed to spend money. With that goal in mind, the publications offer consumption as an answer to almost every need. The key to enhancing one's inner and outer beauty is through purchase of must-have clothing and makeup. Features offer suggestions on ways to enhance one's body type and then provide brands, prices, and Web site addresses where appropriate gear can be bought. I was most amused by a magazine cover that included the headlines: "Your best body: the diet, the workout, the clothes," "Get sexy hair," along with "How to spot a fake person." These magazines do tackle important issues. However, even the more serious pieces still incorporate consumption. For example, an article on preparing for college includes a checklist reminding youngsters to buy new clothes and items for the dorm room (Internet site provided). A piece on health and society's unrealistic expectations for female thinness is interspersed with dozens of ads containing very thin models. The message to accept yourself seems overpowered by seductive visuals peddling self-improvement through consumption.

Parents should also talk with their children about the values these media espouse. Youngsters need to understand that these publications promote consumerism and external indicators of success. Further, youngsters should be keenly attuned to messages on women's and men's roles in society. As noted, many of these publications advance women as passive, ornamental consumers most concerned with attracting males rather than developing their inner strengths. According to Kilbourne, "One of the most powerful antidotes to destructive cultural messages is close and supportive female friendships."[35] During adolescence, friendships have the power to maintain self-esteem and contribute to healthy identity development, characteristics that help to ward off the seductiveness of materialism and the influence of the Mimic.

DEFEATING THE MIMIC

Maintaining vigilance over one's own consumer behavior is one obvious way to shape children's attitudes. Recall the research on celebrity role models. While these models do influence children, parents still possess a great deal of influence over their youngster's choices. Use this influence to help buffer your children from developing materialistic values. Fran describes her struggle to model responsible spending for her son:

> The way I try and run my own life might bring that across to him. I grew up very thrifty; my parents were a product of the

depression. So I try to do keep a medium ground between denying myself everything but food and water, *maybe* bread, and bingeing on stuff [laughs]. I mean, I'm exaggerating but that's how it felt to a young girl . . . the way I was brought up, you had a couple of pairs of pants, a couple of shirts, a coat, a good pair of shoes, and that was it. Definitely not overspending, keeping within your budget. When I was younger, I tended to go to extremes; first denial, denial, go without, and then binge. Now I try to keep a medium ground and stay within the budget. I try to model that for him.

Tammy Lynn also models responsible spending for her three children:

I have to live within my means, I can't live the way someone else might live. I learned this on my own, just knowing that I'm an adult, that I can't run to Mom and Dad to bail me out because I've spent all my money on this or that, I have to be responsible. If it's meant for me to have then I'll save up and get it. In my early twenties I got into some trouble with credit cards, so it's a process of trying to rebuild credit and have the things that I want without going too far. I'm the same way with the kids. They know when we go somewhere like Wal-Mart that they're not getting extra stuff. We just buy what we've gone there to buy.

Lynette describes how she practices what she preaches with her two young daughters:

I have this station wagon that I bought used. It has stickers and dents all over it, and every now and then I think, "Oh wouldn't it be nice to have a fancier car," but then again, the station wagon's paid for, and the kids can mess it up as much as they want. With a new car you have payments and higher insurance; I don't like that alternative.

Her husband adds:

You put money where it makes sense. You don't go to GapKids to buy the kids jeans, you go to Target to buy the jeans. But if you're going to the snow then you go to REI to buy good snow boots because they're going to keep their feet dry and warm. It's not always buying the best of everything, it's being selective. We did a co-op preschool because it was cheaper. We don't thrive on luxury. We don't buy things because they're luxurious, we buy them because they have good value.

I was struck by how so many of the parents have had to learn through experience to live within their means. Several learned the hard way how to manage emotional spending. No one mentioned discovering the subtleties of consumerism or even responsible spending at home or during their school careers. I talk more in Chapter 8 about how parents might consider lobbying schools to include more relevant consumer education in their curricula.

As discussed in Chapter 3, parents can also involve themselves more in their children's consumer lives. Parents who talk with their youngsters about purchasing decisions and who shop with their children raise consumer-smart kids who can think independently. A mother explains how she shops with her children:

> I plan. I tell them we're going shopping on this day, and this is what we're going to look for and this is where we're going to go. Sometimes we'll go to the mall and just roam and meander, and I'm happy to do that now and then. It doesn't happen very often. It just gets to be system overload, and then the kids are like "Oh, look at that" and "Oh, look at this" . . . They get really amped, and that's when I say, "We're done." When the kids say, "Wouldn't it be great to buy this?" I say, "Yeah, it would be nice and it would look really pretty on you, and unfortunately it's not something we're going to be able to afford right now," or I'll say, "Think about your savings from your summer job." I want them to learn about budgeting and buying things that you have really, really thought about.

Involvement includes monitoring media consumption. As one mother I interviewed said, "You need to be proactive, not reactive, with children. We should know what they're watching, what Web sites they visit, what they're seeing so we can protect them."

Increasing children's media literacy can help ameliorate some of
the effects of advertising and thus materialism. Being media literate involves the ability to think critically about media.[36] Children
need to understand, for example, the business of media, the goals
of those who produce television programs and movies, and how
programming affects emotions and behaviors. In the electronic
age, media literacy is as important as reading literacy to raising
children prepared to enter adulthood as competent consumers.
Media literacy includes these components:

- Understanding how and why particular programs or films are
  produced. Some basic knowledge about how and why media
  gets produced helps increase comprehension of the underlying message(s) conveyed in the production. Who is the target
  audience? Is this a big-budget summer film with lots of financial backing, or did the producer struggle to get the piece
  made? Does the film seek to entertain and to promote action
  figures and other products, or does it pitch a particular point
  of view or topic? There is a difference in message, for example, between *Batman Returns* and *Hotel Rwanda*. Using these
  questions as a basis for discussion will help augment children's critical viewing skills.
- Understanding one's emotional reactions to programming.
  Recall the research showing that women felt less attractive
  after viewing cosmetics advertisements of beautiful models.
  Media of all kinds has the *potential* to manipulate emotions
  and self-concept. Knowledge about how media does this will
  help families to avoid its manipulative effects. Sometimes individuals choose to be manipulated. There's nothing like seeing a wonderful drama and having a good cry. In other
  words, sometimes individuals want a particular experience
  when they engage with media: They may want to experience
  intense emotion, to learn more about a particular time in history, to be energized or inspired. When children lack media
  literacy, however, they lack the ability to make informed

choices and more readily buy into the media's interpretations and perspectives of the world.

- Appreciating programming from an aesthetic perspective (think Ebert and Roper). The media has so much to offer viewers, and children should learn to have a critical appreciation for this as well. For example, rather than merely saying "That was a good show," encourage children to talk specifically about what they liked and didn't like about a program.

- Understanding the underlying morals contained in media programming. Children need help grasping the implied values in media programming. Does the show promote sex or abstinence? Is violence presented as an acceptable way to resolve problems? Does the program promote consumer values by idolizing wealthy lifestyles, expensive clothing, and beautiful homes? Shows like *Lifestyles of the Rich and Famous* and VH1's *The Fabulous Life* are obvious examples, but many shows and films emphasize the desirability of wealth in less transparent ways.

Anyone can be skeptical. We've all encountered the doubter who doesn't trust something or someone for less than solid reasons, such as "All politicians are crooks; everyone knows that" or "I just don't like the way he looks." Cultivating uninformed skepticism does little to build children's media literacy. They are more likely to develop an *informed* skepticism of media by furthering their critical thinking skills. Parents can promote a more analytic orientation toward the media by watching ads with their children, encouraging them to express their opinions and to consider other perspectives on the meanings and messages contained in programming.[37] Again, consider whether zero exposure to television advertising best promotes youngsters' literacy skills.

Given time constraints, you may not be able to personally monitor everything your children watch. In this case, talk with them about the programs they watch. Ask questions that get them to think about what they're watching. What do they like best about the shows? Why do they think the characters behave as they do? What do they think is pretend, and what do they think is real? What kinds of products do the shows advertise? Why? These questions can be part of informal discussions during dinner, before bedtime, or while running errands in the car.

Some final notes on media literacy. Through careful monitoring and family discussions, you may raise the most highly developed, media literate child ever. However, that doesn't mean that he or she will be immune to media bias and materialism. Children also need to build an awareness of what media does for them emotionally. I know that advertisements showing healthy-looking people eating tantalizingly photographed chocolate bars are simply trying to get me to spend money on a product that has little nutritional value. Depending on my mood, the commercials still can influence my behavior. Take a stressful day and a hard-to-resist image of a chocolate bar, and I'm halfway to the market before the commercial has ended. Depending upon one's weak spot, almost any product has the power to override reason. The point is that in addition to learning how to examine messages contained in the media critically, children—and adults—need to be aware of their emotional needs and how advertisements might satisfy them. Marketers also have access to child development research and use this knowledge to appeal to youngsters' soft spots.

Your children's developmental level and temperament should also inform your media literacy efforts. Infants, for example, attend primarily to attention-getting sounds and images. They also respond positively to soothing music on the television, and some shows *do* promote language learning. However, to reap the benefits of television, parents must actively interpret program content for their infants. According to some researchers, until about the age of two years, youngsters should not watch any television.[38]

As discussed previously, preschool children (ages two through six years) have difficulty distinguishing between regular and commercial programming. Parents can foster media literacy by teaching this age group about advertising goals and tactics. While advice on time limits varies, many experts recommend no more than two hours of quality programming or videos a day for children over two years.[39] Parents can take advantage of the positive aspects of programming as well. For example, some television shows can promote academic and social skills, particularly when children build on programming material through dramatic play.[40] Youngsters might expand on a storyline from a favorite movie by involving friends or family members in their "productions." One researcher provides an example of using media to facilitate play: "A boisterous 'Peter Pan' was flying around the daycare center while a chubby little 'Wendy' was pretending to cook supper for Peter and his lost boys, two other four-year-olds who were busy sorting out blocks, the pretend utensils for their supper. . . . We were surprised to learn that the children had drawn the story ideas from a television special that had been aired the previous evening."[41]

Parents should also assess their children's temperaments when considering media exposure. People react differently to the same stimulus. A mother shared the way her two children reacted to the movie *The Wizard of Oz*. Her four-year-old daughter sat through the whole show, "even the scary parts," with no discernible distress. Her seven-year-old son, however, would not sleep with the lights off for a week following the movie. The differences in the way these two children responded might constitute differences in temperament. Researchers find that temperamental styles appear early:

> Some babies are easier to manage and learn self-regulation more quickly. Other babies become easily overwhelmed, overreact to stimuli, and require a longer time to be soothed. As infants grow into toddlers, their characteristics of shyness, natural curiosity and ready exploration, and even aggressiveness become more apparent. The effect of watching a scary movie on a shy 3 year-old child or shy 7 year-old child might be different from the effect on a 3 year-old who already exhibits aggressive tendencies or a 7 year-old known for her daring behavior.[42]

SUMMARY

Human beings are natural mimics. We copy behaviors without realizing we're doing it. The Mimic takes advantage of youngsters' copycat ways, coaxing them to emulate materialistic values and behaviors that offer false promises of happiness and increased self-worth. Parents can lessen the Mimic's influence by modeling behaviors consistent with less materialism. They can also devise creative ways to foster less materialistic values. Promoting children's media literacy will go a long way toward equipping them to handle consumerism and materialistic urges. Media literacy efforts should be directed toward all media: television, radio, movies, music videos, and print. Pay attention to teen magazines. Youngsters who regularly read these publications and who use the information to guide their notions on beauty and identity report poorer self-esteem and body image than those who do not rely on them. The magazines also promote consumerism as the panacea for every dilemma. Children need to discover that they can depend on themselves, their good friends, and their family to help them cope with life's challenges.

LET'S DISCUSS IT

Use the following items below to stimulate a group discussion. Each family member should have an opportunity to address each question or statement.

1. The clothes you wear say a lot about who you are. How much do you agree or disagree with this statement? Why?
2. The three people I most want to be like are _____. Why do you admire these individuals? What qualities do they possess that you want to emulate? (To parents: Pay close attention to the people and the qualities that your children most admire. Do they focus on both external and internal attributes? Are the qualities they esteem attainable? For example, do they strive for the "perfect" body or incredible wealth? In a nonjudgmental way, explore with your youngsters why these aspirations might be important to them.
3. Most people judge you based on what you own and what you wear. How much do you agree or disagree with this

statement? Family members might also talk about times
when they have felt judged, positively or negatively, based
on superficial aspects like appearance.

4. The things that make me the happiest are _____.
   Why do they make you happy? (To parents: Attend to the
   types of things children name. Explore the meanings children attach to their possessions. Are material possessions admired simply because they are new or the latest? Do they
   love things that remind them of special people or moments in
   their lives? Or do their possessions connote power, belonging, hipness, or beauty?)

5. My life would be better if I owned certain things I don't
   have. How much do you agree or disagree with this statement? If you agree, how or why would your life be better?
   Are there other things that could improve your life besides
   material goods?

The family discussion should be an opportunity for parents and children to share their views. Try to remain nonjudgmental. The point is
not to tell people what they're doing wrong; rather, aim to discover
more about your family members' beliefs, their emotional needs, and
how they typically try to meet them. Then consider alternatives for
behaviors that aren't working well.

CHAPTER 5

THE COMPARER AND THE LONELY ONE

Can you remember your most embarrassing moment as a child? Perhaps you wore the "wrong" outfit to school or made a fool of yourself in front of your friends. One young woman, Sara, told of the time she secured an invitation to a party with the hip group. Many of the partygoers were older than her sixteen years, which made the event even more exclusive. Sara's mother dropped her off at the party and they agreed on a pickup time. The party certainly lived up to Sara's expectations. Just as she settled in for a good time with her new friends, a voice announced over the loudspeaker, "Sara, your mother is here!" Oh, the shame! Another young man reminisced about the time he wore too-short pants to school and endured ribbing for weeks about his "flood" jeans. Children want to fit in with their peers, and when they don't fit, the effects can be devastating. During early and middle adolescence, youngsters acutely feel the desire to conform. To do this, adolescents must learn new rules of group acceptance—the dos and don'ts that determine whether they will experience rejection or popularity. Material goods play a pivotal role in the rules of acceptance. Choosing a particular brand of apparel reflects youngsters' growing identity. A child who wears the right athletic shoes or clothing also stands a better chance of social approval than a child who gets it wrong. Unfortunately, youngsters who can't afford the "required" products can be at a disadvantage in terms of group acceptance. Brands, labels, and the ability to purchase signal one's status in the peer group and in the school culture.

The Comparer force has particular pull over preadolescents and adolescents because of the importance of conformity and peer acceptance at this age. In the first part of this chapter, I discuss the developmental and situational challenges that this age group faces in trying to resist the Comparer. In the second part, I discuss children susceptible to the Lonely One. Like those vulnerable to the Comparer, these children also crave social acceptance. However, the struggle these kids experience with low social confidence or shaky social skills makes them particularly sensitive to the persuasions of the Lonely One.

THE COMPARER

Academics have coined a term to describe one of the afflictions facing youth today: *perceived clothing deprivation* (PCD).[1] Think of perceived clothing deprivation as akin to a Carrie Bradshaw-*Sex and the City* syndrome. It's like facing a closet full of clothes and thinking, "I have nothing to wear." PCD sufferers believe fervently in the importance of wearing appropriate, often costly apparel as a means of fitting in with one's social group. In the case of Carrie Bradshaw, the social group included New York clubbers and the fashion elite. For children, particularly preteens and teens, the social group encompasses a desired circle of peers—those with whom they play sports, shop, watch movies, study, or eat lunch.

In the world of adolescence, the appropriate uniform can determine social acceptance or rejection. Just consider the theme of so many teen movies. In the film *Clueless*, the designated outcast wore bizarre clothing and maintained eccentric habits. Once she underwent a makeover, which included new clothes and hairdo, she became an acceptable member of the popular group. Or consider the many "Cinderella" tales that are aimed at young people. The unattractive, rejected girl clad in dowdy clothing suddenly becomes noticed by the gorgeous alpha male once she gets her presentation together. Movies like this push the notion of "retail intervention." That is, the idea that purchase of certain apparel, makeup, cars, or other merchandise will guarantee acceptance and happiness. True, many teen movies do focus on the desirability of sincerity and "just being yourself." But the tales touting happiness through retail abound. These movies, such as *She's All That* or *Never Been Kissed*, do reflect real life for many youngsters. Peer group acceptance really can hinge on external presentation. A mother describes how imitating friends can be both positive and negative:

> Whatever their friends have they want. Everyone's into knitting now, so that's a good thing. So I did go out and buy her knitting yarn. If something is useful and educational I'll do it. I try to stay away from materialism though . . . when they're more wanting the name brands. My kids do get caught up in it a little bit. For instance, they wanted a pair of Birkenstocks because everyone else was wearing them last summer. They were $120! I told them I wasn't going to spend that kind of money but they could have something similar, an imitation. But that's not what they wanted, so we ended up not buying anything, which is fine with me.

Children experience particular pressure to conform to peer culture through the purchase of luxury goods. These luxury items include publicly displayed, expensive articles—especially clothing and athletic shoes. Group membership typically depends on goods that imbue the wearer with elite status, whether because of price or exclusivity of the item. As with adults, luxury goods have special meaning for children. These expensive goods signify social status and provide the ticket to membership into a desired group. Fran describes the importance of "luxury experiences" to belonging:

> It's more the feeling that I want to be "part of." It's not about the items themselves, it's more that I want to be a part of the group . . . . I've been in situations where everyone is, say, talking

about their trips to Europe. Well, I haven't been, I can't afford it. It immediately tags you as not belonging, at least that's how it feels.

Here, Fran has identified two critical points related to luxury goods: (1) Certain status items or experiences can signify full membership in some social groups, and (2) the critical aspect of the item isn't so much the ownership but what it can do for the owner. For example, belonging to one social group might entail subscribing to specific magazines (the contents of which are discussed at dinner parties), owning a hybrid car, spending money on books and fine dining, and traveling overseas. This group might actually frown on wearing an expensive watch, driving a Jaguar, or carrying a Vuitton bag. Similarly for children, acceptance into one social group might require expensive athletic shoes, while another group might require designer jeans. Just any old luxury item won't do. Children must learn to discern the subtleties of consumption and social acceptance. The Comparer tries to convince children that they *must* obtain specific, costly items in order to maintain standing with their friends. In this way, the Comparer fosters development of a materialistic orientation by encouraging acquisition and equating worth with the cost of one's possessions.

Poverty and Materialism

Unfairly, economic circumstances do influence standing among peers. Like adults, children often attribute characteristics to a person based on the leanest of evidence. To illustrate this phenomenon, researchers showed adolescents snapshots of people designated as "poor" or "wealthy."[2] All of the people in the snapshots wore similar clothing and accessories. The teens described the "wealthy" individuals as more intelligent, happy, popular, and academically successful compared with those labeled poor. Other studies support the notion that ownership of specific clothing and brands—and by default economic wherewithal—influences one's standing in the peer group.[3]

The consequences for wearing the wrong thing range from chiding and teasing to bullying and social ostracism. Trudy, who shops at Target, lives in a "designer clothing" community. She recalls the treatment her daughter received for wearing "unauthorized" jeans:

> I get Linda's jeans at Target and she doesn't have a problem with that, but I know some of her friends at high school were absolutely appalled. She went to school all excited, telling her friends, "My mother got me these great jeans!" and their response was "Your mother shops at *Target?*" It was mean and hurtful, and it really bothered her. But the ultimate lesson was that it was just indicative of what kind of people those girls really were.

Given the cost of luxury goods (athletic trainers upward of $200), social acceptance presents a special burden for low-income youth. Two British researchers studied the consumption behaviors and beliefs of poor preteens in England.[4] These children knew that the inability to buy pricey goods put them at a disadvantage with their schoolmates, and they vigorously believed in the "power of Nike" to deliver them from social Siberia. For example, the youngsters felt strongly that wearing expensive, branded athletic trainers was critical to garnering a decent social standing. Several of the children implied that wearing cheap, no-name brands invited social rejection. Children discussed fears of "being beaten up because of not being in the 'in crowd', a group one could not enter without the appropriate footwear."[5] One young girl regarded her branded trainers as insurance "to try and prevent the other children from picking on her."

The beliefs of these British youngsters about wealth are similar to those of the American youth in the snapshot study. The Brits used words like "happy," "nice," "rich," and "young" to describe kids who wore branded trainers. Children described the unfortunate owners of affordable, unbranded footwear as "old grannies" who would be unwelcome in their playgroups. Clearly, sentiments about material goods can span nationality and economic circumstances. Many children hold beliefs about expensive possessions that reflect the classic materialism discussed throughout this book—the conviction that expensive items imbue an owner with more positive characteristics; that the high regard of others comes from possessing branded goods; that owning great stuff ensures happiness.

Poor youth in the United States also face tremendous burdens to acquire name-brand items. American children associate certain brands with greater status and acceptance. In the late 1990s, for example, urban African American children became enamored of the "preppy" look as exemplified by the Tommy Hilfiger brand.[6] Many associated the preppy look with the privileged class and sought to project the status of the upper crust by buying polo shirts and slacks. The Hilfiger company took advantage of African Americans' interest and marketed their pricey products directly to them. This situation creates tension for poor children (and their families) who long for expensive, branded products but can't afford them.

Some schools concerned about commercialism and children's focus on clothing styles have instituted school uniform policies. Educators at these schools believe that uniforms can lessen the impact of the pressure, teasing, and social exclusion that many youngsters experience when they don't wear clothing "social approved" by their peers. Research shows that younger children—those in grade 6 or below—like wearing uniforms and feel less pressure to dress in a certain way.[7] Many adolescents however, do not appreciate school uniform policies. This attitude complements the research discussed thus far, which indicates that adolescents are particularly interested in expressing group membership through clothing and accessories. One mother whom I interviewed said that school uniforms did not seem to impact her children's desires for name-brand items. At their junior high school, students were required to wear uniforms but had the freedom to wear any type of shoe. This mom's youngsters found ways to consume luxury brands by focusing on buying designer shoes.

The Comparer holds significant sway over poor minority children. One reason is that these youth watch more television relative to their peers, which means greater exposure to characters with nice clothes, homes, and toys. The television programs provide constant reminders for these children of what they don't have. Children Now, a national organization dedicated to children's needs, conducts an annual survey of prime time television to gauge the types of programming to which youngsters are exposed.[8] The organization found that during the 2003–4 season, seven sitcoms had not one character of color in any role. Young people tend to watch situation comedies the most; unfortunately, these programs are the least racially diverse shows on prime time. The survey also found that Asian, Indian, and Arab Americans continue to be severely underrepresented on network television. Latino Americans were four times more likely to portray domestic workers compared to other ethnicities, and Arab Americans were most often rendered as criminals. Limited, stereotypical roles contribute to children's poor self-esteem and self-concept. When children "do not see characters 'like themselves' on television [they] are learning a fundamental lesson about their group's importance in society."[9] The Comparer has the potential to influence poor children in two ways: (1) The children face reminders in their real lives on a daily basis, that they have much less than other youngsters, and (2) television programming compounds the sense of deprivation. The Comparer uses these circumstances to persuade children that the way to soothe low self-esteem is by overvaluing material possessions.

Helping economically disadvantaged children to cope with the Comparer now can reap lifelong benefits. The lack of economic wherewithal during youth, and the feelings of inferiority that this can produce, can influence youngsters' lifestyles and attitudes as adults. For instance, a study comparing the consumption practices of economically advantaged and disadvantaged young men (mid-twenties to early thirties) found that financial power and self-empowerment go hand in hand.[10] Economically advantaged men included those working in professional fields such as accountants and lawyers (Young Professionals). Less economically secure men tended to work in manual or untrained labor (Young Workers). The two groups spent and saved their money differently. Young Professionals described themselves as intelligent, competitive, powerful individuals capable of achieving their life goals. They were very careful about managing their money. While not necessarily frugal, many believed in growing their money through investments. None of the Young Professionals described their spending habits as hedonistic or out of control. The Young Workers had what the author called a "disempowered life perspective." Several described a lack of optimism relative to their future prospects and their ability to achieve financial security and career satisfaction. Many described themselves as average, nothing special. Young Workers tended to live from paycheck to paycheck and typically had few long-term investment plans for their money. They were more likely to "blow through" their money or to be unclear as to where it all went by the end of the month.

The results of this study suggest that, in terms of materialism and the Comparer, children experience multiple repercussions from poverty. Because many in our society determine status and belonging based in large part on possessions, low-income youngsters are excluded from certain social groups. For a number of these children, fewer social choices may translate into feeling disempowered and into overvaluing material goods as a panacea for social immobility and emotional distress. As the study just mentioned shows, this pattern of self-concept and materialistic values can last into adulthood.

How does research on the poor relate to materialism? As we know, poor self-concept and materialism can go together. However, for many low-income children, possessing the accoutrements of social acceptance is out of their reach due to family financial circumstances. Many youngsters will do whatever they can to be part of a peer group. Some can become singularly focused on obtaining material goods by working after-school jobs or asking parents for unaffordable products. After-school work can negatively impact academic performance. A number of studies report that teenage employment is linked to less time spent on homework, greater absenteeism from classes, and less time available for nonacademic pursuits.[11] Some researchers and educators also express concerns that employment increases children's materialism and decreases their emphasis on academics and achievement. Pressuring parents for unaffordable items can affect family dynamics. In some cases, parents' inability to provide their children with goods can result in family conflict and disappointment. In other circumstances, parents will work harder to afford expensive goods for their children. Some studies have found, for example, that children from low-income and single-parent families receive larger allowances than those from more affluent backgrounds.[12] As in most families, parents in these circumstances earmark any extras for their children.

Poor families in America face a profusion of challenges: securing decent education for their children, obtaining healthcare, finding safe housing, keeping young ones safe from violence, to name a few. This discussion is not intended to trivialize the significant burdens that these families encounter. Nor am I suggesting that low-income children should not strive to make their lives more materially comfortable or to be happy with the little they have. The point here is that materialism spans ethnicity, economics, and gender. Materialistic attitudes don't suddenly kick in once an individual reaches a certain tax bracket; they reflect the culture as a whole. For low-income youth, the Comparer exacts a toll. At its worst, it can cultivate feelings of low self-worth and disenfranchisement. Materialism represents a much more complex notion than simply buying a lot of things. It is a deeply embedded value in this culture that affects multiple aspects of children's lives and their development. The fallout from materialism—depression, loneliness, discontentment—affects us all.

Peer culture, with its enthusiasm for brand name wares, weighs heavily on low-income youth. However, all children, from the very poor to the fabulously wealthy, can fall prey to the imperative to acquire luxuries. Even middle-class or well-to-do children can feel materially deprived as a result of exposure to wealthy lifestyles portrayed in the media. The term *relative deprivation* describes the notion of feeling disadvantaged when comparing oneself to those who own more possessions. I recall, for example, talking with a young man who felt "poor" compared to his classmates who drove their own cars to school. This youngster had "to endure" being dropped off in the morning by his mother. For this young man, much like the PCD kids, "poor" meant not having a car in high school. Without perspective, children grow to take their material blessings for granted. Parents can teach youngsters to respect their belongings. One mother says:

> My oldest son really used to take his toys for granted. If something broke he would say his great-grandmother, he called her Nana, he'd say, "Well, Nana will just get me another one." So, I told Nana not to do that anymore, to just buy the kids toys whenever they ask for them. I told my son, "If you break it, it's broken." He learned that if you don't take care of your things, when they break or get lost, we're not going to replace them. They've learned from that to keep their things in order. My son tells his younger brother and sister now to take care of their things.

One explanation for this relative deprivation lies in the media-heavy world where individuals have access to the lifestyles of people across the globe.[13] In the "olden days," humans lived in small clans surrounded by an extended association of relatives. Within this close-knit group, an individual had a better chance of being highly valued for something: hunting, cooking, artistic or athletic abilities. In the modern world, surrounded by millions, there will *always* be someone more talented, accomplished, or wealthier than you. When children (and adults) compare their lives to those they see on television or in the movies, a perpetual feeling of dissatisfaction results. In part, relative deprivation (a form of social comparison) explains the increasing rates of depression researchers have found among children and adults across cultures.[14]

The Comparer weighs more heavily upon some children than others. For example, preadolescents or 'tweens—those "too old for

Ronald McDonald and too young for car keys"—are strongly motivated to conform to their peer group.[15] Not surprisingly, this group
of youngsters concerns itself with the status of ownership, with
"wearing the latest fashions, being in style, and gaining the prestige
of wearing brand names."[16] Developmentally, it makes sense that
'tweens busy themselves with the outward indicators of belonging.
Preadolescence signals the beginning of a new venture: the start of
identity formation, when youngsters search for ways to define themselves apart from their parents. Many of these children still think
concretely about the world. When asked to describe themselves, for
example, a concrete thinker might say, "I have black hair," "I like
U2," and "I love to read historical novels." Several years ago, I was
watching a talk show featuring a well-known celebrity. When asked
what she most appreciated about her fiancé, she responded, "He
cooks great turkey burgers." While her response was probably more
about protecting her privacy rather than concrete thinking, the comment illustrates how preadolescents organize their world. More abstract thinkers describes themselves in complex, relative terms, such
as "I like people, but sometimes I want to be alone," or "I believe in
free speech although I don't agree with everyone's views." The
search for independence coupled with a concrete cognitive style
leads younger searchers to emphasize externals over more substantial criteria in the process of defining themselves.

Shopping provides youngsters with an opportunity to socialize
as well as to learn about the current trends. One study that included
preadolescent to college-age girls (ages twelve to nineteen) found
awareness of the latest trends to be especially prevalent among the
younger group.[17] Researchers conducted in-depth interviews with
African American, Hispanic, and Caucasian youngsters from a
"large Western and a large Southwestern metro area." All of the
middle school and most of the high school girls reported shopping
frequently with their friends, surveying a wide variety of brands and
products as they browsed, and searching for the newest trends to hit
the market. Only a few of the college-age women fit this profile. As
young people mature, the overriding drive to conform via superficial

means falls by the wayside (one hopes). Older adolescents spend less time roaming the malls and put more energy into academics and other self-defining activities. On the positive side, shopping provides younger teens with a chance to form and strengthen friendships. It also offers an education in social membership. Cruising the mall fosters youngsters' knowledge about what to wear in order to fit in with their desired peer group. They learn about what's hip and what's not; about which products really work and which are a waste of money. However, while peers can be helpful to each other, they also encourage materialism. Studies find that shopping with friends increases youngsters' desires to consume; teens spend more money when they shop in groups and tend to make more unplanned purchases.[18] It may be that young adolescents experience more pressure to spend money to fit in with their friends. In this sense, the Comparer has particular sway over these youngsters, encouraging them to make consumption a group activity.

Children rely on friends to learn about the rules of acceptance in their social group. Peers represent a rich vein of social information. Research on social comparison finds that teens tend to choose shopping pals whom they perceive to be relatively expert on goods and services.[19] Most children depend on their counterparts to make decisions about some purchases. A few children, however, show more vulnerability to conformity and peer expectations than others. Children low in self-esteem are intensely concerned with fitting in and trying to meet the expectations of others. These overly conforming youngsters buy products to impress their friends and to ingratiate themselves with others. Inexperienced shoppers rely more on their mates' judgments when making important purchases. Inexperience and a lack of "shopping confidence" can also impel children toward expensive brand names. How do children overcome their inexperience? Girls typically gain valuable consumer expertise through shopping with their mothers or older siblings.[20] Boys, however, get less of this on-the-job training. Boys tend to be less confident about their purchasing decisions and because of this insecurity, they gravitate toward brand names.[21] "Approved" brands ensure

that boys will impress their friends without the risk of making a embarrassing mistake. Imagine the horror of showing off a new shirt
only to discover that the shirt is a cheap imitation!

Parents should be concerned about "buying to impress" for a
number of reasons. When children base their purchases on whether
others will be impressed, they bypass discovery of their personal interests and tastes, an important part of identity development. This
behavior also promotes materialistic values and increases the influences of the Comparer. Children who attempt to make friends by
trying to impress others with their possessions also risk developing
superficial friendships. The ability to make friends based on substantial criteria—such as common interests or experiences—promotes healthy emotional development.

Youngsters most vulnerable to the influence of the Comparer include those low in self-esteem or social confidence, low-income
youth whose lack of belongings puts them at a social disadvantage,
and tweens and teens who shop together and reinforce materialistic
values. These influences certainly represent some commanding
forces with which to contend. However, parents can buffer the impact of these factors in a number of ways. Some solutions have already been discussed. For example, parents can help children to use
their media literacy skills when they encounter compelling TV or
magazine ads featuring favorite celebrities. Nurturing literacy can
encourage children to react analytically rather than emotionally to
consumer temptations.

Certain parent communication styles can help children to think
independently and to grow a thicker skin when confronted with
peers' often very powerful attempts to influence. The goal here is
not to raise children completely closed to outside input. Insight from
friends and adults furthers children's social and identity development. Rather, parents can provide children with an invaluable gift
by enabling them to question rather than conform. Recall the child
in the tale "The Emperor's New Clothes"? An emperor who loved

beautiful clothing fell victim to a couple of swindlers who convinced him that they could weave him the finest and most stunning outfits imaginable. Of course there was a catch. The fine clothing would be invisible to stupid people or to those undeserving of their position. The swindlers claimed to produce "sumptuous robes" of superior cut and color. The emperor saw absolutely nothing but just couldn't admit it. Out of fear of being called stupid and unfit to lead his kingdom, he donned the clothing and paraded through the town— naked. No one questioned that the emperor had no clothes: not his advisors, not his court, not even the townspeople. Everyone feared the humiliation of not seeing what others saw and went along with the status quo. All except for one young questioner who exclaimed, "But he hasn't got anything on!" Children face the same social pressure as the townsfolk to go along with the group. Why was this one child able to question the emperor when no one else would? Perhaps it was due to her parents' style of child rearing.

Parenting style can render some children less susceptible to peer influence. Academics have identified two general styles of family communication that influence children's propensity to conform. One style, the "socio-oriented" style, emphasizes esprit de corps and compliance with parental authority. In a socio-oriented family, parents inculcate in their children the importance of obedience and not rocking the boat; it is a do-it-because-I-told-you-to style of childrearing. Socio-oriented children receive minimal encouragement to question their parents' decisions and opinions. As a consequence, they demonstrate less independent thought and behavior compared to children experiencing other family styles.

A number of studies have found that socio-oriented children are more susceptible to peer influence.[22] One reason for this might be that youngsters raised to conform to parental expectations have learned in general to conform as a way of pleasing people and gaining acceptance from others, including their peers. Research also finds that children raised in socio-oriented environments watch more television and hold more materialistic attitudes than other children. At first glance, this finding might seem nonsensical;

why would communication style relate to media use and materialism? However, socio-oriented families have fewer open, give-and-take discussions. Because the parents focus primarily on avoiding conflict, relatively little discussion involving differing opinions and attitudes on any issue occurs. Researchers hypothesize that socio-oriented children are left to watch television without the critical discussions on consumerism that could help them to understand their reactions to media messages.

In contrast to the socio-oriented communication style, the "concept-oriented" style stresses children's learning and independent problem-solving. Parents in these families draw out their children's opinions, even if these opinions might differ from their own. These parents encourage discussion on any number of issues; they strive to foster their children's development of "their own views of the world" and discourage the unquestioning adherence to parental beliefs.[23] Several of the parents I interviewed reflected a more concept-oriented approach. A subgroup wanted to raise their children differently from the way they had been raised. Sharon, for example, talked about going beyond the do-it-and-you'll-get-a-treat approach:

> I've spent the last year or two reading about parenting, and I've noticed that there seem to be two types of philosophies. One is behavior modification, which relies on rewards and punishments. And the other is a new positive discipline, which is more about teaching kids and using encouragement instead of tangible rewards. I was raised with the rewards and punishment method and, under stress, I do tend to revert back to that [laughs], but my goal is to use more of the positive discipline . . . focusing on what you want them to do and taking the time to teach and acknowledging their good behavior and the natural consequences, whenever possible, of misbehavior. It works really wonderfully with both the kids.

Parenting can influence children's relationships in a number of ways. For example, teens who score high on peer susceptibility measures tend to report feeling disconnected from their parents.

While studies do not always report on the reasons for distant relationships between parent and child, they might exist for a host of
reasons—divorce, personality differences, lack of communication,
feeling misunderstood or unaccepted, or parent substance abuse, to
name a few. Flagging commitment to school and to community also
increases youngsters' vulnerability to peer influence. These children
may no longer care about their school performance and hang out
with others who harbor similar attitudes. In this circumstance,
youngsters can take on the values of their peer group over those of
family or society. This explains in part why youngsters who claim
less closeness with their families more frequently choose friends
who smoke.[24] The same relationship holds true for materialism and
family closeness. For example, the children of parents who encourage expression of their individuality, who express warmth and affection, and who involve themselves in their children's lives score lower
on materialism measures than children of less present and accepting
parents.[25]

Materialistic values are not the only ones impacted by parent
communication style. Not only do teens from socio-oriented families
hold more materialistic values, they are also more likely to deceive
their parents about purchases than are teens from concept-oriented
environments. These teens admit to hiding purchases from their parents and buying items that their parents would not approve of.[26]
This behavior pattern sets the stage for a lack of honesty and trust in
intimate relationships. Children of less warm and involved caregivers may feel more insecure about their ability to be loved and valued. This insecurity provides a breeding ground for materialistic
values. A child might reason, for instance, that "If I buy these expensive and coveted athletic shoes, people will admire me and want
to be my friend." Parents can combat this way of thinking by allowing their children to express their views respectfully even when they
differ from their own. Listening to a child's opinions does not mean
you have to agree with them or act on them. Providing a safe, nonjudgmental (as is possible) space for children will help them to artic-
ulate and clarify their emerging values.

Allowing children to question, to develop their individuality, and to resist conformity certainly aligns with western cultural beliefs. Some parents may not be comfortable fostering so much questioning and independence. The "nonconformity" approach is just one way that caregivers might address concerns about materialism and peer influence. In addition to communication style, family structure can impact children's purchasing decisions. A few studies have explored the differences in influence between the traditionally western nuclear family and the extended family system characteristic of many cultural ethnic groups. One study compared purchasing behaviors and peer influence of college students from the United States and Thailand.[27] The majority of students in Thailand lived in a multigenerational, communal society where they cohabited with several generations—parents, grandparents, aunts, and uncles. The students from the United States lived primarily in nuclear families, typically comprised of one or two parents and siblings. According to the study's investigators, Thai students were significantly more influenced by their elders and were less swayed by peer opinion when making luxury purchases compared to the American youth. The results of this cross-cultural study suggest that constant exposure to influential adults can serve to ameliorate the effects of the Comparer. American youth were not immune to input from their elders. Parents did have more pull over privately consumed items, such as toothpaste, and bedroom furnishings, and VCRs. When it came to big ticket items, such as athletic equipment, however, peer opinions were number one for American youth.

The study's researchers suggest that identity development might differ for children in communal or collectivist cultures. These children fashion two important identities: an individual self who makes decisions based on one's personal needs and goals, and a family-based self whose objectives take into account the needs of the group. With a dual identity, children can be strongly influenced by both peers and family. American families can help attenuate the influence of the Comparer by emphasizing both collective values and individualism. When children can rely on the opinions and

guidance of extended family and other adults, they are less susceptible to peer pressure to spend.

In the western, noncollectivist culture, families are often spread
out across the country, which makes raising children in an extended
family environment difficult. Families can create this experience
early in their child's life by fashioning an extended network of relatives, friends, and neighbors committed to remaining involved in
each other's lives. One mother describes her efforts to create supportive relationships:

> I was a single parent for four years and in that time I made a lot
> of friends. Older women who don't have grandkids yet . . . we
> have three surrogate grandparents in addition to the grandpas.
> We've got aunties who aren't blood relations, single gay friends
> who aren't going to have kids and want to be a big brother with-
> out the real responsibilities, [laughs] . . . it's beyond being re-
> lated, it's a chosen family.

The Comparer exercises its power through media portrayal of
wealth and status, by creating envy and desire in children. It oper-
ates by persuading children to compare themselves to others constantly as the primary way of defining themselves and gaining
social acceptance. Its influence can lead even the economically
comfortable child to feel deprived. The Comparer can take already
vulnerable children and heighten their concerns about how others
view them, leading them to worry excessively about pleasing people and impressing them with material goods. Combating the Comparer involves nurturing children's ability to question, to
respectfully express themselves, and to make independent decisions. A warm, nurturing parenting style that motivates children to
think independently helps foil the Comparer. A readily available,
extended network of relatives, friends, or neighbors also helps
children to consider the opinions of more than just their peers. The
Lonely One shares some characteristics of the Comparer. Both
forces work on children who are insecure about their social connections. In the next section, I consider the situation of materialism and friendlessness.

THE LONELY ONE

Children's materialism intensifies when they try to gain friendships, belonging, and admiration through consumerism. Children most vulnerable to the Lonely One turn to material goods as a substitute for relationships. Many cultures have fables that chronicle the hubris of the rich man who values money over people. In western culture, for example, we have King Midas whose love of gold cost him his family. In more modern adaptations, movies like *The Kid*, which highlight professionally successful businessmen who mess up their social lives, illustrate the dangers of single-minded ambition. These ancient and modern tales reflect a belief that a love of money and humanitarianism do not mix. A number of parents whom I interviewed considered materialism to be antithetical to relationships and community. Says one mother:

> I think it's a bad thing because you get so concerned with attaining these materialistic things that it takes away from time you could put into your community or caring about other people, which we want our kids to learn.

A father adds:

> Materialism is making yourself feel better by buying things rather than spending time with friends or taking a vacation with your family. Your money and your time go elsewhere, so it impacts other aspects of your life.

Like adults, children have conflicting views on wealth. On one hand, young people imbue the affluent with positive characteristics, such as sophistication, culture, discipline, and intelligence, and many admit that they would love to live in affluence. On the other hand, they also stereotype the wealthy as inconsiderate and "lacking the type of genuine warmth, kindness, and concern for others that might characterize a true friend."[28]

There may be some truth to the notion that the love of possessions and quality relationships don't always make the best match.

Numerous studies, for example, have uncovered a relationship between materialistic attitudes and feelings of alienation. When asked
about their important relationships, college students "who strongly
focused on the pursuit of wealth, fame, and image reported lower-
quality relationships with friends and lovers."[29] Other studies have
also discovered that materialistic values and poor relationships or a
paucity of friendships go hand-in-hand. In another inquiry, materialistic-oriented students agreed with such statements as "I often feel
detached from my social environment," and "In order to relate to
others, I often have to put on a mask."[30]

Clearly, many people find it difficult to sustain both quality relationships and a wholehearted pursuit of wealth. Why are these two
values in such conflict? It may be that children who lack social confidence turn to materialism as a way of compensating for their soli-
tude. In this situation, the Lonely One convinces a lonesome child
that money and possessions increase self-confidence or attract others to them. Youngsters may also become so consumed with the pursuit of material goods and status that they neglect and devalue their
relationships. The Lonely One persuades these children that the joy
of acquiring material goods far outweighs friendships. Either scenario is possible. However, whichever comes first, materialistic values or poor relationships, these externally oriented, alienated
children experience less happiness and more depression and anxiety
than socially oriented youth.

Relationships provide youngsters with a long list of benefits.
Friendships buffer children from stress and adversity. Children who
have at least one close friend suffer less from exposure to parental
conflict or divorce than children with no friends.[31] Even one close
friend can protect a child from the rejection of other peers. Close
friendships give children opportunities to practice and perfect their
social skills, which lead to social competence. Children with friends
perform better academically, enjoy school more, and feel happier,
more confident, and more positively about themselves compared to
friendless children.[32] Companionless children report feeling unhappy, lonely, anxious, and depressed. They prefer to avoid school

because of the rejection or disregard that they experience in the classroom or on the playground. For lonely children, daily ostracism and isolation serves to reinforce their poor self-esteem and social competence. Relationships offer long-term protection as well. Friendless children evidence higher rates of delinquency, drug abuse, suicide, and educational underachievement in adolescence and into adulthood. Obviously, friendships provide very powerful protection against the Lonely One, which is most effective with social isolated youngsters.

The benefits of friendship apply to *constructive* relationships. Children who fraternize with peers who hold antisocial views don't necessarily enjoy the advantages of friendship. The requirements of membership in peer circles vary depending on group norms. Some groups endorse academic achievement, cooperation, and involvement in productive pastimes. Many service groups in elementary and high school, for example, emphasize philanthropy and community service as well as having a good time. However, when youngsters spend time with angry, aggressive children, or with those who deride academic excellence, those behaviors get reinforced. Some children, for example, feel compelled to hide good grades from their friends or to underperform to avoid teasing and contempt.[33] In past years a number of stories in the news have demonstrated that deviant peer relationships can lead to trouble. For example, when analyzing what caused some of the recent deadly school shootings, students and school personnel have reported that the troubled aggressors had endured tremendous peer rejection. Shunned by mainstream youth, the beleaguered youngsters hung out with other children on the fringe, many of whom espoused angry, violent beliefs. While school violence presents an extreme example of the impact of peer rejection, it does illustrate the importance and the power of positive, supportive relationships.

If relationships provide so many rewards, why in the world would any child opt for the less satisfying pursuit of material goods and status? Researchers have identified differences between children who thrive in their relationships and those who do not. Aggressive children, for example, experience more conflict-ridden relationships and, perhaps because of their dissatisfying social life, report less interest in other people. These children tend to think about relationships differently than more socially accepted children. Recall the child who assumed malfeasance when a youngster knocked over his block tower? Pugnacious children assume the worse; they stand ready to take offense at the slightest infraction.

Rejected children view the *causes* of their social difficulties differently than other children as well. When faced with peer disapproval, these youngsters more readily blame others. Similar to comedienne Flip Wilson's claim that "the devil made me do it," aggressive youth are less apt to take responsibility for their behavior and more likely to blame it on the actions of others. "I had a right to shove her," the reasoning goes. "She shouldn't have been making faces at me." Perhaps because of this skewed perspective, these youth feel less self-reproach and depression and more anger and indignation than other rejected children. Aggressive children also demonstrate a lack of introspection about their social standing. They tend to overestimate their popularity; they don't always realize how disliked they are.

Lonely, withdrawn children also experience social rejection. These are the children who wander on the fringes of the playground, get picked last for teams, or eat lunch alone. In the research literature, lonely children typically distinguish themselves in three ways: They have low self-esteem, they perceive themselves as socially unskilled, and they blame themselves for their isolation.[34] Loneliness tends to increase with age, so that adolescents experience more loneliness than elementary or preschool-age children.[35] Loneliness during the teenage years is of particular concern as this is a time of growing independence when youngsters often rely more on their friends than parents for reassurance and approval. Lonely teens can easily fall prey to the Lonely One who steps in and persuades them that the pursuit of material goods will provide them with friendships and identity.

Unlike their aggressive counterparts, withdrawn children blame themselves for their social failures. Consequently, they report significant levels of anxiety, depression, and loneliness.[36] Withdrawn-rejected children fully realize the extent of their poor peer status, which causes them emotional pain. These solitary children have a distinct way of interpreting their social predicament. When they experience some social success, they attribute the reasons to factors beyond their control. For example, when a child includes a usually isolated youngster in her play, the lonesome youth reasons that "it must be because she's in a good mood today," or "she asked me to play because the teacher made her." Further, the reasons given for social success tend to be unstable. A child might think, "She may include me today, but who knows what will happen tomorrow?" Yet, an isolated child more often makes internal and stable attributions for social failures. For example, "No one asks me to play because I'm a nerd. I'll always be a nerd and I'll always be alone, why bother trying?" This explanatory style, often termed a depressed attribution style, damages children's emotional well-being. It leads them to believe that they have little control over either their social triumphs or their setbacks. This style of thinking conjures up a sense of hopelessness, and the feeling that things will never get better segues to depression and low self-esteem. One of the things that materialism provides for children is the *perception* of control. When emotional distress sets in, they might buy food or a new item that will alleviate their mood. Children can also control their image by purchasing and wearing particular clothing and accessories.

A good deal of research has been conducted on attribution style and social and emotional well-being.[37] Attribution theorists maintain that the way people *think* about things influences their *emotions*, which then drive *behavior*. In the psychology literature, researchers refer to this as the thought-emotion-action sequence. Consider this example. Imagine that you are house-sitting for a friend. The house is large and quiet, and you are alone. At around 2:00 A.M. you hear a loud crash coming from somewhere in the home. What is your first thought? What are you feeling? What do you do? If you imagined an intruder skulking about the home, you might feel fear, which could lead you to call 911, lock the door, and hide under the bed. However, if you thought, "Maybe it's the cat knocking over a vase," you probably feel more annoyance than fear, and roll over and go back to sleep. Attribution theory contends that the way we interpret behaviors greatly affects our emotional outlook and actions.

Most people employ a self-serving attribution style when explaining life's circumstances.[38] So, for example, if a student does well on an exam, she might think, "I studied really hard," or "I'm very good at math." If she doesn't do so well on the test, she might tell herself, "The teacher doesn't like me," or "The test was unfair" (rather than "I should have studied more"). Essentially, most of us take credit for the good stuff and blame other people or the situation for the bad stuff. While not always accurate, a self-serving bias does link with better emotional health. Lonely children, however, tend to utilize the depressed attribution style just described. In attempting to explain their isolation, they typically utilize internal, stable, and uncontrollable causes, such as "I am unattractive or stupid" as opposed to "My classmates are busy."

Readers might recognize that some attributions are more amenable to change than others. Conditions perceived as permanent (stable) and uncontrollable (nothing I do can make this better) lead to greater emotional difficulty than other attributions. Children who truly believe that they are stupid, ugly, unworthy, or otherwise unappealing to their mates will believe that they have few options in terms of rectifying perceived deficits. The Lonely One has particular pull on children with the depressed attribution style. Less likely to rely on their own inner resources (which they don't trust), these children might view purchase of a coveted gadget, new clothes, or athletic shoes as the way out of their isolation. Depending on material goods to compensate for perceived shortfalls in personality or appearance strengthens the sense of personal inadequacy. The Lonely One does nothing to increase children's confidence in themselves.

Clearly, withdrawn and aggressive children are not the only ones who experience social rejection. In fact, most of us know what it feels like to be excluded—perhaps through not being invited to a party or asked to a dance. Bullied children also report feeling socially anxious, depressed, and insecure.[39] In fact, peer victimization intensifies rejected children's already fragile emotional problems. Racial differences can provoke social rejection. Studies have found that African American children attending predominantly Caucasian schools experience less social acceptance than majority children. Even African American children characterized as popular by their White peers experience some social immobility.[40] Despite being well liked, these children are less likely to be considered leaders compared to their popular counterparts who attend predominantly African American schools. A similar phenomenon is true for Caucasian youngsters attending predominantly African American schools.

Essentially, a number of paths lead to poor social acceptance among children. How youngsters and their parents cope with these obstacles determines whether children emerge more resilient as a result of their experiences. Isolated, companionless children are particularly vulnerable to the guile of the Lonely One. This force convinces children that consumerism and the pursuit of status will lead them out of their isolation. Other youngsters might like them more if they, say, wore hip T-shirts or owned an X-Box. One parent told me about a lonesome child who brought his GameBoy to school as a way to make new friends. Unfortunately, other boys in his class ended up playing with it while he looked on, once again on the fringes. Lonely children need more sophisticated ways to improve their social status. Parents might consider these tips:

- As discussed, rejected children use a depressed attribution style to explain their social status. Parents can support their children by working with them to change the way they interpret social situations. In many cases doing this involves widening the child's perspective. For example, when a child says, "I asked some kids if I could play with them and they didn't say anything! Nobody likes me," a parent can have the child come up with other explanations for why this might have occurred. Perhaps the youngsters didn't hear the child; perhaps she needs to try a different style of approach. Even popular children experience social rebuffs now and again. Popular children, however, are more likely to try again, often using a different strategy. Isolated children give up more quickly, possibly because they have already decided that they will not be successful.[41] Parents can also counsel children who assume the worst to question their assumptions. Is it possible, for example, that Steve knocked over the blocks accidentally? When children can restructure the manner in which they view the world, they gain more control over their social lives.

• Children need to clearly understand the connections between their behavior and how people react to them. For example, hostile children should understand that most youngsters avoid aggression and conflict. At the same time, they need a wider repertoire of responses. The suggestions offered here are in no way meant to imply that children are solely responsible for negative treatment they might experience from their peers. Some problems, such as bullying behaviors, need to be resolved with the help of teachers and the school administration. When a child lashes out or withdraws due to outside circumstances, such as family problems, however, other interventions such as family therapy might be more appropriate.

• Consider a social skills group. Schools, private practitioners (psychologists, licensed social workers), and community mental health centers often offer groups where children of like age can practice their skills and gain social confidence. Isolated children do not get many opportunities to practice and develop their social skills. Without these opportunities, lonesome children risk social immaturity and awkwardness that may not be remedied in the long term. Youngsters can also improve social competence through participation in structured after-school activities, such as gymnastics, karate, drama, and the like. The activity should be structured and adult-supervised so that the child does not float to the edges of the social group, thus compounding social isolation.

SUMMARY

The Comparer works on children by convincing them that the key to group membership lies in ownership of the appropriate material goods. This force ignores the importance of one's interior: personality, talents, achievements. Passive, less independent youngsters with low self-esteem are particularly vulnerable to the Comparer. Also, children with little consumer experience depend more on their friends and on the cachet of brand names when making purchasing decisions. Parents can lessen the influence of the Comparer by encouraging independence and critical thinking skills. They can surround their children with positive adult role models and demonstrate responsible consumerism.

Dissatisfaction in other areas of one's life can prompt an overconcern with the material world. Consider the plight of the lonesome youngsters who are ostracized, teased, and bullied by their peers. These children might choose effective or maladaptive means of easing their emotional pain. Parents can help their children avoid the force of the Lonely One by presenting adaptive strategies to improve social success. Earlier suggestions on increasing media literacy can also help to combat the Comparer and the Lonely One.

LET'S DISCUSS IT

Use the following items to stimulate a family discussion about materialism and peer influence. Every family member should respond to the questions and statements in this section. Please state whether you agree or disagree with the statements.

1. How happy are you with your friends? Do you feel as if you have:
   Not Enough   Just Enough   Too Many friends
   (Circle one and discuss.)
2. I sometimes feel pressure to dress or act in a certain way. When do you feel the most pressure? The least?
3. My friends like me because_____
   (Complete the sentence. List characteristics about you that make you appealing to your friends).
4. My family loves me because_____.
   (As with item 3, list characteristics that make you lovable to your family). Are there differences in characteristics listed in item 3 and 4? Why or why not? This question can lead to a discussion on differences in feelings of acceptance among family, close friends, and acquaintances.
5. The times when I feel as if I don't fit in with my friends or with other kids/adults are_____. How do you feel, and what do you do when this happens?
6. The times when I feel as if I don't fit in with my family are_____. How do you feel, and what do you do when this happens?
7. The thing(s) that make me most unique is _____.
8. Imagine that one day you go to school/work in a brand-new outfit/shoes/jacket (use the most appropriate descriptor). Not one person compliments you on your new acquisition, and you think you might have heard someone snicker behind your back. What do you do? Will you wear the item again? Why or why not?

   Now imagine that you are debating an issue in class (or in a staff meeting). Perhaps you are talking about views on the death penalty or on immigration law. During the course of the discussion, it becomes clear that no one else shares your opinion. As honestly as possible, talk about what you would do in this situation. Why? (Note: These scenarios are de-signed to get people talking about social rejection, fitting in and how to deal with it. Discuss how or why responses to these two scenarios differ).

These questions aim to help people discover the situations where they feel the most pressure to conform to others' expectations. Parents might look out for areas where family members rely on materialism to make themselves more attractive to others.

CHAPTER 6

YOU COMPLETE ME AND THE HUMDRUM, HO-HUM

As I was shopping one day, I overheard an interaction between a saleswoman and her female customer. The customer was searching for sunglasses and wanted a particular name brand. The store didn't carry the brand, so the salesperson suggested that she consider the Guccis instead. The women demurred that she couldn't because Guccis "just aren't me." For most people in this culture, material goods help individuals to express their identities. The parents profiled in this book provide lots of examples of the notion of uniqueness through belongings. One mother termed herself a "jeans and T-shirt person." Another mom described herself as someone who "shops for classic, quality goods, not fads." A third mom declared that her son wasn't a "toy kid" but enjoyed reading. We believe that the types of things we buy say something about us. The first mother considers herself to be a casual, laid-back, nonmaterialistic person and accentuates this through her garb. The second mom portrayed herself as a nonextravagant woman of discerning tastes. Perhaps mom number 3 sees her son as a future intellectual.

Material goods help children and adolescents to discover and express their sense of self—through the clothes they wear, the music they listen to, the magazines they read, or the shows they watch. Possessions can help build identity; however, the use of goods can also backfire. Just recently I happened upon a television program devoted to the social and emotional development of teenage girls. Several of the girls profiled on the program wanted to be "just like" Britney, Lindsay, or Paris. In pursuit of this goal, they dieted to look like their idols and shopped for clothes and makeup that emulated the teen stars. While a bit of identification with celebrities may be harmless, this overidentification is part of what contributes to body image dissatisfaction, overspending, and materialistic attitudes. One young teen said that she shopped frequently for clothes but had no idea how much she spent. "If I spend too much, my dad lets me know." Striving to emulate a contrived media image does little to help young people discover their own uniqueness. The You Complete Me stokes materialistic desire by convincing youngsters that they *absolutely must* buy certain items to be worthwhile. In the first section of this chapter, I discuss the ways in which self-esteem, identity, and materialism interact and how young people can be wide open to the influence of You Complete Me.

The second section chronicles the influence of the Humdrum, Ho-Hum. Adolescents' impulsivity and their desires for new sensations, coupled with their relative difficulty in delaying gratification, make them particularly susceptible to this force. This formidable cocktail can get youngsters into trouble. One study found that by the time they reach college age, many youngsters have already amassed credit-card debt of over $1,500.[1] Parents can dilute the impact of the Humdrum, Ho-Hum by providing children with alternatives. Options discussed include encouraging youngsters to build their intrinsic interests and offering structured extracurricular activities that foster development of social skills and prosocial values.

YOU COMPLETE ME

Self-esteem. Thousands upon thousands of research articles, magazine pieces, books, movies, commercials, and more have been devoted to describing self-esteem and proposing ways to improve it. Truly nondiscriminatory, struggles with self-esteem impact everyone—children and adults, males and females, and people of varied cultural backgrounds. In this chapter I consider two aspects of self-esteem. *Personal self-esteem,* also termed *personal identity,* refers to how people identify and evaluate their individual qualities and capabilities.[2] A child might describe himself as "handsome," "ugly," "smart," "introverted," or "creative." An individual's values also make up personal self-esteem. A youngster might believe that "helping others is important to me," or "I value owning really nice things." Personal self-esteem, then, involves aspects of identity (who am I?) and evaluation (do I like who I am?). The second aspect of self-esteem covered is *social self-esteem,* sometimes termed *social identity,* which refers to people's identification with and evaluation of the social groups to which they belong.[3] Most of us belong to multiple social groups; we are parents, sons, daughters, males, females, nephews, nieces, shoppers, students, employees, computer whizzes, and the like. A child could identify as a female and a student who belongs to the computer club at school. Further, she might evaluate being a female positively (girls are smart and responsible) or negatively (girls don't do well in science, or girls' opinions are not respected). As with personal self-esteem, social self-esteem involves both identity and evaluation. For the purposes of this chapter, self-esteem and identity will be treated as synonymous constructs. I will discuss how You Complete Me acts by persuading youngsters low in personal or social self-esteem to compensate for their perceived deficits through consumption.

Most people have healthy self-esteem. Consider these three qualities: attractiveness, driving ability, and intelligence. If you were to rate yourself on these characteristics relative to the general population, where would you fall? Average? Above Average? Superior? For many attributes such as these three, most people rate themselves as (at least) above average. One poll found that the majority of the respondents rated themselves above average on attractiveness.[4] Since the term "average" implies that in a normal population, this is where the majority of people fall, some of those respondents might be fooling themselves. Researchers have identified the tendency for people to rate themselves above average on positive traits or behaviors and below average on negative qualities as the *better than average effect* (BTA).[5] The BTA effect helps to protect one's ego. A child who overrates his artistic abilities or who believes that most people like him will have higher self-esteem than a child who underestimates his social or creative skills.

Individuals who are low in self-esteem utilize the BTA effect differently than those with higher self-esteem. One study found that, like most people, adolescents low in self-esteem enhance their positive traits (e.g., disciplined, sophisticated, idealistic). The low self-esteem youngsters agreed, for example, that they were much more disciplined, sophisticated, and idealistic compared to the average person. However, these same youth overemphasized their negative qualities. Relative to those high in esteem, low-esteem youth more readily believed they possessed characteristics such as sarcasm, clumsiness, naiveté, and insecurity. This fact suggests that while youngsters low in self-esteem can identify their positive qualities, they may focus too much on their perceived faults. This negative focus leaves children vulnerable to You Complete Me. A child who truly believes that she is more unattractive and less socially skilled than her peers may more readily turn to consumer goods to improve upon her perceived flaws.

Many youngsters vulnerable to You Complete Me have contingent self-esteem. The term "contingent self-esteem" describes the notion that feeling good about oneself can vary depending on the regard of others or on what one has accumulated.[6] Contingent self-esteem leaves individuals vulnerable to the vagaries of the outside world. A child might feel great about herself one week after acing her exam and winning praise from her teacher and terrible the next week when she receives a B+ on a paper. Contingent self-esteem applies particularly to those who strongly value materialistic goals. Materialistic-oriented individuals use possessions and social status to form an identity, increase their sense of security, and feel better about themselves relative to their peers and others in the society.

During preadolescence and adolescence, relying on material goods can be useful or it can indicate a problem. Material goods can help young people to express their unique selves. Think back to your childhood bedroom. What posters hung on the wall? Which keepsakes took up space on your shelves? What did you do in your sacred space: listen to music, watch television, gab for hours on the telephone? To learn about children's evolving identity, walk into their rooms and note the belongings that they choose to display. Mass communication researchers Jeanne Steele and Jane Brown did just that in a study on adolescent room culture.[7]

Over the course of several years, the researchers interviewed Caucasian, African American, Hispanic, and Native American teenagers in their bedrooms. They discovered that teens use mass media to help shape their emerging identities. In many of the bedrooms studied, posters of rock stars, television sets, and artwork shared space with stuffed animals from childhood. The youngsters used the objects to fantasize about possibilities for the future, to improve their mood, or to emulate admired celebrities. A child experiencing social problems, for instance, might disappear into his room to play music or to imagine how his role model might have handled the school bully.

Brand names also become an important part of the adolescent's developing personalities. Just like the sunglass shopper who wouldn't buy Guccis, youngsters incorporate merchandise brands into their identities. For instance, a study on brand names and identity explains one girl's identification with The Gap: "The clothes there are me because they are really nice and not so showy—real down-to-earth."[8] Material wares can certainly play a positive part in children's lives. They help them to define their likes and dislikes; emphasize (or downplay) their attachment to family or their membership in particular peer groups. Goods also chronicle youngsters' development from child to adolescent to young adult. An overreliance on possessions as a means of self-definition, however, can signify problems. You Complete Me champions the use of goods to define the self, and youngsters with low esteem and confidence are particularly susceptible to this message.

Some individuals seem to be more vulnerable than others to low self-esteem and a shaky identity. Being female represents one risk. As discussed in Chapter 4, before puberty, the rates of depression for boys and girls are roughly equivalent. (In some studies, boys even show slightly more depression than girls.) However, once youngsters reach puberty, the rate of depression for girls moves to twice that of boys. Even into adulthood, females continue to experience more self-reported depressive symptoms than males. Once they reach adolescence, girls also show lower self-esteem than boys. Adolescence does present challenges for girls in terms of body image and attractiveness. However, young women's susceptibility to low self-esteem goes beyond appearance. Some social scientists hypothesize that gender stereotypes and the devaluing of women in this culture also accounts for females' lower self-esteem.[9] Traditional masculine or androgynous characteristics link with greater emotional well-being than traditionally feminine traits. Both girls and boys who express behaviors typically characterized as "male"—assertiveness, athleticism, and competitiveness for example—fair better emotionally. This finding suggests that something about being female puts young women at risk for low self-esteem and depression.

One group of researchers has proposed that girls' social identity as female helps to explain their emotional well-being. Participants in the study included Caucasian, African American, Asian American, and Latino American female and male college students. The research group discovered a number of interesting patterns. Although females believed that their "womanhood" was one of the most important aspects of their identity, males were less likely to say that "being male" was one of the most crucial components of their identity. Not surprisingly, young women endorsed more depressive symptoms and lower self-esteem than the men. In particular, women who believe that society devalues females evidenced more depressive symptoms. Finally, an attribute termed "unmitigated communion" predicted depression in the women. Unmitigated communion simply describes the quality of showing great concern for other people and putting their needs before one's own. I think readers will recognize that this quality describes many women (and some men) in this culture.

The results of this study imply that society's devaluing of girls and women and female's traditional role as caretaker contribute to their self-esteem difficulties. It may be that those adolescent girls who, in the throes of identity exploration, begin to take on the traditional attributes ascribed them also acquire the low self-esteem and depression that go along with a less valued role. This stance of low self-esteem and intense concern about the welfare and the regard of others represents an ideal situation for You Complete Me. Many girls may feel as if they need external accoutrements such as stylish clothing or smart hairdos to experience positive self-worth and the approval of others. Females can buy in to the notion that their worth depends on how they look rather than who they are. This view is certainly reinforced by media as well as other individuals and groups in this society. For example, take a look at your newspaper. My local paper regularly has ads for plastic surgery almost exclusively aimed at females. It should be no surprise that procedures such as breast implants are becoming more and more common among teenage girls.

Much attention has been paid to the difficulties girls experience once they reach puberty. A host of studies corroborates the fact that compared to males, females do report more psychological difficulties during adolescence. However, this does not mean that boys navigate adolescence unscathed. Boys frequently do not admit to depression or anxiety as readily as do females. Males learn early on that expressing certain emotions—fear, sadness, tenderness—results in disapproval from peers and even some adults. By the time he reaches elementary school, a boy who cries or admits vulnerability leaves himself open to ridicule and ostracism. In a television program devoted to boys and emotion, one thirteen-year-old boy says: "We are equally sensitive to girls but society allows girl to show their emotion. And, if a guy steps out of that box and becomes supersensitive, they might be called names or criticized."[10]

Thus, boys keep their pain to themselves. Many psychologists believe that the high rate of completed suicide among adolescent boys—what some consider an epidemic at approximately five times the rate of girls—as well as school violence and shootings—primarily perpetrated by males—stems in part from the difficulty young men experience in realizing a full emotional life.[11] Essentially this research that suggests the huge sex differences found in emotional well-being and self-esteem might be misleading.

Given these gender differences in self-esteem and well-being, one might expect to find sex differences in materialistic orientation as well. The findings, however, have been mixed. Some studies have shown that the percentage of males and females with materialistic attitudes is roughly the same.[12] Those who have uncovered differences indicate that males score slightly higher on materialism inventories than females. At first blush, this finding appears contrary to expectations since females report lower self-esteem. However, as mentioned, sex differences in self-esteem might be misleading. Also, some social scientists believe that a few values, particularly those associated with traditional female roles, conflict with materialistic values. Researchers Ann Beutel and Margaret Marini contend that women are more likely to hold values related to caregiving, compassion, and responsibility for the well-being of the less fortunate.[13] In addition, they strive to find meaning in their lives beyond material success. These authors contend that males value goals of competition and financial profit over the well-being of people in the workplace. Men show their compassion and caring differently from females through "heroic and chivalrous behavior, including non-routine and risky acts of rescuing others."[14]

Beutel and Marini tested their assertions by assessing the opinions of high school students across the United States. They found that young women did indeed attach more importance to practicing compassion and discovering meaning in life over materialism and competition. For example, young women tended to agree with such statements as "I would agree to a good plan to make a better life for the poor, even if it cost me money"; young men agreed more with such statements as "It's not really my problem if others are in trouble and need help." In terms of materialism, females endorsed items including "In the United States, we put too much emphasis on making profits and not enough on human well-being." Males tended to disagree more with this statement. These findings imply that boys endorse greater materialism in part due to differences in socialization. However, we know that *both* males and females can be materialistic.

How can we explain the complex relationship among gender, self-esteem, identity, and materialism? For one thing, boys may outscore girls on measures of materialism because of differences in the way the construct is measured. Different studies define materialism in different ways. For example, studies have construed materialism in terms of competition, social status, identity, and security. It may be that some aspects of materialism resonate more with boys and some more with girls. At this point, there is not enough research yet to confirm this possibility. Also, males and females may express their materialistic leanings differently. I recently heard a mother on a talk show chronicle efforts to curtail her family's out-of-control spending. She "discovered" that most of her impulse shopping was on clothes for her children (to the tune of $250 per month). Consistent with women's propensity to do for others, their materialism might express itself more on purchases for family and friends and less on items for themselves. Mothers quoted throughout this book have admitted that most of their economic resources go toward the children. These parents have talked about materialism in terms of providing youngsters with lavish birthday parties, summer camps, and educational enrichment programs. Sex differences in materialism may reflect differences in spending patterns. Of course men also spend money on their children; however, the propensity to shop for clothing and toys might be a more typical for females.

Despite the fact that this is the twenty-first century, males and females do still experience differences in socialization. The culture generally designates females as "the shoppers." They are expected to do most of the shopping and "are taught at a young age that shopping and buying are enjoyable activities . . . something to do to feel better about oneself or when one is bored."[15] This reminds me of an "experiment" conducted by a talk show where the wives and the husbands switched roles for a day. In one instance, a husband was videotaped trying to do the grocery shopping. Hilarity, of course, ensued as this man spent hours (yes, hours) trying to locate the right potato chips and orange juice. He was saved by his young daughter, who seemed to know more about the market than he did. No one found it surprising that a man might not know how to shop for groceries. Girls and boys are also socialized differently in terms of appearance (see Chapter 4). Girls express greater concerns about their appearance, and these concerns translate into more interest in clothing, fashion, makeup and the purchase of these items to augment self-esteem.[16] It's not a huge leap for mothers to shift their focus and efforts onto their children. One mother, a single parent on a tight budget, says:

> He [son] is never hurt for anything. In fact, the money that used to go to my clothes is going to classes—enrichment classes or swimming classes. Any extra money that I might have or save usually goes to him.

Obviously, these buying patterns do not describe the behavior all males and females. Theories on socialization patterns help to explain overall gender differences in materialism and self-esteem found in the research literature. Clearly, You Complete Me can influence both boys and girls who struggle with low self-esteem and poor self-concept.

Other aspects of identity, beyond gender, can influence consumption and materialistic values. Children who try to meet everyone's expectations are particularly susceptible to You Complete Me. The term "high self-monitor" describes individuals who tend to change their behaviors, tastes, and attitudes depending on the situation. These people express great concern about image, status, and how others view them and may appear to be social chameleons, adjusting their opinions and demeanor depending on who they happen to be with. In contrast, "low self-monitors" place a premium on behaving in a way that is consistent with their values, regardless of the situation. Low self-monitors "rely on their own attitudes, feelings, and dispositions when making decisions or behavioral choices."[17] High self-monitors tend to use material goods in order to bolster their image. They respond more favorably to commercials that promote products by promising enhanced status and will even pay money for a product that might improve their standing with others.[18] Low self-monitors more frequently attend to the quality and reliability of a product when making purchasing decisions.

High self-monitors are particularly susceptible to the influence of You Complete Me. They buy in to the notion that certain products augment their worth. From an advertisers' point of view, these individuals are ideal customers for luxury products. Consider "the cheese experiment," in which researchers presented college students with two different cheeses. One cheese, a cheddar, had a pleasant taste, while the other, an Edam, was not as tasty.[19] One group of participants were told that the less pleasant tasting cheese originated in Mulberry, Kansas. A second group were told that this same cheese came from France. For most people, at least in terms of cheese, France carries greater status than Mulberry, Kansas. The results of this study illustrate the power of suggestion on consumer choices. Individuals who scored high on self-monitoring characteristics rated the cheese that they believed came from France as tastier than the cheese from Kansas. Low self-monitors rated the cheddar as tastier, regardless of where they believed it originated. The results imply that high self-monitors depend on status in determining their enjoyment of an item.

Compliments also enhance the desirability of some products. In another study, college students tested perfume.[20] As with the cheese study, one perfume smelled good and the other did not. Half of the participants received a compliment on the scent (e.g., "that smells good on you"). High self-monitors rated the perfumes more positively when they received a compliment. Low self-monitors rated the pleasant scent as better smelling than the less pleasant scent whether they received a compliment or not. When high self-monitors perceive that a product might cause others to admire them, they come to value this item, regardless of whether it appeals to them personally. Perhaps these chameleons convince themselves that they truly do prefer the higher-status merchandise.

Most of us care to some extent about how we come across to other people. Don describes how easily anyone can be seduced into believing that expensive is better:

> I was going to get [my son] a bicycle for Christmas, so I took him down to the bike shop, he rode the bicycles around the shop. So he liked this one bike and it was $130. I thought, "I bet Wal-Mart would have a cheaper bike." So I went and found one for $75. Then, I admit it, a piece of me thought the $130 bike must be better . [laughs] So I ended up getting the $130 bike because he really liked that one, that's what I told myself. So then Christmas morning comes and we put the bike together and put a big bow on it. He starts tearing open gifts and we finally had to tell him, did you notice the bike? He thanked us for the bike and went on opening stuff. It didn't matter to him whether it was Wal-Mart or the designer bike.

Many readers can probably relate to Don's story. We've all been schooled to presume that expensive items are somehow better than bargain brands. This is one reason why luxury goods hold such cachet. However, adolescents are particularly susceptible to high self-monitoring and status-focused advertising. Their increased susceptibility in part stems from their self-consciousness; as mentioned, youngsters of this age imagine that everybody's looking at them and evaluating them.[21] Add to this self-consciousness, greater self-doubt and fears about fitting in, and you end up with youngsters prone to turning to status brands as a way of addressing their insecure identities and wavering self-esteem.

Consistently using externals to augment social desirability leaves children wide open to the influence of the You Complete Me.

The goal for high self-monitors becomes gaining social acceptance and admiration, either through status goods or by assessing and trying to meet the expectations of others, rather than developing their personalities through discovery of deeply held values. These chameleons actually change personalities to gain the acceptance of others. Relying primarily on this strategy does not serve self-esteem or identity development, however. Instead of allowing other people to determine their identity, youngsters gain greater control over their lives by deciding for themselves which values and behaviors matter most to them. Sticking to one's beliefs regardless of prevailing opinions also develops integrity and fortitude and discourages youngsters from looking outward for approval. Personal control, fortitude, and integrity all are foils for You Complete Me.

People's ability to confidently and effectively communicate who they are to others ties in with greater self-esteem and self-assuredness. Children need to feel as if they have some control over how they present themselves to others and over how others perceive them. Note that this is different from self-monitoring. With self-monitoring, children attempt to gauge what others want and then mold their behavior to fit this assessment. In contrast, we want children to interact with others based on their own internal compass. Children who can communicate their desires effectively develop self-efficacy, confidence, and the ability to resist peer pressure (and You Complete Me). In my past work with young children, I noticed that some youngsters have particular difficulty influencing their peers' opinions of them. In particular, youngsters with social skills problems often were very frustrated when other children refused to see them as potential playmates or to recognize any of their positive qualities. Many of these children resorted to self-defeating behaviors, such as attempting to "buy" friends by giving them gifts or by bringing expensive belongings to school to share with classmates.

The ability to influence others impacts self-esteem. In one study, adult participants were asked to compare their ratings of their competence with their guesses as to how others might rate them.[22] For example, they were asked how well educated they consider themselves to be and how well educated they think *others* consider them to be. A large discrepancy between these two scores indicates less validation by others of one's identity. Less validation affects one's level of self-esteem. Many females, minorities, and homosexual youth experience this discrepancy between their self-concept and the evaluation of others due to stereotypes about their group membership. For example, stereotypes of racial minority individuals as being less intelligent or able than Caucasians can impact their emotional well-being and academic performance.[23] A female student once told me that she walked into a college-level math class on the first day of the semester, only to be met with the comment, "Oh look at the cute little blonde!"—from the course instructor. Despite her excellent performance throughout the semester, the instructor never acknowledged her mathematical abilities. Toward the end of the semester, she felt "so disgusted, [she] I didn't feel like trying." Young people need validation of their strengths and talents for positive self-esteem and self-concept.

The results of the above study indicate that certain groups of people receive greater support for their self-perceptions than others. Participants with more education experienced greater validation of their identity and greater self-esteem and self-efficacy. Education is an indicator of status in this society, and experiencing this status appears to increase people's social confidence. I highlight this study with adults because researchers so far have not examined the relationship among social status, self-concept, and external validation in children in great depth. However, the results are relevant to children as well. Children's self-esteem and self-efficacy will be enhanced when they feel themselves to be competent, important, and an integral part of their family and community. Children who feel disenfranchised or unappreciated will be more prone to self-destructive behavior. As discussed in Chapter 5, youngsters who feel disconnected from their families gravitate toward materialistic values and other self-destructive behaviors.

Large discrepancies between one's real self (who we perceive our-selves to be now) and one's ideal self (where we'd *like* to be) also leave children vulnerable to the You Complete Me. Materialists ex-perience greater discrepancies between their real and ideal selves. For example, an individual who badly wants a wealthy, well-trav-eled, and widely admired lifestyle, yet struggles to make ends meet, experiences a large discrepancy between her ideal and real selves. Many psychologists believe that self-esteem is based on people's comparisons of their real and ideal selves. When there is little differ-ence between the real and the ideal or if a person perceives some progress toward the ideal, positive self-esteem results. However, self-esteem suffers when people feel that the discrepancy is insur-mountable. This comparison process works in many areas of our lives. An individual may feel high satisfaction when it comes to fam-ily, social, and spiritual life and less satisfaction with her standard of living (e.g., her material life). Some researchers propose that materi-alists value the material domain significantly more than other areas of their life.[24] This material fervor translates into a belief that wealth and status—more than a happy family life, emotionally satisfying ca-reer, or spiritual faith—are critical to achieving happiness. Material-ists put more energy into this area of their lives, and You Complete Me acts on this energy. As we know, materialists focus on external goals in their search for happiness. They also express less content-ment with their lives.

Consumer researcher Joseph Sirgy proposes that materialists experience less life satisfaction because they hold higher expecta-tions for their standard of living and feel deserving of a materially comfortable life.[25] Materialists hold these beliefs for a number of reasons. For one, materialist-oriented children engage in social comparison more intensely than do other children. This comparison creates an atmosphere of competition, as the child strives to equal or best other youngsters by owning the best or achieving the most. Materialistic-oriented children also watch television and compare their lives to those on the screen. As we know, the television world presents an unreal universe where disproportionate numbers of people live in affluence yet spend remarkably little time working. How does a person decide whom to use as a point of comparison? When individuals compare themselves to those who have less than they do, they feel good about their lives. When people choose to model their goals after individuals with great wealth or accomplishments, they may feel less satisfied. Because materialists value wealth and status so highly, they more readily choose to compare their lives to those of the rich and powerful. Given media's unrealistic portrayal of work and wealth, shaping an identity in this manner poses a danger to children who feel entitled to material goods or success without the commensurate effort. Entitlement may be a modern-day affliction. Some researchers have concluded that "compared with their counterparts in the 60's and 70's, young people today place more emphasis on earning a lot of money but less emphasis on work."[26]

You Complete Me has particular influence over children and adolescents with low self-esteem and an insecure identity. These difficulties could be due to sex-role socialization and to the belief that others do not value one's gender. In addition, girls receive greater inducements to express themselves through appearance and material goods. Many boys are taught to repress their emotions and to express themselves through competition and financial success. You Complete Me is particularly persuasive with high self-monitors and with those who lack the skills and confidence to communicate who they are to peers. Finally, when children's ideal self does not match their current circumstance, they are more likely to experience dissatisfaction and to turn to materialism as an answer to their problems.

Fortifying your children's self-esteem and self-concept will help you contend with You Complete Me. Consider the ways in which you treat your children's emotions. Do you encourage your daughters to express anger and assertiveness as well as sadness and tenderness? Do you attend to the full emotional lives of your sons? Remember that much of our socialization behavior is unconscious and therefore requires extra vigilance. For more information on this topic, I provide a brief list of suggested readings on boys' and girls' identity and emotional development at the end of the chapter.

BEATING THE HUMDRUMS

When do you get bored? My peak moments of monotony usually involve tedious meetings that feel eternal. During interminable meetings, confined to 300 square inches of metal chair, I typically daydream or make mental to-do lists to lighten the monotony. Almost everyone experiences boredom now and then, and children discover both good and bad ways to deal with it. Take drug use, for example. Early research on this topic concluded that much drug use by children and adolescents was due to peer pressure. However, recent research has found that children cite boredom as a leading reason for drug experimentation and continued use. In one study, almost 50 percent of preteens (ages ten to twelve years) surveyed indicated that boredom led to their use of marijuana and other illegal substances.[27] The children commented on how the drugs made them happy and saw the substance use as a social activity, something fun they could do with their friends. The youngsters in this study also indicated that they had very few options for extracurricular activities, citing inadequate facilities for sports and other organized pursuits. Those children in the study who avoided drug use were more likely to be involved in organized pastimes, such as sports teams, dance classes, or drama club. Additional studies have also uncovered boredom as a leading contributor to impulsive behaviors like shopping, overeating, and Internet addition.[28] The literature clearly indicates the importance of teaching children how to manage boredom and of making structured activities available to them.

The ability to manage boredom has implications for the Humdrum, Ho-Hum.

Boredom accounts indirectly for adolescents' inclination toward sensation seeking and impulsive buying. Throughout adolescence, the brain experiences tremendous changes in structure. The areas of the brain that regulate emotion and biological drives, such as sexual behavior, undergo a significant increase in volume.[29] Thus teens experience greater urges for exciting, novel, complex experiences (perhaps not a surprise to their parents). At the same time, executive functioning, regulated by brain structures in the prefrontal lobe, remains relatively less developed until late adolescence. Executive functioning refers to behaviors such as planning, attention, and self-control. In adults, executive functioning can inhibit the portions of the brain that control emotion and impulsive behaviors. This means that when an adult really wants something that she can't afford, her executive function can help her reason that "I need to wait on this purchase until I've saved more money." The immaturity of executive function areas in adolescents helps to explain why they exhibit more impulsive, risk-taking behaviors. Teenagers "experience more intense urges, [but] the skills required to control these urges are in short supply; such skills do not develop with the onset of puberty but rather improve gradually with age and experience."[30] Teenagers' desire for novelty and their less developed ability to control impulses makes them particularly vulnerable to the Humdrum, Ho-Hum.

Teenagers also experience frequent shifts in mood (again, no surprise to parents). During adolescence, youngsters show an increase in negative emotions such as anger, depression, and anxiety.[31] Fluctuations in mood might be due to hormones and to the many life changes that youngsters undergo at this stage. Changes in friends, schools, body, social rules, and self-consciousness, not to mention acne, combined with physiological changes could put anyone into a funk. Many adults may find youngsters' reactions to small occurrences to be gross overreactions. However, for many young people, discovering a pimple or having "nothing" to wear truly does feel devastating. Research finds that negative mood, in children and adults, is predictive of impulsive behavior.[32] When youngsters find themselves in an emotional slump, their goal is to do whatever they can—shopping, drinking, eating—to lessen their distress. In this situation, controlling impulses takes a backseat to mood enhancement (and this is where the Humdrum, Ho-Hum can take over). Thus the research on adolescent brain physiology and social development suggests that teenagers are particularly primed for impulsive shopping and materialistic inclinations.

Teens may interpret their hunger for new experiences as boredom. And impulse shopping can certainly provide the rush that some youngsters crave. However, impulse shopping results in deleterious consequences. In this society, young people with access to credit cards have amassed high levels of debt. Since 2000, the median level of credit card debt among college students has increased approximately 43 percent.[33] Remember the teen mentioned at the beginning of this chapter. She took no responsibility for budgeting or managing her spending. She relied on her father to let her know if her spending habits were problematic. Practices like this do nothing to foster responsible attitudes toward money management. This problem of credit card debt is evident among my college students. Several have told me that they received unsolicited credit cards in the mail when they were in high school. By the time they reached college, they had to work just to pay off their outstanding balances.

Some researchers have identified characteristics associated with irresponsible spending. In one study, investigators examined individuals' propensity to consider future consequences.[34] Imagine going shopping for socks. In the course of your sock expedition, you come across a beautifully made jacket that happens to cost $700. You *really* want it. While you can't afford the jacket right now, you could charge it on your credit card. What do you do? Researchers found that people more prone to consider the future consequences of their spending are more likely to put that jacket back on the rack. Those who are low in this quality more frequently buy now and put it on plastic. Less consideration of future consequences links with greater impulsivity. These less future-oriented individuals were also more apt to comment on the excitement of buying on impulse. Again, the excitement of impulse spending is part of what lures youngsters into debt.

In this same study, young people were asked to imagine receiving a $900 windfall. The participants could spend this money by paying off credit card debt, making a purchase, going on a trip with

friends, or saving it. Those less likely to consider future consequences more frequently allocated the greater part of their "money"
to a special purchase and less to paying off debt. Again, the results
reinforce the notion that giving in to instant gratification can backfire for youngsters in the long-term. The Humdrum, Ho-Hum uses
the promise of excitement and gratification to encourage materialism in youngsters.

All teenagers do not give in to their impulses. One quality that
differentiates young impulse shoppers from those who resist is
emotional intelligence.[35] Individuals with high levels of emotional intelligence are adept at understanding and regulating their own and
others' emotions. They have greater insight into how feelings can
lead to particular behaviors—for example, how a slight by a friend
or a poor grade might lead to a shopping spree. They also have a
better grasp of how their behavior impacts the feelings and behaviors of others. Emotional intelligence (also known as emotional understanding) has implications for children's emotional health as
well as for the quality of their relationships with others. In one
study, investigators traveled to shopping malls to assess the emotional intelligence and impulse-buying behavior of teenagers.
Items assessing emotional intelligence included statements like "I
can tell how other people are feeling by listening to the tone of
their voice," and "I know why my emotions change."[36] Teens who
scored low on emotional intelligence were also more likely to admit
to impulse shopping.

The research indicates that helping children to understand their
emotions, where they come from and how they affect behavior, represents an important investment in their future. Emotional understanding links with greater psychological health, social competence,
and, as discussed, less impulsive behavior. Fortifying a child's emotional intelligence could also protect them from developing materialistic values. Children with insight into their behavior are more likely
to address their distress directly rather than blindly buying something to feel better. Emotional education should start early. Young
children of parents who engage their youngsters in discussions

about their emotional lives have a greater grasp of the kinds of situations that lead to happy, sad and angry feelings.[37]

There do appear to be gender differences in the way many parents approach emotions with their children. As discussed earlier in this chapter, because of societal expectations that males be strong, confident, and certainly not "wimpy," many parents (and teachers and other adults) treat their son's feelings differently than they do their daughters'. Adults dwell less on emotions with their sons and jump more quickly to solutions. With girls, many of us feel comfortable exploring exactly how they felt in great detail when discussing both happy and sad occasions. It's easier to talk about feelings with girls. They're socialized to attend to this area of their lives and feel much more comfortable in the world of emotion. Boys present a greater challenge as most don't receive this kind of training. Just visit the playground of an elementary school. Girls can be found clustered in small groups discussing just about anything. Boys typically congregate in large "swarms" and come together over athletic activities. They are much less likely to talk about feelings or even what might be going on in their lives.[38]

Boredom can lead youngsters to seek inappropriate ways to create excitement in their lives. For teenagers, changes in brain structure and hormone levels increase their vulnerability to impulse buying and the influence of the Humdrum, Ho-Hum. Parents can ameliorate its impact by helping youngsters to develop their emotional understanding. They can also encourage young people to develop productive pastimes that will keep them engaged and interested in life. I discuss ways to develop intrinsic interests next.

GOING WITH THE FLOW

One powerful antidote to boredom is *flow,* the experience of being so engrossed in an activity that one loses track of time.[39] People usually flow when they pursue an activity simply out of joy or interest, or for the challenge. Flow activities include the obvious and the not so obvious: making collages, painting pictures, hiking in the mountains, playing Frisbee, knitting a scarf, reading a book, surfing the Internet, gardening, talking with friends, going for a bike ride, picking berries, riding the waves, sewing, writing poetry, baking bread . . . Flow can appear at the workplace. People have reported flow experiences working on assembly lines, doing computer work, and performing surgery.[40] Psychologist Mihaly Csikszentmihalyi has conducted research and written extensively about the flow experience, which he describes as "providing a sense of discovery, a creative feeling of transporting the person into a new reality."[41] According to Csikszentmihalyi, flow stems from intrinsic motivation. Individuals pursue flow activities out of interest, not for praise or material rewards. While rewards might be an added outcome, the primary motivation comes from intrinsic desires. Think of flow as the antithesis of materialism. A materialistic framework encourages individuals to act based on the philosophy of "What's in it for me?" Flow inspires individuals to get involved in activities based on a credo of "What can I learn?"

Flow experiences include several elements: challenge, goals, and keen concentration. First, the activity provides some degree of challenge. Whether learning to crawl or mastering chess, human beings love a challenge. Our inherent curiosity and desire to push ourselves explains the popularity of mind teasers, crossword puzzles, and games. Challenge keeps boredom at bay in part because individuals devote their attention more fully to tasks that require effort. To flow, people must also have the skills for an undertaking. This combination of skills and challenge, in part, constitutes flow.

Humans' genetic makeup includes the propensity to seek out challenging experiences. Researchers have determined, for instance, that even infants prefer moderate levels of challenge. For example, when presented with a 2-by–2 checkerboard pattern and a 24-by–24 checkerboard pattern, four-month-olds initially prefer the 2-by–2 pattern. After practice examining the more complex board, however, they come to prefer the 24-by–24 pattern. The researchers concluded that "as the children's ability to deal with complexity increased they preferred more complexity."[42] The *moderate-discrepancy hypothesis* describes the notion that humans have a penchant for situations that go just a little bit beyond their current capabilities. When an activity is too difficult, people tend to get frustrated and give up. Yet an exceedingly easy pursuit leads to boredom and disinterest.

Flow activities usually involve clear goals and immediate feedback. For example, when an individual begins knitting a sweater, she has an idea of what the finished product will look like (the goal). She gauges her progress as a sleeve or the neckline starts taking shape (feedback). If she misses a stitch, she knows she must start over again (more feedback). People derive great joy from meeting their objectives. Flow activities reap other benefits as well. Setting and following through on goals helps to build self-discipline, self-esteem, autonomy, and identity. Further, when people engage in flow pursuits, they forget about others' judgments and opinions. As we know, youngsters with strong materialistic values care very much about appearances. When individuals find their flow, they focus on what makes them happy, not on what others think. I discovered the "physics of flow" several years ago when I start taking yoga classes. For the longest time, no matter how hard I tried, I could not maintain a headstand in class. I would manage to hoist myself into the air, balance precariously for a split second, and then come tumbling down, embarrassed and frustrated. During the week, I tenaciously practiced headstand at home, holding the pose relatively easily. But sure enough, Saturday class would come along, and once again I'd find myself toppling to the ground. I realized that in class I thought so much about my performance that I really wasn't concentrating on my yoga practice. Once I decided to forget about the other students and even the instructor and turn my focus inward, I found a love of yoga (and I held the headstand). Individuals flow when all of the elements come together: "Concentration is so intense that there is no attention left over to think about anything irrelevant, or to worry about problems. Self-consciousness disappears, and the sense of time becomes distorted. An activity that produces such experiences

is so gratifying that people are will to do it for its own sake, with little concern for what they will get out of it, even when it is difficult,
or dangerous. "[43]

People who flow get more enjoyment out of life. So why don't
we all flow all the time? Despite our inherent curiosity and zest for
life, a great deal of the time, people prefer comfort and relaxation.[44]
While flow activities make for peak experiences, they also require
energy and drive. The dilemma calls to mind the archetypal conflict
between good and bad. Imagine trying to resist a piece of chocolate
cake. The angel on your left shoulder whispers, "Don't do it. Sweets
aren't good for you, and remember your resolution to lose weight
this year." On your right shoulder the devil cajoles, "Oh come on.
It's just one piece of cake. Think about how amazing it's going to
taste!" Humans' wavering drive toward flow resembles the conflict
between naughty and nice, except that the angel represents an active, joyful spirit and the devil looks more like a couch potato. Once
people tune out their inner couch potato and convince themselves to
put on their hiking boots or grab the surf board, they report feeling
happy and alive. This active engagement in life also provides protection from the influence of the Humdrum, Ho-Hum.

When do children flow the most? The Csikszentmihalyi team
equipped high school students with pagers so that they could check
in with them at various times during the day and night.[45] When the
pagers sounded, youngsters reported to the research team on their
activities and their mood. This study found that flow experiences
generally contained both high challenge and high skills. Flow activities included productive pursuits, such as classwork and homework,
and extracurricular activities, such as hobbies, sports, and after-
school jobs. When students flowed they reported greater happiness,
enjoyment, motivation, concentration, and self-esteem. Low-flow
activities included passive pursuits like watching television, staring
out the window, household chores, and riding the bus to school.
During low-flow periods, students reported more apathy and less
happiness and motivation. Teens also reported enjoying relaxing activities such as spending time with friends, listening to music or eat-

ing. Researchers characterized these pastimes as containing high skill and low challenge. The teens in this study spent the majority of their time happily relaxing (32 percent of the time). Approximately 17 percent of the time they reported feeling anxious; at this time typically they were engaged in activities that required more skill than they felt they possessed (e.g., taking tests or very difficult courses). A quarter of the time, they reported feeling apathetic, spending time sleeping or staring out the window (a prime situation for Humdrum, Ho-Hum). About 26 percent of the time, they engaged in flow activities. The group of teens who reported the greatest flow spent more time in productive activities and less time hanging out with friends and watching television.

Even though teenagers in this study report the highest levels of well-being while engaged in flow activities, note that they spent only about a quarter of their time pursuing them. Like many people, teenagers chose to relax rather than to engage in more challenging activities. Parents need to motivate their youngsters to get off the couch or hang up the phone and flow. It's not an easy task, but it's certainly worth the effort. Increasing flow experiences and, by definition, intrinsic motivation can decrease children's reliance on material goods as a way of alleviating boredom. As one mother attests, children can certainly put up a fight when asked to make that stretch:

> At first, whenever it was time to go to karate class, Carlo would start complaining, "I don't want to go, I don't like it there, I want to stay home." When he got to class he always had a good time. I remind him of this whenever he starts resisting. I wish my parents had done this for me; who knows, maybe I'd be a dancer or a gymnast now.

Participation in challenging pursuits and active leisure activities generates multiple benefits. Active leisure includes structured activities that require some level of skill (sports teams, the debate squad, service clubs). Passive leisure—watching television or shopping for instance—ask very little of an individual. Children who participate in

active leisure display higher self-esteem, higher academic performance, more interest in school, and better overall mental health. These
active, engaged youngsters flow more often and also say that participation in their chosen activity is important to their emerging identity.[46] Self-defining pursuits include organized sports, social activities,
performing and fine arts, religious groups, and altruistic activities.
The point is to help your youngsters find their flow while avoiding the
overscheduling treadmill. Remember that finding a flow activity
should be based on a child's genuine interest, not your own. Writer
David Sedaris chronicles the pitfalls of living through one's child:

> "Hold on to your hat," my father said, "because here's that guitar
> you've always wanted." Surely he had me confused with some-
> one else. Although I had regularly petitioned for a brand-name
> vacuum cleaner, I'd never said anything about wanting a guitar.
> Nothing about it appealed to me, not even on an aesthetic level. I
> had my room arranged just so, and the instrument did not fit in
> with my nautical theme. An anchor, yes. A guitar, no. He wanted
> me to jam, so I jammed it into my closet.[47]

Integrating more flow into life can help children to avoid the influence of the Humdrum, Ho Hum. Flow experiences foster increased energy and direct children's attention onto gratifying
pursuits and away from over concern about the opinions and judgments of others. Flow promotes positive self-esteem and a more
complex self-concept. Best of all, people who flow are happy.

SUMMARY

The You Complete Me presents a challenge for most youngsters.
However, it has particular pull for those low in self-esteem and those
acutely sensitive to the impressions they make on others. Because of
gender stereotypes and expectations, adolescent females are prey to
depression and low self-esteem and therefore wide open to the influence of You Complete Me. Boys socialized to restrict emotional expression of "unmasculine" feelings such as fear and sadness and to

pursue competition and financial gain also have vulnerability to You Complete Me. The Humdrum, Ho-Hum presents particular challenges for youngsters because of their difficulties regulating impulsive behavior. Those who have trouble connecting their feelings with behavior are also more likely to engage in impulsive spending, which soothes distress and satisfies the need for sensation and new experiences. To ameliorate the impact of materialistic forces, parents can enhance satisfaction through fortifying emotional intelligence and promoting flow activities.

LET'S DISCUSS IT

This section includes statements and questions designed to stimulate discussion on notions of materialism most impacted by You Complete Me and Humdrum, Ho-Hum. Every family member should have an opportunity to respond to the items. Please feel free to add your own questions.

1. How would your friends describe you? How would your family describe you? Which three adjectives would you use to describe yourself?
2. Do you own certain possessions that best reflect who you are (e.g., an item of clothing, something used as part of a hobby, photos, artwork, books)?
3. The situations that make me feel really down are _____ _____. (Parents: If youngsters have difficulty answering this question, you may need to offer some suggestions. Examples include being ignored by a friend, doing poorly on a test, too much homework, etc.)
4. When I feel down I respond by _____. Do your strategies help you to feel better or worse?
5. The one or two things that I "flow" in are _____. How often do you participate in this activity? What obstacles keep you from the activity? What can you do to lessen the impact of these obstacles?

SUGGESTED READINGS:

J. Garbarino, Lost boys: Why Our Sons Turn Violent and How We Can Save Them (New York: The Free Press, 1999).

M. Gray, In Your Face: Stories From the Lives of Queer Youth (New York: Harrington Park Press, 1999).

D. Kindlon and M. Thompson, Raising Cain: Protecting the Emotional Life of Boys (New York: Ballantine Books, 2000).

M. Pipher, Shelter of Each Other (New York: Ballantine Books, 1997).

W. Pollack, Real boys: Rescuing Our Sons From the Myths of Boyhood (New York: Owl Books, 1999).

R. Savin-Williams, Mom, Dad. I'm Gay: How Families Negotiate Coming Out (Washington, D. C.:American Psychological Association, 2001).

S. Shandler, Ophelia Speaks: Adolescent Girls Write About Their Search For Self (New York: Harper Paperbacks, 1999).

CHAPTER 7

INSPIRING WONDER

When you think of the word "spirituality," what comes to mind? Do you picture a certain religion? Maybe you consider certain qualities, such as faith, goodness, compassion, or dedication. Perhaps you envision a particularly virtuous soul: Mother Teresa, Martin Luther King, Jr., Gandhi, or Archbishop Tutu. The term "spirituality" means different things to different people, and in this sense it constitutes a very personal concept. For some individuals, personal spirituality might encompass a dedication to art, nature, or music. It can be any area that allows people to experience a sense of veneration and a greater connection to themselves and others. Americans today profess a deep interest in faith and spiritual connection. In 2005, *Newsweek* magazine took on the topic of spirituality in America, concluding that citizens are eager to experience *transcendence*—going beyond the concrete realities of regular life to experience communion with a higher power.[1] True to our individualistic nature, Americans have discovered many different paths toward the spiritual: Evangelical Protestant, Roman Catholic, Hindu, Buddhism, Kabbalah, Islam, Baptist, and Pagan, to name a few.

In her book *Megatrends 2010*, Patricia Aburdene identifies spirituality as the most significant cultural trend in businesses today.[2] Aburdene considers the rise in conscious capitalism to reflect the importance of spiritual-based values to both consumers and businesses. Conscious capitalism refers to business practices that incorporate integrity and social responsibility into attention to the bottom line. It springs, in part, from spiritual values such as generosity, love, and social justice. Companies that practice conscious capitalism are typically active in the community—whether that means helping to preserve the environment or providing scholarships to low-income youth. According to Aburdene, conscious capitalism affects company profits. People prefer to frequent businesses that embrace humanistic practices. She finds that "the majority of people (90 percent) would consider switching products to avoid doing business with companies that have a reputation for poor corporate citizenship."[3] Spirituality in business, then, reflects its growing importance in society.

Research concurs with the popular literature. The majority of American adolescents, (over 90 percent), "believe in God or a universal spirit," and over half attend religious services at least monthly.[4] For most teenagers, part of the search for identity includes a strong push to discover their spiritual nature. Their spiritual undertaking includes a search for meaning and purpose in their lives. Younger children also seek spiritual or divine experience. Some researchers and psychologists maintain that little ones do not possess the cognitive capacity to truly have a spiritual life. They contend that young children's conceptualizations of spirit are limited to memorized prayers or to a man who lives in the sky. Others disagree with this portrayal. Tobin Hart, whose work I discuss later in this chapter, asserts that young children's openness to the world around them and their less linear cognitive style make them particularly primed for spirituality and transcendent experiences in particular.[5]

I decided to include a chapter on spirituality in part because both research and theory suggest that materialistic values lie in opposition to the values espoused by many spiritual traditions. For example, self-interested individuals, focused on personal advancement and materialistic goals, less frequently endorse the values of social responsibility and compassion.[6] Self-enhancement and self-tran-

scendence are fundamentally different. Values such as desires for social status, sensual gratification, and personal success are considered
contrary to values such as understanding and appreciation of people
and nature.[7] Individuals who esteem both sets of values more frequently experience psychological stress compared to those who
favor one or the other.

I also included this chapter based on parental comments. All the
parents I interviewed expressed, in some way, their desire to inculcate spirituality into their children's lives. However, their notions of
spirituality varied. Sasha describes her hopes for altruism in her six-
year-old son:

> My biggest fear is that he'll grow up feeling that he has a *right* to
> things, that he has something coming, that he's entitled. I talk
> with him about rich and poor and how important it is to give to
> people in need, and he gets it. The other day he announced that
> "if I were president, I would give money to the poor people."
> When we go to events and they pass around the hat, I make sure
> that he's the one who puts in the money.

Mandy discusses the importance of generosity, ritual, and belonging to a community:

> We believe in reusing and try to instill that in him [son]. We
> want him to think about giving to others. He got this really cool
> truck for Christmas. Every time one of his good friends, Parker,
> came over to play, Parker always wanted to play with the truck.
> On Parker's birthday, my son decided to give the truck to him. It
> was his decision . . . and it was great! We do some religious ritu-
> als like lighting the menorah, we did that every night. And we're
> talking about joining a synagogue . . . we were both raised that
> way and we would like him to be exposed to that and have some
> kind of religious affiliation. . . . I'm not terribly religious, but I
> want him to have that in terms of the traditions and the identifi-
> cation, I think it's important and I don't want to turn my back on
> it. The affiliation and the community, that's the part I really want
> him to get.

Lina and her husband believe that religious education will help their children to cope more adeptly with life's challenges :

> We've been feeling like we need to tell them more, so he's [husband] started teaching them Hindi . . . and we have been talking with them more about Indian mythology, just introducing it to them . . . we don't do that much and so the kids aren't as grounded in the religion and they do need to have some kind of foundation. Then they can do what they want with it, but at least they'll know a little bit about the heritage and what Hinduism is even about. It's an ancient religion, more of a philosophy, with certain premises about reincarnation, and the importance of our actions that I think will help them in life. The idea of detachment, that you do your best at what you do, but don't get too attached to the outcome, I think they need that foundation.

Although Thelma and her partner don't practice an organized religion, they want their girls to feel free to choose their own spiritual path:

> I think that connecting to something larger than ourselves and the little universes of our lives is really important for kids. Neither of us had great experiences with religion . . . so we were looking for a way to bring spirituality into our lives and expose the kids to many religions, so as they grew older, they could pick one or develop their own sense of spirituality.

Fran, a single parent of a five-year-old, expressed concerns that her son learns about civil rights and "understanding about race and inequality." The notions of spirit described by these parents encompass a number of characteristics and beliefs: equality, generosity, responsibility to relieve the misery of others, staying open to experience, valuing community, and religious tradition.

Clearly the word "spirituality" means different things to different people, and trying to define it proves difficult. For this chapter, I draw on Tobin Hart's notions of spirituality.[8] Hart explains that, first, the concept represents a way of viewing the world as steeped in spirit. It's the feeling of spirit (e.g., God, a higher power, the divine) existing in everything that surrounds us—nature and people, the things we love and the things we dislike. Second, spirituality is an important part of identity development, which includes discovering meaning in life, setting goals based on ideas of purpose, and possessing the desire to contribute in some way to improving the lives of others. The interpretation here reflects both the internal and the external. Spirit is both personal and introspective, social and altruistic.

The definition of spirituality I present is intentionally broad and includes both religious and secular beliefs. The parents whom I interviewed construe spirituality in myriad ways. You will find views and experiences of families from traditional religious disciplines as well as less mainstream perspectives. I also report on how this topic has been covered in the literature. I provide examples of religious rituals and practices not intended as endorsements, but rather to give readers new perspectives and ideas. The first section of the chapter covers the ways in which spirituality contributes to children's happiness and overall social and emotional development. The second section includes ideas on how parents can nurture their children's spirituality.

I believe spiritual development is extremely important for children (and adults) and that it should receive the same attention that other areas of growth—social, emotional, and physical—receive. Unfortunately, research on spiritual growth is relatively less robust than the research on other facets of development. As with the topic of materialism, spirituality receives a relatively short shrift in the child development literature. Further, I believe that maintaining caring connections with other people, a quality that many religions hold dear, is essential to children's personal development and to society as well. This value reflects a belief in the importance of collectivism to optimal human and community functioning. A final note: The literature often uses the terms "spirituality" and "religion" interchangeably; therefore "spirituality" as used in this chapter refers both to beliefs affiliated with organized religion and to more individualistic or unaffiliated ideologies. We begin our discussion with the theory of caring and try to answer the question of why spirituality matters so much to so many.

SPIRITUALITY AND PSYCHOLOGICAL WELL-BEING

Many philosophers maintain that a happy life depends on good character.[9] The argument goes that the happiest people try to live a virtuous life, show compassion toward others, and contribute to the well-being of society. A bold claim? You might be thinking "What about So-and-So. He's not so nice, but he is successful or wealthy. He must be at least a little happy!" Others might think, "I should be so miserable." Happiness, as I describe it here, goes deeper than the momentary pleasure gained from indulgence or entertainment. Enduring happiness requires work and rests in large part on how we feel about and treat our fellow citizens.[10] Open-mindedness, critical thinking, empathy, tenderness: a contented, well-lived life all contribute to the desire to care for others. Many social scientists believe that parents who wish to foster happiness in their children must commit to promoting not only intellectual, moral, and social development but youngsters' ability to feel compassion for others.

Education philosopher Dr. Nel Noddings calls this set of beliefs *the ethics of caring*.[11] This theory maintains that living a truly moral, and ultimately fulfilling, life involves constantly evaluating one's actions relative to how they impact others. Parents encourage these values by compelling children to think about how their behaviors serve to help others and strengthen relationships. Actions that weaken relationships not only harm others but also compromise a person's moral and spiritual character. Moral development goes beyond consideration of individual rights. Children's emotional understanding, their ability to walk in another's shoes, helps them to develop empathy. For example, when youngsters contribute to the care of homeless people, they increase their understanding of the complex reasons for the plight of these individuals.[12] These youngsters are less prone to blaming and dismissing those in dire straits. The parents featured in this book shared a number of strategies for breeding the values of caring. One couple tries to teach their two boys compassion through the ritual of prayer:

> We always hold hands at every meal and we say grace. And then at night we say our prayers. We created our own prayer that we added on to the standard prayer. We start out with the standard "Now I lay me down to sleep . . . God bless Mama, and Papa, and Auntie, and all the sick people, all the lonely people, all the people who have AIDS. Amen." Every time something happens in the world, like Hurricane Katrina, "God bless all the people affected by Katrina." And then we'll say, "Remember the tsunami? God bless all the people killed by the tsunami." And so on . . . I want them to have compassion for others outside of our household. Things that happen globally, we still care about those people. We may not know them, but we feel their pain. It may sound trite, but they remember . . . out of the blue they'll ask, "What about the Katrina people, how are they doing?" I think of it as our compassion list.

Learning through observing presents powerful lessons for youngsters. One mother describes how she teaches her son to feel good about giving:

> When friends of ours have babies, he picks a toy, a favorite stuffed animal, to give them, so it's really nice because we wash it and he gives it to the baby and tells the baby the story of it: "Oh, that used to be my giraffe." The first time or two he wasn't all that happy about it, but now he looks forward to it. I want him to know that the greatest reward for doing something that feels good is how good you feel . . . he'll say, "I'm making good choices today!" I'll ask him, "Don't you feel really good inside yourself?" and he'll say "Yeah, I feel really good." I want him to feel good about doing good things for others. The other day he made a special dinner for his father. It was his idea totally. I helped him but he did it, so you know it was basically chicken nuggets, but that's okay! He set the table, he served his dad, it was absolutely wonderful and it was such a marvelous gift, and he felt good about it. And he didn't need a whole lot of external praise.

Mandy gives an example of indirectly teaching her son about valuing people from diverse backgrounds:

> We've made choices not to live where he's going to be exposed to a lot of materialism . . . making a lot of money, driving expensive cars, and showing it off. If we lived in a more affluent area we'd be getting a better school, but we'd also be getting a whole lot of other stuff that we don't want him to be around. We had talked about moving and briefly considered [wealthy area] . . . but even in the public schools there is no diversity at all; there are very few working moms, there is no mix of kids racially . . . we don't want that for our son. He's still young but we try to explain this to him.

Children can also learn about good works through religious teachings:

> They go to Catholic school and it's Lent right now. My son isn't giving something up for Lent; instead he's doing a "goodwill" chart. It has things like help your sister, or help a family member, or say thank you to your teacher today. He has to do goodwill . . . I want them to be thankful for what they have and to be moral and good.

The literature on the ethics of caring complements research on happiness and relationships. Recall that multiple studies support the notion that cultivating supportive, quality relationships contributes greatly to happiness. Noddings and her colleagues take this finding a step further by asserting that individuals must seek to "maintain positive relations with others" in all aspects of their lives. This directive sets up the formidable challenge of not only caring about the well-being of family and friends, but extending compassion to those in one's community, to strangers, even to difficult-to-love people.

How do positive relationships relate to spirituality? Connection with other individuals, with one's community, and with humankind embodies a facet of a spiritual life: "Relational spirituality is about communion—a profound sense of interconnection with the cosmos; connection—a sense of intimacy with someone or something; community—a sense of belonging to a group; and compassion—the drive to help others."[13] Fostering a spiritual life, particularly as it relates to connections with other people, is important not only because it elevates the existence of those around us, but because it improves the quality of our lives. Elevating values such as relationships and charity also keeps materialistic values from being too primary in our lives.

Many spiritual disciplines consider caring and connectedness to be vital to a harmonious existence. For example, a number of Native American groups look to the medicine wheel to help guide their behavior and inform their views on life. The specifics of the wheel vary from group to group, but for most tribes, it is divided into four quadrants.[14] Adherents believe that attention must be paid to all four quadrants in order to achieve harmony or balance in one's life. *Connection* embodies the east side of the wheel and represents the importance of family and community to a balanced life. Here, the east implies that all individuals in a group essentially "belong to one another" and as such should be treated with compassion and respect. The term "family" often has a very broad interpretation and may include relatives, friends, and neighbors.[15] In this sense, when making decisions about one's life, individuals must consider the impact of their behavior on themselves, their immediate family, their larger community family, and even the earth. Gail provides one example of how purchasing a car becomes a spiritual endeavor when she and her husband based their decision on environmental concerns rather than cost or luxury:

> At first we decided to buy a hybrid SUV. We had even gone down to the dealer and put down a deposit, the whole deal. My husband and I got home and we looked at each other and we both agreed that we really weren't "SUV people." We didn't see ourselves driving around in a huge car, and we really care about things like the environment. We canceled the order and bought a Prius instead.

The south side of the wheel represents *life tasks*, including developing competence in one's life (e.g., maintaining a spiritual life, learning self-control, getting along with others, and developing a healthy self-concept). Spirituality is equal in importance to social and emotional development. In fact, rather than representing discrete entities, the medicine wheel views the emotional, psychological, social, and spiritual as intricately woven together. To accomplish competence, individuals must be willing extend themselves and to take risks. A risk might be as small as trying something new and as life-altering as changing an academic major or career, severing a destructive relationship, or venturing out to interact with people from very different backgrounds or circumstances. Taking risks and the willingness to make mistakes or look foolish leads to personal growth. According to the tenets of the wheel, living a life without risk or exploration means living an unrealized life. Psychological research supports the importance of venturing outside of one's comfort zone as a way of advancing empathy and acceptance of differences. For example, young people who involve themselves in community clubs or activities report more positive views about people who differ from themselves compared to uninvolved youngsters. Further, they feel better about their communities and exhibit more willingness to help remedy the problems in their neighborhoods.[16] This fact suggests that attention to one's south side and to individual life tasks also encourages a collectivist perspective. Individualism and collectivism do not have to be in opposition.

While less relevant to our discussion on happiness and spirituality, the remaining two quadrants of the wheel, *uniqueness* and *values and goals*, do contribute to people's life decisions. *Uniqueness*, an individual's idiosyncratic lifestyle choices, sits to the west. This quadrant represents an individual's personal experiences that help to shape choices on how to live. Personal experiences may inform decisions about whether one marries or has children, sexual choices, or how to spend money. The wisdom of the wheel suggests that one cannot judge another's decisions without understanding their personal experiences (e.g., family background or formative life events). Experiences such as family circumstances and associated emotional well-being can influence the development of both materialistic attitudes and spirituality. The north represents specific values and goals that individuals hold that give life meaning and direction. Materialistic goals as well as goals related to family and career would orient on the north. According to some Native American beliefs, erroneous convictions about happiness guide people in their goal-making endeavors. Individuals, for instance, who believe that money and possessions bring happiness are destined to live unfulfilled lives pursuing wealth rather than gratifying relationships or work. In one Native folktale, the main character learns about "the eight lies of Iktumi," problematic beliefs that lead to discontent.[17] Some of these "lies" relate to the chimera of materialism: "If only I was rich, then I'd be happy," "If only I was famous, then I'd be happy," and "If only I was more attractive, then I'd be happy." Native American culture uses folktales to teach what seems to be a universal understanding: pursuing material goods and status does not bring lasting well-being.

Empirical research has also discovered multiple associations between spiritual beliefs and psychological adjustment.[18] Many of these studies do not differentiate between spirituality and religiosity, which makes it impossible to determine the specific experiences that lead to psychological outcomes. What's clear, however, is that involvement in some form of spiritual experience—whether it is an organized religion or a set of personal beliefs—can yield rewards for children and adolescents. (Some negative outcomes associated with religious involvement are discussed later in this chapter.)

Young people involved in spiritual pursuit report greater meaning in their lives, which contributes to identity development. For example, spiritually engaged teenagers have thought more about their personal values, beliefs, and life goals compared to nonengaged youngsters. Spiritual youngsters report that life takes on greater meaning through helping others and contributing in a positive way to social ills, such as poverty, racism, and illiteracy[19] These young people practice what they preach by working more on community

service projects than youngsters who report less spiritual inclinations. The notion of community service is germane to our focus on
materialism. Many materialistically oriented individuals are less involved in their communities and more committed to furthering their
own interests.[20] A focus on community needs can help to balance
material goals.

While research shows a correlation between community service
and spirituality, I do not mean to imply that nonspiritual or nonreli-
gious children do not make significant societal contributions. While
many spiritual disciplines encourage development of values related
to social responsibility, this is obviously not the only factor that can
foster community values. Individuals with absolutely no spiritual associations have made great contributions to the well-being of others.
In fact, one self-described "not very spiritual" mother discussed in
detail her commitment to values of compassion, community, and
kindness toward the earth. Since her children were young, she in-
sured that they "understand their responsibility toward helping people," through canned food and toy drives and participation in
neighborhood events. Clearly, many paths lead to the dedication to
altruism, humanism, and community action.

Developing a sense of purpose in life is another crucial piece of
identity formation. Purpose, as distinguished from meaning, involves setting relatively long-term goals (e.g., raise a family or work
to find a cure for cancer versus hang out with the gang this Saturday) and includes a desire to make a difference in the world.[21] Of
course, people can harbor goals that don't contribute to society.
Similarly, goals that harm others in some way also, technically, constitute purpose. However, based on the interpretation of purpose
presented here, neither of these goals provides youngsters with the
meaning they need in life to flourish socially and psychologically.
Further, it has been shown that self-centered or destructive goals
link with greater depression, addictions, social difficulties, and general psychological malaise.[22]

When asked to identify the most meaningful aspects of their
lives, relationships are the most crucial to the majority of preadoles-

cents, adolescents and young adults studied.[23] In addition, many young people do not consider materialism or hedonistic pleasures to be significantly meaningful or important to their lives. However, there are differences between young people who profess a sense of purpose and those who do not. Possessing a sense of purpose links with greater happiness and spiritual and religious involvement and fewer antisocial and impulsive behaviors. Youngsters low in purpose endorse greater desires for hedonistic pleasure and excitement. It makes sense that aimless individuals might turn to short-term gratification as a substitute for long-term aspirations. Adolescents clearly enjoy exciting new happenings, and hedonistic pursuits like partying and shopping are part of the teenage scene for many young people. However, as youngsters mature, so should their life goals. In terms of these goals, self-absorption and materialistic pursuits lie in opposition to a strong identity and sense of purpose, the valuing of relationships, and spiritual beliefs.

The strong identities of spiritual youngsters' come as a result of much thought and exploration about their passions and their desires for accomplishment. This last point is important. Some young people may take on an identity based on minimal exploration or questioning. For example, a girl may decide to pursue law because her parents expect it or because everyone in the family is a lawyer. A boy may opt to go into the family business without ever considering whether this is truly what he wants to do. Some evidence suggests that youngsters who go through this process of questioning feel more positively about their futures and have higher self-esteem than those who "settle" on an identity or who never define for themselves the person they would like to be.[24] Spiritual involvement has the potential to move young people toward a stronger sense of self. Through their involvement in a spiritual community, individuals may come to define themselves as altruistic and compassionate, as strong leaders and community activists, or as deeply contemplative and intuitive.

Spiritual involvement may influence children's orientation to community in a number of ways. For one thing, it presents service to others as a cultural norm. Part of belonging to a particular organization or taking on a specific belief system usually involves agreement with the cultural norms of the group. As mentioned, members of collectivist cultures tend to consider group welfare and group identity more strongly than do those from individualist cultures. Most people who belong to sports clubs believe in the importance of physical health and the thrill of competition. Similarly, individuals who ascribe to certain religious tenets usually believe in the importance of altruism and sacrificing one's own needs to help others. Again, this value opposes a materialistic orientation. Part of what binds people together in groups is common values and interests. This doesn't mean that individuals unquestioningly take on every practice and belief of a group, but some commonality of purpose does exist.

Children also learn about the value of community through interaction with their elders. Spiritually involved youth, particularly those who belong to an organization, interact more with nonfamily member adults. Exposure to adults from various generations provides youngsters with mentors from whom they can learn about values and receive support.[25] In part because of this, spiritually involved children report fewer risk-taking behaviors—less substance abuse, violence, and capricious sexual activity.[26] Children also learn firsthand the rewards of giving to others through the example of adults around them. Sasha, for instance, has spent her adult life involved in charity efforts. Her child has watched his mother provide support to others all his young life. His declaration that "if I were president, I would give money to the poor people!" supports the notion that children profit from observing. These lessons can last a lifetime. Lina says that her beliefs about respect for all come from her parents:

> In my country there is a big class difference, this is quite common. Very few people would treat them [household helpers] as equals. . . . For me, people are people, but keeping boundaries is important there. When we lived over there we had a lot of help. We had a night guard, a housekeeper, a cook . . . my mom had someone who helped her in the kitchen all the time, but she would do a lot herself. He [kitchen worker] would make tea for

me, but I would make tea for him too. He was like a family member. My parents invited all of his friends over and made dinner for them. We'd celebrate everyone's birthday . . . it's how we were raised. Because that's what I saw, that's what I try to give to my children.

Possessing the spiritual value of social responsibility increases young people's sense of trust in others. The word trust denotes the feeling that most people are dependable and fair; that others are not out to take advantage of us. Today, the younger generation (people between eighteen and twenty-five) have less trust in others than do older generations, due in part to a decline in faith of our politicians.[27] Clearly some skepticism helps people to avoid gullibility and naïveté. However, a lack of trust can signify insecurity and difficulty maintaining intimate relationships. In fact, trust springs in part from the early, secure relationships people form with their caregivers and their supportive relationships with peers. Youngsters who profess a lack of trust live more socially isolated lives and watch more television during their free time.[28] Most television does little to promote community values. Isolated youngsters involve themselves less in community service efforts—those same efforts that not only increase life satisfaction, but also serve to build greater trust and appreciation for other people. Further, social trust and materialism are incompatible. Young people who value materialistic life goals have more suspicion of others' motives. Perhaps they consider their fellow citizens to be competitors rather than potential friends or collaborators.

FAMILY RELATIONSHIPS

Family life has great potential to enhance children's spiritual development. Lana describes family rituals that she practices to promote spiritual awareness in her daughters:

I teach my girls about the rhythms of life. We have a nature table in the house and, depending on the time of year, we'll have flowers, branches, bugs, once we even had a dead mouse . . .it didn't stay there very long. [laughs]. I talk with them about life and death and how humans are connected to every living creature, even the bugs.

A spiritual core can help families through difficult circumstances. Research has found, for example, that religious beliefs and praying help to maintain hope in families with an ill child.[29] Retrospective research shows that children learn about spirituality in much the same way that they learn about other concepts—by watching their parents.[30] What do children learn from their elders? They learn about the importance of rituals. Bedtime prayers, lighting the menorah during Hanukkah and observing the Advent calendar pass family values onto children. Rituals can help families to cope with life's challenges. Thelma's family for example, has periodic "family circle" time where everyone joins hands and each person shares their good fortunes or concerns they might be experiencing. Rituals also have the effect of "slowing time and heightening our senses."[31] They call attention and give meaning to small moments that we might otherwise not acknowledge: the changing of the season, the spiritual aspects of the holidays, mealtimes, and the like.

Discussions about religion and spirituality also help to create a spiritual foundation. Parents can promote children's growth by asking them to elaborate on their opinions and to explain their reasoning regarding spiritual phenomena. Mothers have particular sway over children's spiritual development, and not just in the United States. Studies examining religion in Christian and in Jewish homes in England and Australia find that mothers are children's primary religious educators. Why do mothers take the lead in the children's spiritual education? For one thing, they talk with and explore emotions more with their children than do fathers.[32] Perhaps because of this, mothers attend more to the "north side" of the medicine wheel (the meanings children make of their world). When a child expresses confusion about a moral dilemma, for instance, mothers are more likely than fathers to ask "How does that make you feel?" as opposed to "What are you going to do about it?" I recall talking with a couple a few years ago about their parenting styles. The father good-naturedly ribbed his wife:

> [She's always] having to understand *why* the girls behaved badly, what are you feeling, why did you do it, and *every* little detail of why they were getting punished. An hour later and they're still talking. I say punish them and it's done!

Fathers of course, can have a significant influence on their children's spiritual development. In studies where fathers participated more in their children's religious education, the boys in particular report a closer relationship with their father. Perhaps because of this support and role modeling, these boys are less likely to father children outside of marriage.[33] Most likely, all parents, male or female, who participate in their children's spiritual education are also more involved in their emotional lives.

In addition to the benefits discussed thus far, spiritual practice reaps even more rewards. Evidence suggests that church attendance is associated with enhanced academic achievement, higher educational attainment, and more highly developed leadership skills. These findings may be particularly true for poor and ethnic minority youngsters, as religious services and its prosocial teachings can help to protect them from the risks inherent in low-income neighborhoods.[34] Social support as well as moral teachings delivered through sermons and religious education boost children's ability to excel despite the influences of poverty and violence. Support might come directly in the form of adult encouragement and involvement in children's academic careers. It might manifest indirectly as well, through inculcation of the faith that a higher being cares about and looks after people and that everything will work out for the best.

Studies have found that religious affiliation can boost children's resilience.[35] Literature on the topic typically focuses on identifying factors that help people to flourish despite adversity. Children have survived and even thrived through a host of traumatic conditions, from physical abuse and neglect, to extreme poverty to war.[36] A

number of psychological and environmental factors have been identified as particularly effective in protecting these survivors; one such
factor is religious faith. Religion may fortify children through its influence on attachment. A strong attachment to a parent or other dependable adult promotes security in children and enables them to
thrive socially, emotionally, and cognitively.[37] Researchers hypothesize that when children truly perceive an attachment to God or a
higher being, they feel more secure, which increases their confidence and ability to cope effectively with life's challenges. In the
case of abuse or neglect, this divine bond might be enough to compensate for a poor relationship with a parent. For youngsters living
in relatively normal circumstances, enhanced resilience can bolster
their self-concept and give them the confidence they need to resist
unhealthy peer pressure.

Religious affiliation may also contribute to resilience due to social support and moral education. Churchgoers tend to report a
large social network that can be called on for emotional succor or
even financial assistance in times of need. In terms of moral education, religions generally provide their faithful with codes of conduct — guidelines for living that can imbue life with purpose. Many
religions provide direction regarding wealth and materialism. Buddhism, for example, cautions against attachment to material indulgences; despair "emerges from craving for life to be other than it is,"
whether that means wishing for a wealthier lifestyle or greater status.[38] Many religions preach against coveting wealth or the neigh-
bor's belongings, for that matter. A universal creed runs through
many spiritual practices that equate greed and the love of things
with sinful or problematic behavior.

Our discussion so far has focused on the many benefits of religious or spiritual involvement. Religion does not appeal to everyone,
however, and certainly religious affiliation is not a prerequisite for
raising a well-rounded and resilient child. As with altruism and religion many roads lead to resilience. The presence of an encouraging
parent, relative, or teacher; peer support; participation in extracurricular activities; and a close, supportive family can all provide chil-

dren with the strength they need to overcome difficult circumstances. Religious and spiritual practice gives parents another way to cultivate confidence and tenacity in their children.

For some people, religious affiliation has been less than positive. Religious groups that advocate hatred or intolerance of others do not provide the positive benefits of religious involvement. Using faith to justify cruel or bigoted behavior distorts the premise of spirituality and compassion. Lack of conformity to the edicts of one's religious organization can also lead to negative outcomes. For example, unwed teen mothers who attend religious services report greater postpartum depression than unaffiliated youth.[39] In this case, young women did not receive the emotional and social rewards that religious involvement generally offers. Likewise, gay and lesbian teens report that they experience conflict between religion and sexual orientation. For many, religious teachings and prejudice from other churchgoers has led to feelings of shame and depression.[40] To truly benefit spiritually and emotionally, parents and children must choose a compassionate practice consistent with their own beliefs.

The African American church provides a fitting example of how spiritual practice can inform social and emotional development.[41] The "African American" church refers generally to institutions located in predominantly African American communities that meld African and European American Christian belief systems.[42] Historically, these churches have provided numerous benefits to their congregations. A primary goal of this church, as with most religious organizations, is to offer spiritual guidance. In addition, the importance of community is woven throughout every aspect of the church and its teachings. Now and in the past, community has been crucially important, lending support in a world that has been hostile toward Black Americans. The church served as the bedrock for the civil rights movement and for the work of Martin Luther King, Jr. The African American church has also served as a sanctuary from racism.

In her in-depth study on the African American church, Wendy Haight cites examples of children who learn to cope with racially motivated name calling and harassment by internalizing teachings on nonviolence and forgiveness.[43] According to Haight, the ability to remain calm in the face of racial attacks enables children to endure and to survive hateful behaviors. Church elders interviewed as part of her study believed that responding in kind to attacks compromised children's safety and went against church teachings. Haight also describes the church's reactions to institutional racism—when, for example, teachers ignore the history of African American children. In one instance, a school principal claimed that attention to Black history was unimportant because there was only one African American child in the school. Church members regarded this incident as an opportunity for education. The principal was informed that all children should learn about Black history, not just African American children. Church elders responded to racism in the schools by acting on both the educational institutions and the children. In one situation, the church lobbied schools to institute multicultural education for the White teachers and administrators. Religious teachers believe in the power of spiritual teachings to instill self-worth in the children so that they do not internalize the negative messages about their race picked up in school. During Sunday school, children not only studied the Bible, but also enriched their literacy and study skills. Children learned how to value and protect themselves by observing their elders, by improving their academic skills, and by developing a strong identity.

Through religious teaching, mentorship, self-esteem building, and identity enhancement, church elders promote development of a number of skills and characteristics: transcendence through spiritual practice, resilience, a respect for community, emotional self-regulation, and a desire to connect with the good in all people. The church also admonishes against greed, exhorting children to share with their neighbors. These positive benefits are not unique to African American churches; any religious organization or set of beliefs that promotes prosocial virtues can be enormously useful to youngsters. Perhaps you subscribe to Islam, Catholicism, Judaism, or Hinduism; maybe you believe in the universal power of nature or follow the teachings of yoga. At their best, all of these belief systems instill in youngsters skills and the character development that will help them to withstand the forces of materialism.

THE ECSTASY!

Some philosophers and religious scholars suggest that spirituality might be viewed as personal or institutional. Institutional devotion "implies approaches to spiritual growth formed around doctrines, various practices or rituals, and standards of behavior."[44] Essentially, institutional practice centers most on worship within the organized context of the church, temple, synagogue, or mosque, with its attendant teachings on how one can live a virtuous and holy life.

Personal spirituality centers on intimate, transcendent experiences. These occurrences "are direct, personal, and often have the effect, if only for a moment, of waking us up and expanding our understanding of who we are and what our place is in the universe."[45] Spiritual experiences might be the awe one feels when gazing at newly sprouted daffodils, a sense of intense connection with those around us, or a feeling of great joy and gratitude for simple things. According to Tobin Hart, spiritual experiences include wonder, which maintains the sacred in even the most small and mundane aspects of our lives.[46] It involves experiencing love, gratitude, respect, and awe for everything around us: bugs, soil, plants, and animals. Most of us don't experience wonder on a constant basis; it visits us now and then, often unannounced. Children are primed for wonder as they are especially open and sensitive to things that many adults no longer notice. I remember one day my nephew became very distressed when my husband started pruning a tree. He began crying "You're hurting it! You're going to kill it!" Only after my husband explained that pruning a tree helps it to grow stronger did my nephew calm down and actually help with the operation.

Children take great pleasure and fascination in the seemingly small and insignificant. They get sidetracked by the ant colony pouring out of the sidewalk, bugs (dead or alive!), the shape of a rock, or a cow mooing. They can spend hours absorbed by discarded "junk" or mud puddles. Experiencing wonder can happen anytime, without warning. As I write this chapter on a chilly afternoon, it has begun to snow (a rare and amazing occurrence for moderate northern California). Watching the soft, wet flakes drift down fills me with joy and gratitude. I feel as if I'm nestled in a cabin in some faraway place, like Vermont, on a lazy afternoon. This relatively brief snowfall was transcendent for me because of the unselfconscious joy I felt in the moment.

This ability to maintain wonder is in many ways materialism's opposite. Wonder involves reverence for nature, people, or occurrences without attempts to own or manipulate them. A materialistic attitude views objects or people as commodities to possess or to impress. Sasha describes the way she tries to instill wonder in her son:

> I talk to him about how important it is to be open to what life brings. I know people who try to plan every little thing about their lives: what school they'll go to; how old they'll be when they get their first job as a banker; or a stock broker, or a lawyer; when they want to get married; how many children they'll have. There's nothing wrong with planning, but if you don't stay open, flexible, you might miss your great love. I do think being open is related to materialism . . . it's the intangible, being willing to go down a road even if it may not give you money or what have you.

Flow moments provide opportunities for spiritual development. Recall that flow involves losing oneself in a pursuit. This ability to lose sense of time and to absorb oneself completely in the present moment lays the foundation for spiritual experiences, or ecstasy.[47] Children still possess that "natural capacity for absorption, their intuitive style of knowing, the perception of novelty all mixed with the mystery of life."[48] Their natural ability to absorb themselves fully can be channeled toward beneficial or less beneficial pastimes. A mother describes her efforts to break the "television trance":

In some ways it's [television] like his martini, he wants to come home and unwind. We won't let him watch a whole movie, and sometimes I wonder if even that's okay, because it's still screen time . . . and I don't like all the screen time, it's completely mesmerizing. It's like when you talk to him, he doesn't hear anything that you say, he doesn't talk, he doesn't see you; it's almost like a trance, where everything else on earth stands still.

Parents can nurture children's spiritual nature by encouraging their natural propensity for engagement, curiosity, and receptivity. We can also learn from youngsters; they can help us to broaden our focus from the traffic jams, the schedules, the deadlines, the all-consuming responsibilities of daily life, to the small delights that lie close at hand. One father, Ned, told of the time he drove home with his daughter at the end of the workday. As he motored along, preoccupied with the evening's work—cooking, eating dinner, finishing the chores, getting the kids bed—his daughter cried, "We missed the giraffe!" Giraffe? What giraffe? It turned out that two giraffes were painted on the side of the freeway and his daughter enjoyed greeting them everyday as they passed. Thereafter, Ned made a point of slowing down to appreciate the art with his daughter. He moved from a state of "doing" to one of "being."

While children are particularly open to moments of wonder, many adults have famously found ways to maintain their fascination with small spirit-enhancing "gifts"—the unnoticed, the inconsequential, the taken for granted. For example, contemporary artists make creations out of "found objects" from dumps, or roadsides or garages. They find meaning in items that many of us consider used-up trash. A collage composed of scraps of fabric, newspaper clippings, candy wrappers, and bits of cork might represent the universality of western life for one individual or the beauty of shape, color, and composition for someone else.[49] An art piece composed of a wire hanger and some yarn, while bizarre to some viewers, possesses great meaning to the artist (and presumably to the major art museum showing it). I once viewed a sculpture made entirely of car parts, metal scraps, and broken dishes created to convey the throw-away society in which we live. The point really isn't whether we like or dislike a particular form of expression. The crucial point is that these artists have found a way to express themselves—their joys, fears, their nature—by staying open to possibility. Many artists describe their work as a spiritual endeavor that furthers their search for meaning. Others try to create an atmosphere that helps "free viewers from the material world."[50]

Art is only one way to experience life's wonders. I believe that the key to experiencing wonder is first silencing your critic—the part of you that tells you not to take risks because people will laugh at you, they'll think you're dumb, no one else does it, you're not good at it, this isn't going to look right, this is a waste of time. . . . Have I left anything out? The second key to encouraging wonder is to help children to follow their interests. Like flow experiences, pursuits that engross youngsters lay the groundwork for wonder and a greater appreciation for life. The third bit of advice falls into the stop-and-smell-the-roses arena. It is important move your mind off autopilot and experience the present. I once attended a gestalt therapy training seminar. The instructor was an expert in helping clients to stay in the present rather than living in the past or projecting into the future. This instructor lived so much in the present that she claimed to carry almost no "emotional baggage"—the grudges and perceived insults that people hold onto without ever discussing their grievances with the offender. You know the kind: the "I'm never talking to her again, see if I forgive him, I'll never do another favor for her, see if I ever stick my neck out again" variety. A perspective that emphasizes confronting emotional issues as they arise can be helpful for parents and their children. Dealing with anger, sadness, disappointment, and other unpleasant feelings rather than ignoring them, burying them, and allowing them to fester will help both children and adults to avoid unhealthy expression of emotions. Unexamined feelings can preoccupy adults, taking the focus away from the present and from the enjoyment of parenting. Children who have accumulated several years of hurt feelings are more likely than emotionally unburdened children to soothe themselves by purchasing an item that promises happiness and acceptance.

As I have emphasized throughout this book, children learn by watching. Parents can spark spirit in their youngsters through their own actions. Observing their parents do good works, both large and small, increases the likelihood that youngsters will internalize this behavior as part of their own repertoire. Including lots of singing and laughter in the home can also bring family members closer to their spiritual natures.[51] Many spiritual practices incorporate singing or chanting as part of their worship in the belief that it brings one closer to the divine. Laughter and a sense of humor provide people with perspective. It allows them to move out of the poor-me rut, freeing energy to focus on other more productive pursuits.

Adults can also kindle youngsters' awe and wonder by encouraging the "whys" and the "how comes." Children are typically bursting with questions — "Why is the sky blue?," "Where do babies come from?," "What does God look like?" According to Tobin, maintaining a questioning stance toward life breeds curiosity and an openness to experience. The ways in which we respond to children's questions can also help them to tolerate ambiguity. As we all know, questions don't always have clear answers. One mother tries to encourage her son to question:

> I know that everything I say doesn't sink in, but the point is to evoke his curiosity. I want him to know that it's not about having the right answers or even that there is such a thing as the right answer. He should know that things are out there to be questioned.

In his book, *The Secret Spiritual World of Children*, Hart lists five conditions, or what he calls "freedoms," that set the stage for spiritual development.[52] Children must have the freedom to play, to pursue their own interests, to experiment and to make mistakes, to have private thoughts and feelings, and to behave and hold beliefs that differ from those of their parents. These freedoms essentially give children the space to discover themselves and, in the process, their spiritual nature.

SUMMARY

Evidence from a number of sources indicates that the majority of Americans believe spirituality to be essential to a life well lived. A well-lived life might mean happiness, balance, harmony, contentment, or self-actualization. Both young children and teenagers seek spiritual experience, which includes traditional organized religion and personal spiritual beliefs. Generally, spiritual practices involve valuing connection with and compassion for people, animals, and nature. Spirituality might also involve moments of wonder and feelings of communion with the world. In this sense, young children are particularly open to spirituality. In their pursuit of fortune and fame, materialistic individuals risk losing harmony and well-being in their lives.

CHAPTER 8

TAKING THE NEXT STEP

Everyone has too much stuff, even comic strip characters. In one of my favorites, *Sherman's Lagoon,* a crab offers to lend some of his stuff to a turtle. The story starts with the turtle minding his own business, sitting in his rocking chair and reading the paper. It seems that the crab wants to move some of the clutter out of his crab hole so that he can buy more junk. When the turtle refuses his advances, the crab regroups and tries to buy the chair out from under the turtle.[1] A perfect illustration of the difficulty of turning away from consumerism.

Clearly materialism is a complex concept that can both facilitate and hinder well-being and identity. A mother of two boys, describes materialism as a two-edged sword:

> It is a positive thing in the sense that as you get older, you may want to have more ambition because you want to work to obtain the things you enjoy. That will give you some ambition, especially if you've never had anything . . . to try and better your life. The bad thing is, and I am a victim of this in my own life, you feel that you're lacking something in your life and you feel like you need to fill it. . . . Little kids call that feeling "I have an empty feeling in my tummy." So sometimes when I have that empty feeling, I might fill it up by buying say, cheap stockings or books. That's the negative thing with materialism because you

always want stuff. When my kids come to me and say, "I want a snack," I tell them, "You just ate, you're just bored, and your way of dealing with your boredom is to eat something." I think it annoys them, but you've got to know this so you don't do it when you're an adult.

Material goods can play *a part* in teenagers' efforts at developing an identity. However, we do not require a surfeit of material comforts to fashion a happy and meaningful life. Once individuals meet basic needs for food and safety, possessions do not provide the path to contentment nor do they furnish a life purpose that can sustain people emotionally. As we have seen, a materialistic orientation can lead to negative outcomes. Children who look to material goods as a solution to the normal developmental challenges of identity building, self-esteem, and social belonging risk shortchanging their potential. Materialistic values connect with poor relationships, a lack of social confidence, low self-esteem, and emotional difficulties. Materialistic individuals evince less concern for the well-being of the community and the environment. Youngsters with a materialistic orientation motivate themselves through external factors, such as money or status, rather than intrinsically generated values. This decreases the likelihood that they will experience deeply satisfying, emotionally sustaining flow or spiritual activities.

Imagine how our communities might transform if everyone critically examined their level of materialism. More people, from the grassroots level to the highest rungs of government, might make greater efforts to protect the earth and its natural resources. In a world where many people complain of feeling isolated and disconnected from others, less materialism and greater valuing of relationships and altruism could bring more caring and supportive neighborhoods. There would be less pressure to impress others through high status schools, jobs, and possessions. Children would be less overscheduled with resume-building pursuits and more free to discover their passions without the overwhelming pressures to earn straight As or take a full slate of advanced placement courses.

Parents would be less burdened with oppressive work hours and with getting ahead.

A shift in priorities would benefit individuals, communities, and the earth. Is this "new world" a pipe dream? Certainly the forces of materialism in this culture are both powerful and ubiquitous. However, lessening your materialistic focus does not necessarily entail huge life changes. The suggestions included in this chapter range from the small to life-altering. I profile parents who have devised creative solutions to potentially materialistic-ridden events such as birthdays and holidays. Parents also share ways in which they confront the influences of media and advertising. On the other end of the spectrum are the *voluntary simplifiers*, who have made significant changes to their lifestyles, their careers, and their incomes. Think of this chapter as a makeover guide, somewhat like the *Oprah* show where people come in looking scruffy and out-of-date only to be transformed into more polished versions of their former selves. Instead of a spiffy haircut or a new wardrobe, the ideas in this chapter can help you gain greater satisfaction and a lifestyle more in line with your intrinsic values. You must decide for yourself whether you just need a quick trim or a completely new look.

STARTING SMALL

Most of the parents I have spoken with over the years have mentioned the "relative factor" as a common concern. That is, what to do about well-meaning relatives and friends who pile on the presents during the holidays or who gift children with very expensive or impractical items. Parents' solutions ranged from doing nothing to actively working with extended family to keep gift giving from spiraling out of control. For example, one mother keeps gift giving balanced by reining in the purchases that she and her husband make for their two girls:

> We try to get them what they want for Christmas as long as it's not too crazy. It's not as though they ask for much; a soccer ball

and a skateboard, that's not too bad. They get a lot of stuff from my mom. Their great-aunts send them tons of stuff and their cousins too, so there's already way too much. We just don't do a ton ourselves. It's important to us to keep things reasonable . . . . I think it has to do with how I was raised. I also don't want them to feel as though they have to spend a ton of money on clothes and stuff to be accepted.

Another mother devised a creative idea for managing her son's rapidly growing menagerie of toys and games:

Oh my gosh, this kid has so much stuff . . . I could go five years without buying anything and he'd still have plenty to play with! We have a big family . . . and it means lots and lots of gifts and lots of stuff piling up. He [son] doesn't feel as overwhelmed about it as I am. I have a box and if I come across toys and I haven't seen them being played with for five or six months, they go in a box. If he doesn't ask for them in the next couple of months they're rotated out. They get donated or used in art projects at work.

Her six-year-old son came up with his own solution for keeping toys under control:

He decided that he wanted to earn some money so he decided he wanted a garage sale. He routed through his things and came up with a whole box of stuff where he was putting on tags; $2.00, .50, what have you [laughing] . . . the box is kept under his bunk bed and so far he hasn't pulled it out to take toys back out of the box. Once he gets enough things collected, we'll put on the garage sale.

Like many of the parents interviewed, Don and Theresa become inundated with a glut of gifts during Christmas and birthdays. Their son never uses many of the toys. Theresa decided to take the direct route with her friends and relatives:

Sometimes we'll get things that are really not at his age level or that he's already outgrown. Things from relatives across the country who don't really see what kinds of toys he's playing with. So I said to them, you know, instead of just giving him gifts, these random gifts, why don't you give us the money to put toward his gymnastics class or toward his activities or towards his college fund . . . giving him two more trains when he's already got 250 of them, you know, 252 isn't going to make a big difference. I'll also tell people specifically what he needs. If there is something, I'll tell them specifically the toy, the brand, the character. That way we don't get random gifts that we end up throwing in the closet, it's more useful and fits with what he's playing with now.

A few parents have tried to make substantial changes in the way they orchestrate rituals and celebrations. Motivated to teach her child to enjoy life without relying on material goods, Sasha experimented with a gift-free birthday party:

That was a big experiment. We wanted to ask people to help us to live closer to our values. This was the birthday party that his school friends attend, this wasn't the one for his family. And I said to parents, "[Son] has a lot of family who will be giving him lots of things for his birthday. Please just come and celebrate with us." And almost everybody honored that. And [son] had a good time at his party and then there was the family party where he got his presents. And *then* he said a couple of weeks later, "I sure didn't get as many presents as other people do at their birthdays" . . . We talked about it and how he felt about that. We also talked about what he gets when it's not his birthday and what he's gotten since then. His birthday is next month and I've expected him to say "Please, don't tell people not to bring presents, Mom." But he hasn't said that yet.

This year Sasha plans to modify the gift-free format. Her son is passionate about the effort to rescue pets from harm, so she will also request that friends bring a gift or donation for the animals in his honor. Partygoers will also have the option of bringing a gift for her son. Sasha's attempts to dematerialize her family's life and to live closer to their values illustrate the challenges involved in going against the tide of consumerism. She found it necessary to balance her beliefs about materialism (which she wanted to pass down to her son) with her child's desire to receive some gifts from his friends.

Other ideas for dealing with overzealous relatives and friends include spacing out the Christmas morning gift opening. Don and Theresa have their son open just a few presents at a time to avoid the frenzied ritual of Christmas morning gifts—when children act like the food-deprived characters from *Survivor* desperately ripping into bags of white rice. By opening just a few gifts at a time, the children have a chance to appreciate each item before moving on to the next. Some philosophers have observed that in some sense materialistic individuals, always on the lookout for more acquisitions, do not treasure their belongings enough. Rituals that allow children the time to take pleasure in heartfelt gifts from family and friends can discourage youngsters from taking their possessions for granted. Parents, for instance, can institute thank you days, when children design and mail thank you notes or make phone calls thanking their benefactors.

Parents can also ask friends and relatives to give *time* instead of material goods. For example, for many years, Lina's close friend would shower her two children with gifts every Christmas. Uncomfortable with her children receiving so much, Lina diplomatically asked her friend to think of an activity she could do with the children to replace the gift giving. Now every year the youngsters look forward to building a gingerbread house with her friend. The possibilities for special time abound and depend on a child's interests: a trip to the zoo, horseback riding, an afternoon spent making cookies, a nature hike, making holiday decorations, a museum excursion, playing basketball, going to a baseball game. As you make decisions about how to dematerialize birthdays and holidays, you may want to keep these points in mind:

- Carefully consider how decisions might impact your children both in the short run and over time. For example, does raising a child who values a day spent playing with friends over receiving lots of presents balance out some disappointment with fewer gifts? Sasha's compromise allowed her son the chance to feel good about helping the animals while still experiencing the fun of receiving some gifts from friends at his birthday party.

- Think about the age and temperament of your child. For example, it would be much more traumatic to institute gift-free birthday parties when children are twelve years old than when they are five or six years old. Also, some children tolerate change more easily than others. Consider your child's temperament before instituting any significant changes.

- Children should be involved in decisions regarding celebrations or rituals. Even young children can help to come up with ideas for fun birthdays that don't revolve around gifts. Youngsters should also understand why parents make particular consumer decisions. Making children part of the decision making process provides an opportunity to discuss issues of materialism and consumerism, which of course is the point.

- Incorporate children's interests and pastimes when planning events. Sasha decided to request donations for rescued pets because this was something in which her son had expressed great interest. Considering your child's interests presents a wonderful opportunity to cultivate a child's identity ("I'm someone who loves and helps animals"), self-esteem and altruism.

DO AS I SAY . . .

As we've seen, advertising represents a significant influence on children's materialistic orientation. We can counteract some of the effects of materialistic messages from the media by developing children's media literacy. Readers might also consider some of the creative ideas that the parents profiled in this book have devised to educate their children about advertising. For example, one mother plays a guessing game with her son:

He watches no unstructured TV at all. TV watching is either
with me or his father. There's always an adult with him. . . . we
find that the commercials are worse than the actual shows. We
either fast forward through them with the prerecorded shows or
we mute the television and we play a game: "What do you think
they're trying to get us to buy now?" We deconstruct it. Now my
son will say, "Mom, look that man is kissing that car. They want
us to buy a car!"

This family began the commercial game as soon as their son started
watching television at around the age of three. According to this
mother, even when he was very young, her son had the rudimentary understanding that commercials are designed to sell products.
Several of the parents I talked with relied heavily on prerecorded
programming, either using the VCR or TiVo. They managed advertising by fast forwarding through the commercials. In a similar
vein, some parents, especially those of young children, allowed
their children to watch only commercial-free television networks
(i.e., Public Broadcasting Service) or movies on video or DVD.
Again, you must weigh the costs and benefits of avoiding commercials altogether. By banning commercial television entirely, you
avoid having to respond to your children's desires and requests for
advertised products. However, you also miss an opportunity to
teach children about the goals and tactics of advertising. One way
or another, children will almost certainly be exposed to commercials at some point; perhaps at a friend's home, on the internet, or
even in school. Watching a few commercials at home gives the parent some control over how children interpret electronic and print
advertising.

Truly impacting children's media literacy requires monitoring
media use outside the home as well (if possible). Some educators
have called for more attention to issues of materialism, consumerism, and media literacy in school settings. Some schools in
the United States, Canada, and Europe have instituted media education curriculum — time-limited projects that benefit a relatively
small number of students.[2] These projects have focused on facili-

tating children's critical viewing skills, increasing knowledge about the media industry and the forces that influence production of programming, teaching children to analyze media content, and encouraging insight into individual values and needs and why people use media.[3] Many of these curricula have succeeded in increasing youngsters' media competence. For example, ongoing discussions of media literacy-related topics in the classroom and incorporation of the issue into multiple subjects throughout the children's school day increased ninth graders skills in media analysis in one study.[4] Educational efforts also help very young children. Researchers demonstrated that kindergartners and third graders trained in critical viewing skills were able to distinguish between fantasy and reality in television programming. As a result of the educational intervention, children's knowledge of television production also increased.[5]

To bring media education into the schools, you might work through parent-teacher associations (PTAs), parent-teacher organizations (PTOs), and child advocacy organizations like Children Now and the Children's Media Policy Coalition.[6] These organizations can help parents to organize campaigns with the aim of getting school districts to develop curricula for the classroom. Most schools' curricula, however, are already packed with required classes. As we all know, many schools have tight budgets, which make adding additional curricula and teacher training quite difficult. You will need to work with teachers and administrators to make sure that media education addresses critical developmental and cultural needs. Although research has shown that materialism, in part fomented by the media, has significant and deleterious effects on children's development, some educators lack awareness of this research and of the importance of addressing the issue at multiple levels: at home, in the schools, and through policy and legislation. We need to do everything we can to ensure that schools attend to this significant developmental issue with our children.

Parents can begin advocacy efforts by gathering research and information on media and child development. The American Academy of Pediatrics Web site is a good place to start; it offers media guidelines for parents as well as readable research articles on advertising and children.[7] The American Psychological Association also has relevant materials on children and the media. Recruit other concerned parents to join your efforts at media advocacy. Parent groups can sponsor awareness campaigns, such as National TV-Turnoff Week, in the schools and in the community (sponsored by TV-Free America).[8] Grassroots campaigns can be highly effective. As I write this book, the school district in my area is seriously considering a policy banning all junk food from their campuses—not only vending machines, but even bake sales and fundraising. The proposed policy comes as a result of efforts from community members and school employees working together for change.[9]

Feeling ambitious? Consider going beyond grassroots advocacy to affect national policy on media-related issues. Current legislation does offer children some protection from age-inappropriate media. In 1990 Congress adopted the Children's Television Act (CTA), which established specific requirements for children's programming.[10] Among a number of things, this act contains restrictions related to commercial programming. For example, both cable networks and broadcast stations must limit commercial time during children's programming to "no more than 12 minutes per hour on weekdays and 10.5 minutes per hour on weekends."[11] Further, stations must ensure that a clear distinction exists between regular programming and commercial programming. On the positive side, the CTA does consider children's developmental capacities in its regulations on television advertising. However, while the act offers children some protection, more work remains to be done. Networks can still air program-length commercials that pitch merchandise directly to children. As we know, the great difficulty young children have distinguishing between regular and commercial programming leaves them vulnerable to these types of shows.

In 2004 Children Now along with the Children's Media Policy Coalition led efforts to amend the Federal Communications Commission's guidelines on educational programming. The revised guidelines, which provide greater protection to children who watch digital television, now require digital television broadcasters to:

- Ensure commensurate levels of educational programming for children
- Provide more information about ratings and education programs to parents
- Prohibit interactive advertising[12]

On a broader scale, you might focus your efforts on other modes of media, such as the Internet, cable television, or satellite radio. Because current regulations do not apply to cable television to the same degree as broadcast stations, cable stations have much more freedom to air programming detrimental to children. Further, the Internet is virtually unregulated in terms of policy on child-oriented fare. Individuals can make a difference by becoming politically involved in efforts to protect children from deceptive and unfair advertising and programming practices in these venues.

Finally, you can confront the issue of media and materialism by avoiding the do-as-I-say, not-as-I-do directive. If we expect our children to limit their media use, to use good judgment in program selection, and to resist the temptations of advertising, then we must do the same. As one father I interviewed put it:

> We never buy off of commercials, none of us, and my son knows this. We really push the idea of doing your research and planning ahead. If we're going to make a purchase, first we decide: Can we afford it? Then we do our research, figure out which brand is going to be the best value. We've always done this . . . and I don't want [son] to think that you see something and then you just blindly go out and buy it.

Working on media literacy and putting your beliefs into practice through role modeling or through advocacy will increase your children's awareness of materialism and consumerism and give them more control over their life choices.

THE SIMPLE LIFE

On the reality series *The Simple Life,* two wealthy young women from the city play at getting back to basics by donning overalls, milking cows, and venturing into bargain emporiums like Wal-Mart. While the two characters eventually trade in their overalls for Gucci and return to their golden lifestyles, today many Americans have chosen to slow down the consumer treadmill and live more simply. For many individuals, "living simply" means buying and accumulating less and focusing more on such areas as family, the environment, spirituality, and personal growth. For some individuals, the desire to live simply comes from intrinsic beliefs about the importance of family or the environment. One father describes his perspective:

> The way I see things is probably the opposite of materialism. Materialism to me is when people make themselves feel better by buying things rather than spending time with friends. I think I'm this way partly because my dad was fairly frugal. Also, when I got out of the navy, my friend had all of this money saved up and I had nothing and I realized I was probably wasting a lot of money on things that I really don't need, so that made me more frugal as well . . . and we just don't have the time. When the weekend rolls around, we'd rather spend it with family and friends, not at the mall. We buy used stuff, consigned furniture . . . when she got pregnant the entire baby's room, all of the furniture, was hand-me-down stuff. Our couch is used, and we give a lot of our things away to friends. We try to share stuff so everybody isn't always buying and buying and buying. We don't want to add to the glut. I always think about how over-filled the dump must be, and I just don't want to be wasteful . . . I'm just that way in general. I read somewhere that if everyone in the world lived like we do [Americans], there would need to be 7 1/2 earths to support all that. It made me think, "Wow, we just waste a lot of stuff." We're totally into the earth and the environment, all of that, we give to Greenpeace. I try to recycle everything, and I'm very conscious about what can be recycled and what can't. . . . We've looked into running the house on solar energy as well. I'm also concerned about all of the packag-

ing that comes with products; everything comes in packaging that's just wasteful. Like the apples at Trader Joe's come in a big plastic container that takes up space in the recycling bin; why can't we just buy things without all the plastic?

For other families, the desire to live plainly is based on practical concerns. According to one busy mom:

It's not that I don't want to buy clothes for myself or do things for myself, it's more that I don't have time. Between getting home from work and having to get dinner ready and grocery shopping and washing clothes and cleaning the house, who has time to go to the mall and window shop and browse? Honestly, I haven't bought new clothes in years.

Another mother says that she doesn't have a particular philosophy about living simply, it's just the lifestyle that she's most comfortable with:

I hate to shop . . . I don't have the patience. I hate going to the mall, the masses of people, the parking, the trying to find the right price. As a young girl, I loved shopping with my girlfriends. But then as an adult, I guess I found better things to do. On a weekend, I'd rather be outside exercising or doing stuff with the family. I'm pretty much a jeans and sweater person. It's *one* of the reasons I went into teaching. I didn't want to wear nylons [laughs]!

While none of these parents identifies as part of an organized movement, many of their beliefs are consistent with the ethos of voluntary simplicity. Voluntary simplicity consists of loosely connected groups of people who share similar anticonsumerism, prosocial, and environmental beliefs.[13] No one description captures the characteristics and beliefs of all voluntary simplifiers. Some people choose to live modestly to spend more time with friends and family. Others decide to downsize in order to economize. Many people who espouse a modest lifestyle may not even identify themselves as part of a "simplicity movement." In general, however, the values that best describe voluntary simplicity include material restraint, compassion and respect for others, self-determination, ecological awareness, and personal growth.[14] Clearly the values of voluntary simplicity are light years away from materialism, which prizes wealth and consumption over humanitarianism and the environment.

Perhaps not coincidentally in this age of affluence, the voluntary simplicity movement is gaining steam and boasts individuals from many countries and cultures. Estimates of those who espouse the simple life range from about 15 to 25 percent of Americans. The voluntary simplicity movement has been characterized as a cause of the middle class and the well-to-do, typically individuals who decide to forgo the high-powered career for more meaningful pursuits. Some literature suggests that people from varied economic levels have decided to live more simply, not just those with financial means.[15] The common thread comes from a concern about the level of consumerism and materialism in the society. However, economics does play a role in decisions to simplify. The notion of *opting* to live modestly implies choice. For many Americans, simple living arises out of financial necessity. This circumstance was illustrated by one single mother I talked with who struggled to support her family on a small income. She was quite concerned that her son not acquire materialistic values and that he learn to value people based on "what's on the inside, not on what stuff they have." At the same time, she wanted a more financially comfortable life, which included the opportunity to "own nice things" and live in a safer neighborhood. While people from many income levels do ascribe to the voluntary simplicity movement, the notion of *trying* to live modestly is more relevant to those with financial resources.

There are three categories of voluntary simplicity.[16] *Downshifting* involves moderate changes in lifestyle, such as buying used goods, eschewing brand-name products, and buying organic produce, for example. Many of the parents profiled in this book have downshifted in some way. Several parents, such as Don, try to live environmentally conscious lives. With an eye toward "decluttering" their living spaces, other parents limit their purchasing or give toys and clothing to other family members or to charity. Downshifting does-n't require huge sacrifices.

Strong simplifiers give up high incomes or status positions in order to decrease stress and reorganize their priorities. Sasha's deci-sion to work for a nonprofit organization that pays significantly less than what she could earn in a more mainstream position exemplifies the strong simplifier position.

The third group of individuals more completely embrace the goals of the *simplicity movement*, and try to live consistent with beliefs about anticonsumerism and compassion for people, animals, and the earth. Many of these individuals actively participate in voluntary simplicity organizations. A number of organizations offer informa-tion and support for families interested in de-materializing their lives. For example, Seeds of Simplicity, sponsored by Cornell Uni-versity, provides families with information on how to join simplicity circles—groups of people who support each other in their efforts to live modestly.[17] The group also conducts research and holds confer-ences on voluntary simplicity. Families attempting to embrace a less materialistic existence need support to stick with the simple life. It's one thing to commit to work against materialism. However, realisti-cally trying to live that decision can prove daunting when sur-rounded by families, schools, and media that hold opposing values. One couple found that practicing a less consumer-centered life re-quires reevaluating one's social circle:

> We noticed that how we deal with other adults, that there's al-most a formula for it. First of course we have to like the parents, and second they have to have kids about the same age as ours, otherwise we're not relating to the teenage kid's issues or we're not really into talking about changing diapers. But the third part is that for us to feel comfortable, we have to have the same spending approach as the parents. Because we find that if we're going to go do stuff, go to dinner, or to a show, or on vacation even, that it's big deal. Maybe they want to stay at the Ahwanee and we want to stay in the tent-cabins at Yosemite. You've got to

get the spending levels about the same, otherwise one or the
other couple is going to feel uncomfortable. Here's an example.
We went out to dinner with this couple who spend much differently than we do, and I'm looking at the menu thinking "$20.00
for what?!" It was really expensive and we were uncomfortable . . . and I'm sure it would be uncomfortable the other way
around where they're wanting to spend more. The other important point is that it's not income level, it's how they choose to
spend money.

Other parents also differentiate between spending and income.
For example, one mother says that her spending habits have remained
the same over the years despite a significant increase in salary:

When I was a single parent I really had to scrimp. When [son] was
young, we used this dresser made of cardboard to store his things.
Now I'm much more comfortable and can buy what I want, but I
find that I buy less now after so many of those tight years.

People choose to simplify for a wide variety of reasons. People
like the parents just quoted may have similar ideas regarding spending based on different rationales. Researchers distinguish those
"who are motivated by concern for the environment and social justice" as *ethical simplifiers*. These simplifiers might make decisions
based on spiritual or philosophical beliefs. For example, an ethical
simplifier might evaluate his job based on whether it contributes to
or detracts from the well-being of the community. However, many
roads lead to simplicity. *Economic simplifiers* may be motivated to save
money or to pay off credit card debt. Many *family simplifiers* have decided that spending time with the children has precedence over
earning a large paycheck or building a career. Choosing to focus on
child rearing over pursuit of a prestigious career is more relevant
today than ever, particularly for women. At this writing, a number
of very high-profile women have shocked their industries by leaving
their positions to be with their families. For example, Phoebe Philo,
the former designer for the Chloe fashion house, quit her position at
the peak of her career to spend time with her infant.[19] Other indi-

viduals opt for better health, less stress, or the opportunity to pursue passions instead of staying on the "earn-and-spend" treadmill. The point is that there is no one *right* reason for dematerializing one's life. Moving toward voluntary simplicity is a personal choice that should be congruent with one's values, goals, and life circumstances. Again, the decision to quit one's job or to downsize financially is an option only for those with the financial resources to do so.

We're just starting to seriously examine voluntary simplicity in the United States. Studies find that the majority of voluntary simplifiers have made the decision to change their lives both because of anticonsumption attitudes and out of the desire to free "one's time to spend with family and friends, to spend at activities that are more meaningful, such as making gifts, or simply to feel in control of one's own life."[20] One recent study compared the characteristics of voluntary simplifiers and so-called nonsimplifiers.[21] Investigators found that simplifiers were less likely than nonsimplifiers to use brand-name goods and fashion as a way to convey status. While both groups enjoyed purchasing books and music, nonsimplifiers more frequently indulged in movies, theater, dining out, and travel. Simplifiers tended to spend money on trips to the museum and the bookstore. In terms of consumption, simplifiers make distinctions between what they consider to be indulgences and purchases that increase children's cultural capital. Among my group of parents, even the staunchest simplifiers made exceptions for books, as one mother explains:

> I tend to be a little weak with bookstores. We have a lot of books, but I have a hard time not letting them each pick a book when we're at the bookstore . . . I love it that they love to read! They're excited about it. And I love to read, I'm vulnerable to bookstores. But with other things, when we go shopping I let them know that we're not buying anything for ourselves today. I try not to just buy them stuff randomly.

Another study identifies specific practices employed by simplifiers.[22] The top practices included avoiding impulse purchases,

recycling, eliminating clutter, working at a satisfying job, buying lo-
cally grown produce, limiting exposure to ads, buying environmentally friendly products, and limiting car use. Essentially, behaviors
encompassed values related to ecology, the community, and personal
well-being. Participants cited lack of time as the biggest impediment
to consistently following through on simplicity commitments. It
takes time, for example, to ride the bus rather than drive or to rein in
accumulating piles of catalogs and junk mail, which seem to grow
exponentially. Twenty-eight percent of the participants voluntarily
reshaped their lives in ways that resulted in a lower income. This
change goes against the grain of what most of us are told constitutes
the American Dream—success and happiness through economic
prosperity. Hearteningly, respondents claimed greater satisfaction
with their lives as a result of their simplifying efforts, offering more
evidence to support the notion that money and happiness do not always go hand in hand.

The voluntary simplicity movement is not limited to individuals
with extreme social or environmental views. Practicing simplicity
does not require moving to a commune or converting to a brown
rice and tofu diet. Voluntary simplicity describes an effort to live according to values that limit consumption and emphasize family, community, environment, and personal growth. The movement is not
without its critics. Some sociologists claim that voluntary simplicity
is elitist and that it really applies just to the well-to-do. The movement has also been accused of being moralistic and judgmental of
"unreflective" people who choose to consume irresponsibly.[23] With
this in mind, you can address concerns about materialism by using
utilizing ideas from voluntary simplicity that make the most sense
for you. Readers interested in lessening the pull of materialism in
their lives may choose to downshift just a bit, or they may decide to
incorporate the voluntary simplicity philosophy into every aspect of
their lives.

A social phenomenon related to our discussion on materialism
deserves some mention. In their book *The Cultural Creatives,* sociolo-
gist Paul Ray and psychologist Sherry Ruth Anderson write about a

growing group of people in the United States who possess similar values related to personal growth, spirituality, relationships, and activism.[24] The authors call this group of people the *cultural creatives*. The creatives believe strongly in authenticity—the notion that one's intrinsic values and one's behavior should be consistent. Essentially, creatives try to live up to the practice-what-you-preach view of life. Cultural creatives are often idealistic and passionate about personal involvement in issues that they care about. Ray and Anderson's research revealed that 75 percent of the creatives engaged in volunteer work (as compared to 60 percent of the general population). Cultural creatives express concerns about global environmental issues and finding solutions to long-term sustainability on the planet. They rate "women's issues" as critical: concerns such as domestic violence and equal opportunities for employment and career advancement. Creatives consider "women's way" of knowing and interacting with the world—through intuition, empathy, and compassion—as equal to, if not more credible, than analytical, linear thinking. Many cultural creatives harbor deeply spiritual beliefs and value personal growth and self-actualization. Consumerism holds little appeal for this group. "They are disenchanted with 'owning more stuff,' materialism, greed, me-firstism, status display, glaring social inequalities of race and class, society's failure to care adequately for elders, women, and children and the hedonism and cynicism that pass for realism in modern society."[25] Ray and Anderson contend that the creatives don't wholeheartedly align with either the left or the right politically, seeking a more innovative direction for the country.

Cultural creatives and simplifiers share a number of values—anticonsumerism, relationships, ecology—and quite a bit of overlap exists between the two groups. An anticonsumerist stance and the realization that overemphasizing status and wealth do not contribute to personal, community, or global well-being go together with characteristics such as compassion, spirituality, and a desire for connection with others. Further, this cluster of beliefs links with greater life satisfaction. Certainly this is a life many of us wish for our children.

CULTIVATING MEANING

The message of this book has been twofold. Addressing materialism is as critical to children's healthy maturation as other more recognized areas of development, such as social and cognitive competency. In fact, the evolution of materialistic attitudes both affects and relies on many aspects of children's development. Youngsters' desires to fit in with their peers, their emerging identity, their self-esteem, their spiritual life, and their materialistic orientation all interact with and influence each other. Further, allowing materialistic attitudes to grow unchecked increases the chances that children will experience depression, anxiety, and weaker connections with others. Single-minded pursuit of status and wealth decreases the likelihood that youngsters will develop a spiritual life or an emotionally sustaining sense of purpose.

The book's message has also been that combating materialism requires focused effort using a multitiered approach. Because materialistic values surround families daily, parents must work at addressing the issue from several angles. We all have to examine our own values and behaviors related to materialism. Children learn about consumerism and develop attitudes about material goods based in part on observing their parents and other close family members. Parents can also rein in materialism by modeling responsible media use, by teaching media literacy skills, and by monitoring their children's intake of advertising and programming.

Helping children to cultivate meaning in their lives goes a long way toward avoiding the allure of materialism. Meaning takes many forms. Providing children with opportunities to experience flow increases emotional well-being, combats boredom, and contributes to positive self-esteem and identity development. Stay attuned to your children's interests. When children can say "I'm great at karate" or "I love animals" or "I'm a writer," they are less likely to rely on designer jeans and athletic shoes to feel good about themselves and impress other people. In a 2006 interview on the *Oprah* show, tennis star Serena Williams stated that she didn't need to obsess about her looks because "I have tennis and I know I'm good at something."[26] The importance of children developing their intrinsic talents can't be overstated. One mother describes her six-year-old budding playwright:

> He's dying to come home from school everyday and work on this project. He's writing a movie. I was laughing the other day because he was writing this story for the movie and we were going to do a storyboard and then play around with some animation on the computer . . . right now he's writing and he sits there at this little table and he's got this black turtleneck on . . . it's just so artsy!

Instead of coming home from school and watching television, this child is creating! In the process, he might also learn a little about how and why scripts get developed, thus adding to his media literacy. Cultivating meaning can also take the form of spiritual practice. A spiritual life—whether that means attending religious services, taking nature walks, or delivering meals—can crowd out materialistic urges and encourage greater connection with people, animals, and the earth.

Finally, parents might consider outside resources for children struggling with social and emotional concerns that leave them vulnerable to materialism and other maladaptive coping strategies. For example, children experiencing significant difficulties making or keeping friends would benefit from a social skills group or other structured social activity. Youngsters struggling with esteem issues can benefit from a consultation with a teacher, school counselor, or child psychologist.

A reminder to readers: Recruit other parents in your quest to dematerialize! In talking with many people during the course of writing this book, I was struck with how so many parents tried to confront materialism on their own. As one mother put it, "We'll all talk about how guilty we feel about giving in, but we never really talk about what to do about it." Successfully confronting the "I want it nows" really does take a village. Use this village to create your own commercial-free zone.

NOTES

INTRODUCTION

1. T. Kasser, *The High Price of Materialism* (Cambridge, MA: The MIT Press, 2002).
2. Throughout the book, I use pseudonyms to protect the families' privacy.

CHAPTER 1

1. H. C. Andersen, *Eighty Fairy Tales*. Translated by R. P. Keigwin (New York: Pantheon Books, 1976).
2. J. Hammerslough, *Dematerializing: Taming the Power of Possessions* (Cambridge, MA: Perseus Publishing, 2001).
3. M. L. Richins and S. Davison, "A Consumer Values Orientation for Materialism and Its Measurement: Scale Development and Validation," *Journal of Consumer Research* 19, no. 3 (1992), 303–316.
4. J. E. Burroughs and A. Rindfleisch, "Materialism and Well-Being: A Conflicting Values Perspective," *Journal of Consumer Research* 29 (2002), 348–370.
5. D. M. Buss, "The Evolution of Happiness," *American Psychologist* 55, no. 1 (2000), 15–23.
6. T. DeAngelis, "Consumerism and Its Discontents," *Monitor on Psychology*, no. 6 (2004), 52–54.
7. J. E. Burroughs and A. Rindfleisch, "Materialism as a Coping Mechanism: An Inquiry into Family Disruption," *Advances in Consumer Research* 24 (1997), 89–97.
8. R. Inglehart and P. R. Abramson, "Economic Security and Value Change," *American Political Science Review* 88, no. 2 (1994), 336–354.
9. Ibid.
10. T. Kasser, *The High Price of Materialism* (Cambridge, MA: MIT Press, 2002).

11. References to "poor" or "low-income" refer to families living at or around the poverty line in the United States. In 2004, that rate was 12.7 percent. Of that number, 24.7 percent of Blacks, 21.9 percent of Hispanics, 9.8 percent of Asians, and 8.6 percent of non-Hispanic Whites met criteria for poverty. The government does not have official classifications for low, middle, or upper income.

12. Burroughs and Rindfleisch, "Materialism and Well-Being."

13. M. W. Allen and M. Wilson, "Materialism and Food Security," *Appetite* 45 (2005), 314–323. T. L. Hartl et al., "Relationships among Compulsive Hoarding, Trauma, and Attention-Deficit/Hyperactivity Disorder," *Behaviour Research and Therapy* 43 (2005), 269–276.

14. Allen and Wilson, "Materialism and Food Security."

15. S. Zukin, *Point of Purchase: How Shopping Changed American Culture* (New York: Routledge, 2004).

16. D. V. Drehle, *Triangle: The Fire that Changed America* (New York: Atlantic Monthly Press, 2003). In the early 1900s, safety regulations for workers were abysmal. Hundreds died in workplace hazards during this time. In the Triangle Waist Company fire, workers were trapped in the inferno because the company bosses locked the exit doors to "restrict unauthorized comings and goings by the workers."

17. J. Spring, *Educating the Consumer-Citizen: A History of the Marriage of Schools, Advertising, and Media* (Hillsdale, NJ: Lawrence Erlbaum Associates, 2003).

18. Ibid.

19. Ibid.

20. J. B. Twitchell, "A (Mild) Defense of Luxury," *Regional Review* 11, no. 4 (2001), 12.

21. T. Meyers, "Marketers Learn Luxury Isn't Simply for the Very Wealthy," *Advertising Age* 75, no. 37 (2004), S2–S10.

22. Ibid.

23. J. U. Ogbu, "Minority Education in Comparative Perspective," *Journal of Negro Education* 59, no. 1 (1990), 45–57. J. U. Ogbu, "Origins of Human Competence: A Cultural-Ecological Perspective," *Child Development* 52 (1981), 413–429.

24. V. D. LaPoint and P. J. Hambrick-Dixon, "Commercialism's Influence on Black Youth: The Case of Dress-Related Challenges," in T. Kessler and A. D. Kanner (eds.), *Psychology and Consumer Culture: The Struggle for a Good Life in a Materialistic World* (Washington D.C.: American Psychological Association, 2003), 233–250.

25. M. M. King and K. D. Multon, "The Effects of Television Role Models on the Career Aspirations of African American Junior High School Students," *Journal of Career Development* 23, no. 2 (1996), 111–125.

26. Ibid.

27. D. E. Levin and S. Linn, "Commercialism's Influence on Black Youth: The Case of Dress-Related Challenges," in T. K. Kasser and A. D. Kanner (eds.), *Psychology and Consumer Culture: The Struggle for a Good Life in a Materialistic World* (Washington, D.C.: American Psychological Association Press, 2003).

28. M.Schoenhals, M. Tienda, and B. Schneider, "The Educational and Personal Consequences of Adolescent Employment," *Social Forces* 77, no. 2 (1998), 723–762. K. M. Zierold, S. Garman,and H. A. Anderson, "A Comparison of School Performance and Behaviors among Working and Nonworking High School Students," *Family and Community Health* 28, no. 3 (2005), 214–224.

29. D. G. Myers, *The American Paradox: Spiritual Hunger in an Age of Plenty* (New Haven, CT: Yale University Press, 2001).

30. Ibid.

31. Children Now, *Fall Colors: 2003–2004 Prime Time Diversity Report* (2004). Online at: www.childrennow.org/media/fc2003/fc–2–3-highlights.cfm.

32. M. Antonucci, "Steamy TV Brings Worry about Teens," *San Jose Mercury News*, November 10, 2005.

33. S. Bertman, *Hyperculture: The Human Cost of Speed* (Westport, CT: Praeger, 1998).

34. K. A. Moore et al., "What Are Good Child Outcomes?" in A. Thornton (ed.), *The Well-Being of Children and Families: Research and Data Needs* (Ann Arbor, MI: The University of Michigan Press, 2001), 59–84.

35. W. Mischel, Y. Shoda, and M. L. Rodriguez, "Delay of Gratification in Children," *Science* 244 (1989), 933–938.

36. K. C. Montgomery, "Digital Kids: The New On-line Children's Consumer Culture," in D. G. Singer and J. L. Singer (eds.), *Handbook of Children and the Media* (Thousand Oaks, CA: Sage Publications, Inc., 2001), 635–650.

37. Blue's Clues Web site, retrieved March 19, 2006, from www.nickjr.com.

38. Children's Television Workshop Web site, retrieved March 19, 2006, from www.sesameworkshop.org/.

39. Montgomery, "Digital Kids."

40. D. Kunkel, "Children & Television Advertising," in Singer and Singer (eds.), *Handbook of Children and the Media*, 375–394.

41. Bertman, *Hyperculture*.

42. A. M. Buchanan et al., "What Goes in Must Come Out: Children's Media Violence Consumption at Home and Aggressive Behaviors at School," *National Institutes on Media and the Family* (2002). Retrieved July 9, 2003, from www.mediafamily.org/research/report_issbd_2002.shtml

43. D. R. Shaffer, *Social and Personality Development*, 4th ed. (Belmont, CA: Wadsworth/Thomson Learning, 2000), 407.

44. K. Subrahmanyam et al., "New Forms of Electronic Media: The Impact of Interactive Games and the Internet on Cognition, Socialization, and Behavior," in Singer and Singer (eds.), *Handbook of Children and the Media*, 73–99.
45. V. Goldman, "The Baby Ivies," *New York Times*, January 12, 2003.
46. D. C. Pope, personal communication, 2004.
47. L. Slonaker and B. Bartindale, "Pressure to Succeed," *San Jose Mercury News*, February 8, 2004.

CHAPTER 2

1. A. Hulbert, *Raising America: Experts, Parents, and a Century of Advice about Children* (New York: Knopf, 2003). The term "preschooler" was created in the 1920s as toddlers became a focus of study among child development experts. J. Spring, *Educating the Consumer-Citizen: A History of the Marriage of Schools, Advertising, and Media* (Hillsdale, NJ: Lawrence Erlbaum Associates, 2003). The word "teenager" is believed to have been created by marketers looking to cash in on the blossoming teen consumer population through magazines such as *Seventeen*.
2. Hulbert, *Raising America*. B. Watson referred to this as "smother love" and believed that it stymied healthy emotional development (see p. 141).
3. T. Gordon, *Parent Effectiveness Training: The Proven Program for Raising Responsible Children* (New York: Three Rivers Press, 2000).
4. G. Cross, "Wondrous Innocence: Print Advertising and the Origins of Permissive Child Rearing in the U.S.," *Journal of Consumer Culture* 4, no. 2 (2004) 183–201. See pp. 183–184.
5. Hulbert, *Raising America*, see p. 27.
6. Spring, *Educating the Consumer-Citizen*.
7. Hulbert, *Raising America*.
8. Ibid.
9. R. Barkley, *Defiant Children: A Clinician's Manual for Assessment and Parent Training* (New York: Guilford Press, 1997). D. Stipek, *Motivation to Learn: Integrating Theory and Practice* (Boston: Allyn & Bacon, 1997).
10. Barkley, *Defiant Children*.
11. Stipek, *Motivation to Learn*.
12. A. Kohn, *Punished by Rewards: The Trouble with Gold Stars, Incentive Plans, A's, Praise, and Other Bribes* (New York: Houghton Mifflin,1993).
13. M. Miserandino, "Children Who Do Well In School: Individual Differences in Perceived Competence and Autonomy in Above-Average Children," *Journal of Educational Psychology* 88, no. 2 (1996), 203–214.
14. T. Kasser, *The High Price of Materialism* (Cambridge, MA: MIT Books, 2002), see chapter 5.
15. R. Eisenberg and J. Cameron, "Detrimental Effects of Reward," *American Psychologist* 51, no. 11 (1996), 1153–1166.

16. J. Cameron and W. D. Pierce, "Reinforcement, Reward, and Intrinsic Motivation: A Meta-Analysis," *Review of Educational Research* 64, no. 3 (1994), 363–423.

17. B. F. Skinner was a noted researcher/psychologist who believed that behaviors could be "conditioned" in children based on the application of positive or negative consequences. His heyday was in the late 1930s and 1940s.

18. Kasser, *The High Price of Materialism*.

19. K. M. Sheldon and T. Kasser, "'Getting Older, Getting Better': Personal Strivings and Psychological Maturity across the Life Span," *Developmental Psychology* 37 (2001), 491–501, as cited in Kasser, *The High Price of Materialism*.

20. R. Eisenberger and J. Cameron, "Detrimental Effects of Reward: Reality or Myth?" *American Psychologist* 51, no. 11 (1996), 1153–1166.

21. Stipek, *Motivation to Learn*, see Chapter 8.

22. Eisenberger and Cameron, "Detrimental Effects of Reward."

23. Cross, "Wondrous Innocence."

24. Ibid., p. 185.

25. Ibid.

26. Hulbert, *Raising America*, see Chapter 8.

27. G. Lerner (ed.), *Black Women in White America: A Documentary History* (New York: Vintage Books, 1992).

28. P. Moen and Y. Yu, "Effective Work/Life Strategies: Working Couples, Work Conditions, Gender, and Life Quality," *Social Problems* 47, no. 3 (2000), 291–126.

29. K. C. Montgomery, "Digital Kids: The New On-line Children's Consumer Culture," in D. G. Singer and J. L. Singer (eds.), *Handbook of Children and the Media* (Thousand Oaks, CA: Sage Publications, Inc., 2001), 635–650.

30. P. N. Stearns, *Anxious Parents: A History of Modern Childrearing in America* (New York: New York University Press, 2003).

31. D. Ehrensaft, *Spoiling Childhood: How Well-Meaning Parents Are Giving Children Too Much—But Not What They Need* (New York: Guilford Press, 1997).

32. Moen and Yu, "Effective Work/Life Strategies."

33. M. Emmons, "Adults Hurting Youth Sports, Report Says," *San Jose Mercury News*, November 10, 2005.

34. P. Sidebotham and ALSPAC Study Team, "Culture, Stress and the Parent-Child Relationship: A Qualitative Study of Parents' Perceptions of Parenting," *Child: Care, Health and Development* 27, no. 6 (2001), 469–485.

35. P. Tyre et al., "The Power of No," *Newsweek* (retrieved from Business source Premier, 2/28/05).

36. C. B. Holst, "Buying More Can Give Children Less," *Young Children* (September 1999), 19–23.

37. *San Jose Mercury News,* November 24, 2005, p. 4A.
38. S. Luthar, "The Culture of Affluence: Psychological Costs of Material Wealth," *Child Development* 74, no. 6 (2003), 1581–1593.
39. Ibid.
40. S. Luthar and C. Sexton, "The High Price of Affluence," in R. Kail (ed.), *Advances in Child Development and Behaviour* 32, (Cambridge, MA: Elsvier, Inc., 2004), 125–162.
41. Ibid.
42. Luthar, "The Culture of Affluence."
43. B. Lane, "Excessive Wealth Leads Teenagers to Spend Money Carelessly," *The Paly Voice* (2005) (retrieved 7/18/2005, http://voice.paly.net/view).
44. Jamie Johnson, dir., *Born Rich,* produced by Shout Factory, 2003, documentary.
45. Luthar and Sexton, "The High Price of Affluence."
46. J. Ogbu and A. Davis, *Black American Students in an Affluent Suburb: A Study of Academic Disengagement* (Hillsdale, NJ: Lawrence Erlbaum Associates, 2003).

NOTES TO CHAPTER 3

1. S. Zukin, *Point of Purchase: How Shopping Changed American Culture* (New York: Routledge, 2004).
2. T. Kasser et al., "The Relations of Maternal and Social Environments to Late Adolescents' Materialistic and Prosocial Values," *Developmental Psychology* 31, no. 6 (1995), 907–914.
3. M. E. Goldberg et al., "Understanding Materialism among Youth," *Journal of Consumer Psychology* 13, no. 3 (2003), 278–288.
4. E. Flouri, "Exploring the Relationship between Mothers' and Fathers' Parenting Practices and Children's Materialistic Values," *Journal of Economic Psychology* 25, no. 6 (2004), 743–752.
5. Kasser et al., "The Relations of Maternal and Social Environments to Late Adolescents' Materialistic and Prosocial Values."
6. Ibid.
7. D. Baumrind, "Rearing Competent Children," in W. Damon (ed.), *Child Development Today and Tomorrow* (San Francisco: Jossey-Bass, 1989), pp. 349–378. J. G. Querido, T. D. Warner, and S. M. Eyberg, "Parenting Styles and Child Behavior in African American Families of Preschool Children," *Journal of Clinical Child Psychology* 31, no. 2 (2002), 272–277.
8. L. Steinberg, *Adolescence,* 6th ed. (New York: McGraw-Hill, 2002), 133–138.
9. R. K. Chao, "Extending Research on the Consequences of Parenting Style for Chinese Americans and European Americans," *Child Development* 72, no. 6 (2001), 1832–1843.

10. L. Carlson and S. Grossbart, "Parental Style and Consumer Socialization of Children," *Journal of Consumer Research* 15 (1988), 77–94.

11. R. J. Faber, "A Systematic Investigation into Compulsive Buying," in A. Benson (ed.), *I Shop, Therefore I Am: Compulsive Buying and the Search for Self* (Lanham, MD: Rowman & Littlefield, 2000), 27–53.

12. D. R. Matsumoto, *Culture and Psychology: People around the World*, 2nd ed. (Belmont, CA: Wadsworth, 2000).

13. Ibid.

14. D. S. Johnson and M. Lino, "Teenagers: Employment and Contributions to Family Spending," *Monthly Labor Review* 123, no. 9 (2000), 15–25

15. J. J. Kacen and J. A. Lee, "The Influence of Culture on Consumer Impulsive Buying Behavior," *Journal of Consumer Psychology* 12, no. 2 (2002), 163–176.

16. Ibid.

17. A. D. Schaefer, C. M. Hermans, and R. S. Parker, "A Cross-Cultural Exploration of Materialism in Adolescents," *International Journal of Consumer Studies* 28, no. 4 (2004), 399–411.

18. Ibid.

19. Ibid.

20. D. Kunkel, "Children and Television Advertising," in D. G. Singer and J. L. Singer (eds.), *Handbook of Children and the Media*, (Thousand Oaks, CA: Sage Publications, Inc., 2001), 375–394.

21. P. Cohen and J. Cohen, *Life Values and Adolescent Mental Health* (Mahwah, NJ: Lawrence Erlbaum Associates, 1996), as cited in T. Kasser, *The High Price of Materialism* (Cambridge, MA: MIT Press, 2002).

22. A. Rindfleisch, J. E. Burroughs, and F. Denton, "Family Structure, Materialism, and Compulsive Consumption," *Journal of Consumer Research* 23, no. 4 (1997), 312–325

23. Kasser et al., "The Relations of Maternal and Social Environments to Late Adolescents' Materialistic and Prosocial Values." Much of the psychological research still focuses on mothers and their children. In part, this is because of the belief that mothers are still the primary caretakers. There is also the convenience issue: Women are more likely to volunteer for research studies than men.

24. T. Kasser and R. M. Ryan, "A Dark Side of the American Dream: Correlates of Financial Success as a Central Life Aspiration," *Journal of Personality and Social Psychology* 65 (1993), 410–422.

25. J. E. Burroughs and A. Rindfleisch, "Materialism and Well-Being: A Conflicting Values Perspective," *Journal of Consumer Research* 29 (2002), 348–370.

26. H. Hesse, *Siddhartha* (Toronto: Bantam Books, 1981).

27. M. Csikszentmihalyi, "The Costs and Benefits of Consuming," *Journal of Consumer Research* 27 (2000), 267–272.

28. M. L. Richins and S. Dawson, "A Consumer Values Orientation for Materialism and Its Measurement: Scale Development and Validation," *Journal of Consumer Research* 19, no. 3 (1992), 303–316.

29. N. Noddings, *Happiness and Education* (Cambridge: Cambridge University Press, 2003).

30. J. Schmidt and G. Rich, "Images of Work and Play," in M. Csikszentmihalyi and B. Schneider (eds.), *Becoming Adult: How Teenagers Prepare for the World of Work* (New York: Basic Books, 2000), 67–94.

31. Ibid.

32. Ibid.

33. M. Cole and S. R. Cole, *The Development of Children*, 3rd ed. (New York: W. H. Freeman, 1999).

34. E. Diener and M. E. P. Seligman, "Very Happy People," *Psychological Science* 13, no. 1 (2002), 81–84.

35. Kasser, *The High Price of Materialism*.

36. T. Kasser, and R. M. Ryan, "Be Careful What You Wish For: Optimal Functioning and the Relative Attainment of Intrinsic and Extrinsic Goals," in P. Schmuck and K. M. Sheldon (eds.), *Life Goals and Well-Being: Towards a Positive Psychology of Human Striving* (Goettingen, Germany: Hogrefe & Huber, 2001), 116–131.

37. D. G. Myers, "The Funds, Friends, and Faith of Happy People," *American Psychologist* 55, no. 1 (2000), 56–67.

38. E. Diener, "Subjective Well-Being: The Science of Happiness and a Proposal for a National Index," *American Psychologist* 55, no. 1 (2000), 34–43.

39. Myers, "The Funds, Friends, and Faith of Happy People."

CHAPTER 4

1. M. Buijzen and P. M. Valkenburg, "The Effects of Television Advertising on Materialism, Parent-Child Conflict, and Unhappiness: A Review of Research," *Applied Developmental Psychology* 24 (2003), 437–456.

2. D. Kunkel, "Children and Television Advertising," in D. G. Singer and J. L. Singer (eds.), *Handbook of Children and the Media* (Thousand Oaks, CA: Sage Publications, 2001), 375–394.

3. Ibid.

4. E. Palmer and C. McDowell, "Program/Commercial Separators in Children's Television Programming," *Journal of Communication* 29, no. 3 (1979), 197–201.

5. Kunkel, "Children and Television Advertising."

6. Ibid.

7. D. M. Boush, "Mediating Advertising Effects," in J. Bryant and A. J. Bryant (eds.), *Television and the American Family*, 2nd ed. (Mahwah, NJ: Lawrence Erlbaum Associates, 2001), 397–412.

8. Ibid.

9. W. J. Potter, *Media Literacy* (Thousand Oaks, CA: Sage Publications, 1998).

10. M. Cole and S. R. Cole, *The Development of Children,* 3rd ed. (New York: W. H. Freeman, 1999).

11. J. H. Flavell, P. H. Miller, and S. A. Miller, *Cognitive Development,* 4th ed. (Englewood Cliffs, NJ:: Prentice-Hall, 2002), 198–202.

12. J. A. Evra, *Television and Child Development,* 3rd ed. (Mahwah, NJ: Lawrence Erlbaum Associates, 2004).

13. K. C. Montgomery, "Digital Kids: The New On-line Children's Consumer Culture," in Singer and Singer (eds.), *Handbook of Children and the Media,* (Thousand Oaks, CA: Sage Publications, Inc., 2001), 635–650.

14. L. R. Vande Berg, L. A. Wenner, and B. E. Gronbeck, "Media Literacy and Television Criticism: Enabling an Informed and Engaged Citizenry," *American Behavioral Scientist* 48, no. 2 (2004), 219–227.

15. J. A. Evra, *Television and Child Development.*

16. D. M. Boush, M. Friestad, and G. M. Rose, "Adolescent Skepticism toward TV Advertising and Knowledge of Advertiser Tactics," *Journal of Consumer Research* 21, no. 1 (1994), 165–175.

17. Ibid.

18. M. Harmon, "Affluenza: Television Use and Cultivation of Materialism," *Mass Communication and Society* 4, no. 4 (2001), 405–418.

19. Buijzen and Valkenburg, "The Effects of Television Advertising on Materialism, Parent-Child Conflict, and Unhappiness."

20. L. J. Shrum, J. E. Burroughs, and A. Rindfleisch, "Television's Cultivation of Material Values," *Journal of Consumer Research* 32 (2005), 473–479.

21. Ibid.

22. K. B. Firminger, "Is He Boyfriend Material? Representation of Males in Teenage Girls' Magazines," *Men and Masculinities* 8, no. 3 (2006), 298–308.

23. L. Steinberg, *Adolescence,* 6th ed. (New York: McGraw-Hill, 2002).

24. Ibid.

25. J. Kilbourne, "'The More You Subtract, the More You Add': Cutting Girls Down to Size," in T. Kasser and A. D. Kanner (eds.), *Psychology and Consumer Culture: The Struggle for a Good Life in a Materialist World* (Washington, D.C.: American Psychological Association, 2003), 251–270.

26. Ibid.

27. M. F. Sypeck, J. J. Gray, and A. H. Ahrens, "No Longer Just a Pretty Face: Fashion Magazines' Depictions of Ideal Female Beauty from 1959–1999," *International Journal of Eating Disorders* 36 (2004), 342–347.

28. A note about the research on body image and eating disorders. Many of the findings relate particularly to middle-class Caucasian girls. Many cultures do not share the larger society's obsession with a thin physique for females. In some cultures, a curvaceous figure garners great admiration. Research suggests that assimilation may increase females' openness to the cult of thin. For example, studies have found that as ethnic minority families move up in socioeconomic status, their notions of the ideal body become slimmer. The introduction of the thin ideal via media can also change the way youngsters view their bodies. When television was introduced on a Fijian island, the rate of eating disorders increased among female adolescents, particularly among girls who watched a lot of television. Before the advent of television, a full figure was considered an attribute. Clearly, a number of media influences, teen magazines, television, movies, and the like affect girls' body image and eating behavior. Other factors such as culture and family circumstances also play a part.

29. NBC News, *20/20*, "The Family Fix: Help I've Got Kids!"

30. Firminger, "Is He Boyfriend Material?"

31. Ibid.

32. T. G. Morrison, K. Rudolf, and M. A. Morrison, "Body-Image Evaluation and Body-Image among Adolescents: A Test of Sociocultural and Social Comparison Theories," *Adolescence* 39, no. 155 (2004), 571–592.

33. Ibid.

34. Ibid.

35. Kilbourne, "The More You Subtract, the More You Add."

36. Potter, *Media Literacy*.

37. W. J. Potter, "Argument for the Need for a Cognitive Theory of Media Literacy," *American Behavioral Scientist* 48, no. 2 (2004), 266–272. Also see Potter, *Media Literacy*, and J. A. Evra, (2004)

38. V.S. Villani, C.K. Olson, and M.S. Jellinek, "Media Literacy for Clinicians and Parents," *Child and Adolescent Psychiatric Clinics of North America* 14 (2005), 523–553.

39. American Academy of Pediatrics, "Media Guidelines for Parents," retrieved March 7, 2006 from http://www.aap.org/pubed/ZZZGVLA PQ7C.htm?&sub_cat=17.

40. D.G. Singer and J.L. Singer, *Imagination and Play in the Electronic Age* (Cambridge, MA: Harvard University Press, 2005).

41. Ibid.

42. Ibid.

CHAPTER 5

1. L. Simpson, S. Douglas, and J. Schimmel, "Tween Consumers: Catalog Clothing Purchase Behavior," *Adolescence* 33, no. 131 (1998), 637–644.

2. D. Skafte, "The Effect of Perceived Wealth and Poverty on Adolescents' Character Judgments," *Journal of Social Psychology* 129, no. 1 (2001), 93–99.

3. H. Dittmar and L. Pepper, "To Have Is to Be: Materialism and Person Perception in Working-Class and Middle-Class British Adolescents," *Journal of Economic Psychology* 15 (1994), 233–251.

4. R. Elliot and C. Leonard, "Peer Pressure and Poverty: Exploring Fashion Brands and Consumption Symbolism among Children of the 'British Poor,'" *Journal of Consumer Behaviour* 3, no. 4 (2004), 347–359.

5. Ibid.

6. V. D. LaPoint and P. J. Hambrick-Dixon, "Commercialism's Influence on Black Youth: The Case of Dress-Related Challenges," in T. Kasser and A. D. Kanner (eds.), *Psychology and Consumer Culture: The Struggle for a Good Life in a Materialistic World* (Washington, D.C.: American Psychological Association, 2003), 233–250.

7. V. LaPoint et al., "Attitudes of Youth of Color on Student Dress and Uniforms: A Case of Commercialism in Schools," *Journal of Negro Education* 72, no. 4 (2003), 406–417.

8. Children Now, "Fall Colors: Prime Time Diversity Report," 2004. (Retrieved from www.childrennow.com, January 2005.)

9. Ibid.

10. J. Joireman, D. E. Sprott, and E. R. Spangenberg, "Fiscal Responsibility and the Consideration of Future Consequences," *Personality and Individual Differences* 39 (2005), 1159–1168.

11. M. Schoenhals, M. Tienda, and B. Schneider, "The Educational and Personal Consequences of Adolescent Employment," *Social Forces* 77, no. 2 (1998): 723–762. K. M. Zierold, S. Garman, and H. A. Anderson, "A Comparison of School Performance and Behaviors among Working and Nonworking High School Students," *Family and Community Health* 28, no. 3 (2005), 214–224.

12. S.M. Danes, "Children and Money: Income and Expenditures," *Children, Youth and Family Consortium* (1991). Retrieved July 22, 2005 from www.cyfc.umn.edu/schoolage/resources/IB1001.html

13. D. M. Buss, "The Evolution of Happiness," *American Psychologist* 55, no. 1 (2000), 15–23.

14. Ibid.

15. Simpson, Douglas, and Schimmel, "Tween Consumers."

16. Ibid.

17. D. L. Hoytko and J. Baker, "It's All at the Mall: Exploring Adolescent Girls' Experiences," *Journal of Retailing* 80, no. 1 (2004), 67–83.

18. T. F. Mangleburg, P. M. Doney, and T. Bristol, "Shopping with Friends and Teens' Susceptibility to Peer Influence," *Journal of Retailing* 80 (2004), 101–116.

19. Ibid.

20. S. Zukin, *Point of Purchase: How Shopping Changed American Culture* (New York: Routledge, 2004).

21. Ibid.

22. M. Buijzen and P. M. Valkenburg, "Parental Mediation of Undesired Advertising Effects," *Journal of Broadcasting and Electronic Media* 49, no. 2 (2005), 153–165.

23. Ibid.

24. K. A. Urberg et al., "A Two-Stage Model of Peer Influence in Adolescent Substance Use: Individual and Relationship-Specific Differences in Susceptibility to Influence," *Addictive Behaviors* 28, no. 7 (2003), 1243–1256.

25. E. Flouri, "Exploring the Relationship between Mothers' and Fathers' Parenting Practices and Children's Materialist Values," *Journal of Economic Psychology* 25, no. 6 (2002), 743–752.

26. T. Bristol and T. F. Mangleburg, "Not Telling the Whole Story: Teen Deception in Purchasing," *Journal of the Academy of Marketing Science* 33, no. 1 (2005), 79–95.

27. T. L. Childers and A. R. Rao, "The Influence of Familial and Peer-Based Reference Groups on Consumer Decisions," *Journal of Consumer Research* 19, no. 2 (1992), 198–211.

28. A. N. Christopher and B. R. Schlenker, "The Impact of Perceived Material Wealth and Perceiver Personality on First Impressions," *Journal of Economic Psychology* 21 (2000), 1–19.

29. T. Kasser and R. M. Ryan, "Be Careful What You Wish For: Optimal Functioning and the Relative Attainment of Intrinsic and Extrinsic Goals," in P. Schmuck and K. M. Sheldon (eds.), *Life Goals and Well-Being: Towards a Positive Psychology of Human Striving* (Goettingen, Germany: Hogrefe & Huber, 2001), 116–131.

30. T. Kasser, *The High Price of Materialism* (Cambridge, MA: MIT Press, 2002).

31. J. B. Kupersmidt and M. E. DeRosier, "How Peer Problems Lead to Negative Outcomes: An Integrative Mediational Model," in J. B. Kupersmidt and K. A. Dodge (eds.), *Children's Peer Relations: From Development to Intervention* (Washington, D.C.: American Psychological Association, 2004), 119–138.

32. Ibid.

33. M. Pipher, *Reviving Ophelia: Saving the Selves of Adolescent Girls* (New York: Ballantine Books, 1994), see Chapter 3.

34. M. J. Sandstrom and A. L. Zakriski, "Understanding the Experience of Peer Rejection," in Kupersmidt and Dodge (eds.), *Children's Peer Relations*, 101–118.

35. Kupersmidt and DeRosier, "How Peer Problems Lead to Negative Outcomes."

36. M. A. Toner and P. C. L. Heaven, "Peer-Social Attributional Predictors of Socio-Emotional Adjustment in Early Adolescence: A Two-Year Longitudinal Study," *Personality and Individual Differences* 38 (2005), 579–590.

37. J.Y. Lau, F. Rijsdijk, and T. Eley, "I Think, Therefore I Am: A Twin Study of Attributional Style in Adolescents," *Journal of Child Psychology and Psychiatry*, 47, no.7 (2006), 696–703.

38. S. Nolen-Hoeksema, "Explanatory Style and Achievement, Depression, and Gender Differences in Childhood and Adolescence," in G.M. Buchanan and M.E.P. Seligman (eds.), *Explanatory Style* (1995), 57–70.

39. D. Olweus, *Bullying at School* (Malden, MA: Blackwell Publishers, 2001).

40. J. A. Graham and R. Cohen, "Race and Sex as Factors in Children's Sociometric Ratings and Friendship Choices," *Social Development* 6, no. 3 (1997), 355–372.

41. C. A. Erdley et al., "Relations among Children's Social Goals, Implicit Personality Theories, and Responses to Social Failure," *Developmental Psychology* 33, no. 2 (1997), 263–272.

CHAPTER 6

1. J. M. Norvilitis, P. B. Szablicki, and S. D. Wilson, "Factors Influencing Levels of Credit-Card Debt in College Students," *Journal of Applied Social Psychology* 33, no. 5 (2003), 935–947.

2. J. Katz, T. E. Joiner Jr., and P. Kwon, "Membership in a Devalued Social Group and Emotional Well-Being: Developing a Model of Personal Self-Esteem, Collective Self-Esteem, and Group Socialization," *Sex Roles* 47, nos. 9/10 (2002), 419–431.

3. Ibid.

4. J. Suis, K. Lemos, and S. H. Lockett, "Self-Esteem, Construal, and Comparison with the Self, Friends, Peers," *Journal of Personality and Social Psychology* 82, no. 2 (2002), 252–261.

5. Ibid.

6. V. Zeigler-Hill, "Contingent Self-Esteem and the Interpersonal Circumplex: The Interpersonal Pursuit of Self-Esteem," *Personality and Individual Differences* 40, no. 4 (2006), 713–723.

7. J. R. Steele and J. D. Brown, "Adolescent Room Culture: Studying Media in the Context of Everyday Life," *Journal of Youth and Adolescence* 24, no. 5 (1995), 551–576.

8. L. N. Chaplin and D. R. John, "The Development of Self-Brand Connections in Children and Adolescents," *Journal of Consumer Research* 32, no. 1 (2005), 119–129.

9.   J. E. Stets and M. M. Harrod, "Verification across Multiple Identities: The Role of Status," *Social Psychology Quarterly* 67, no. 2 (2004), 155–171.

10. Films for the Humanities & Sciences, *The Secret Life of Boys* (1999).

11. W. Pollack, *Real Boys: Rescuing Our Sons from the Myths of Boyhood* (New York: Owl Books, 1999). Approximately 20 percent of male suicides and 14 percent of female suicides occur during adolescence (ages 15–24). See M. Empfield and N. Bakalar, *Understanding Teenage Depression: A Guide to Diagnosis, Treatment, and Management* (New York: Henry Holt and Company, 2001).

12. E. Flouri, "An Integrated Model of Consumer Materialism: Can Economic Socialization and Maternal Values Predict Materialistic Attitudes in Adolescents?" *Journal of Socio-Economics* 28 (1999), 707–724. M. E. Goldberg, G. J. Gorn, L. A. Peracchio, and G. Bamossy, "Understanding Materialism Among Young," *Journal of Consumer Psychology* 13, no. 3 (2003), 278–288.

13. A. M. Beutel and M. M. Marini, "Gender and Values," *American Sociological Review* 60 (1995), 436–448.

14. Ibid.

15. R. J. Faber, "A Systematic Investigation into Compulsive Buying," in A. Benson (ed.), *I Shop, Therefore I Am: Compulsive Buying and the Search for Self* (Lanham, MD: Rowman & Littlefield, 2000), 27–53.

16. S. Grogan and N. Wainwright, "Growing Up in the Culture of Slenderness: Girls' Experiences of Body Dissatisfaction," *Women's Studies International Forum* 19, no. 6 (1996), 665–673.

17. A. N. Christopher and B. R. Schlenker, "The Impact of Perceived Material Wealth and Perceiver Personality on First Impressions," *Journal of Economic Psychology* 21 (2000), 1–19.

18. Ibid.

19. K. G. DeBono and K. Rubin, "Country of Origin and Perceptions of Product Quality: An Individual Difference Perspective," *Basic and Applied Social Psychology* 17, nos. 1/2 (1995), 239–247.

20. K. G. DeBono and S. Krim, "Compliments and Perceptions of Product Quality: An Individual Difference Perspective," *Journal of Applied Social Psychology* 27, no. 15 (1997), 1359–1366.

21. C. R. Lechner and D. A. Rosenthal, "Adolescent Self-Consciousness and the Imaginary Audience," *Genetic Psychology Monographs* 110, no. 2 (1984), 289–305.

22. Stets and Harrod, "Verification across Multiple Identities."

23. C. M. Steele, "A Threat in the Air: How Stereotypes Shape Intellectual Identity and Performance," *American Psychologist* 52, no. 6 (1997), 613–629.

24. M. J. Sirgy, "Materialism and Quality of Life," *Social Indicators Research* 43(1998), 227–260.

25. Ibid.
26. Ibid.
27. J. McIntosh, F. MacDonald, and N. McKeganey, "The Reasons Why Children in the Pre and Early Teenage Years Do or Do Not Use Illegal Drugs," *International Journal of Drug Policy* 16, no. 4 (2005), 254–261.
28. K. Nalwa and A. P. Anand, "Internet Addiction in Students: A Cause of Concern," *CyberPsychology and Behavior* 6, no. 6 (2003), 653–656.
29. C. Pechmann et al., "Impulsive and Self-Conscious: Adolescents' Vulnerability to Advertising and Promotion," *Journal of Public Policy & Marketing* 24, no. 2 (2005), 202–221.
30. Ibid.
31. R. Larson and M. Richards, "Daily Companionship in Late Childhood and Early Adolescence: Changing Developmental Contexts," *Child Development* 62 (1991), 284–300.
32. D. M. Tice, E. Bratslavsky, and R. F. Baumeister, "Emotional Distress Regulation Takes Precedence Over Impulse Control: If You Feel Bas, Do It," *Journal of Personality and Social Psychology* 80, no. 1 (2001), 53–67.
33. Norvilitis, Szablicki, and Wilson, "Factors Influencing Levels of Credit-Card Debt in College Students."
34. J. Joireman, D. E. Sprott, and E. R. Spangenberg, "Fiscal Responsibility and the Consideration of Future Consequences," *Personality and Individual Diffferences* 39 (2005), 1159–1168.
35. K. S. McCown et al., *Self-Science: The Emotional Intelligence Curriculum* (San Mateo, CA: Six Seconds, 1998).
36. C.-H. Lin and S.-C. Chuang, "The Effect of Individual Differences on Adolescents' Impulsive Buying Behavior," *Adolescence* 40, no. 159 (2005), 551–558.
37. K. L. Shipman and J. Zeman, "Emotional Understanding: A Comparison of Physically Maltreating and Nonmaltreating Mother-Child Dyads," *Journal of Clinical Child Psychology* 28, no. 3 (1999), 407–417.
38. J. Markovits, J. Benenson, and E. Dolenszky, "Evidence that Children and Adolescents Have Internal Models of Peer Interactions that Are Gender Differentiated," *Child Development* 72, no. 3 (2001), 879–886.
39. M. Csikszentmihalyi, "Materialism and the Evolution of Consciousness," in T. Kasser and A.D. Kanner (eds.), *Psychology and Consumer Culture: The Struggle for a Good Life in a Materialistic World,* (Washington, D.C.: American Psychological Association, 2003), 91–106.
40. M. Csikszentmihalyi, *Flow: The Psychology of Optimal Experience* (New York: HarperCollins, 1990).
41. Ibid.

42. R. S. Siegler, *Children's Thinking*, 3rd ed. (Englewood Cliffs, NJ: Prentice-Hall, 1998).

43. Csikszentmihalyi, *Flow*.

44. Csikzentmihalyi, "Materialism and the Evolution of Consciousness."

45. M. Csikszentmihalyi and B. Schneider, *Becoming Adult: How Teenagers Prepare for the World of Work* (New York: Basic Books, 2000).

46. J. D. Coatsworth et al., "Exploring Adolescent Self-Defining Leisure Activities and Identity Experiences across Three Countries," *International Journal of Behavioral Development* 29, no. 5 (2005), 361–370. N. Darling, L. L. Caldwell, and R. Smith, "Participation in School-Based Extracurricular Activities and Adolescent Adjustment," *Journal of Leisure Research* 37, no. 1 (2005), 51–76.

47. D. Sedaris, *Me Talk Pretty One Day* (New York: Little, Brown, 2000).

CHAPTER 7

1. J. Adler, "In Search of the Spiritual," *Newsweek*, August 29, 2005, 48–64.

2. P. Aburdene, *Megatrends 2010* (Charlottesville, VA: Hampton Roads, 2005).

3. Ibid., see Chapter 2.

4. A. Mahoney, S. Pendleton, and H. Ihrke, "Religious Coping by Children and Adolescents: Unexplored Territory in the Realm of Spiritual Development," in E. C. Roehlkepartain et al. (eds.), *The Handbook of Spiritual Development in Childhood and Adolescence* (Thousand Oaks, CA: Sage Publications, 2006), 341–354.

5. T. Hart, "Spiritual Experiences and Capacities of Children and Youth," in ibid., 163–177.

6. W. Damon, J. Menon, and K. C. Bronk, "The Development of Purpose during Adolescence," *Applied Developmental Science* 7, no. 33 (2003), 119–128.

7. J. E. Burroughs and A. Rindfleisch, "Materialism and Well-Being: A Conflicting Values Perspective," *Journal of Consumer Research* 29 (2002), 348–370.

8. T. Hart, *The Secret Spiritual World of Children* (Maui, HI: Inner Ocean Publishing, 2003).

9. N. Noddings, *Happiness and Education* (Cambridge: Cambridge University Press, 2003).

10. Ibid.

11. Ibid.

12. Damon, Menon, and Bronk, "The Development of Purpose during Adolescence."

13. Hart, "Spiritual Experiences and Capacities of Children and Youth."

14. R. L. Roberts et al., "The Native American Medicine Wheel and Individual Psychology: Common Themes," *Journal of Individual Psychology* 54, no. 1 (1998), 135–145.

15. Ibid.

16. Damon, Menon, and Bronk, "The Development of Purpose during Adolescence."

17. B. Mills, *Wokini: A Lakota Journey to Happiness and Self-Understanding* (New York: Orion Books, 1990).

18. P. E. King and P. L. Benson, "Spiritual Development and Adolescent Well-Being and Thriving," in Roehlkepartain et al. (eds.), *The Handbook of Spiritual Development in Childhood and Adolescence*, 384–398.

19. Damon, Menon, and Bronk, "The Development of Purpose during Adolescence."

20. Ibid.

21. Ibid.

22. J. E. Burroughs and A. Rindfleisch, "Materialism and Well-Being: A Conflicting Values Perspective."

23. D. G. Myers, "The Funds, Friends, and Faith of Happy People," *American Psychologist* 55, no. 1 (2000), 56–67.

24. L. Steinberg *Adolescence*, 6th ed. (New York: McGraw-Hill, 2002), 274–275.

25. King and Benson, "Spiritual Development and Adolescent Well-Being and Thriving."

26. Ibid.

27. C. Flanagan, "Trust, Identity, and Civic Hope," *Applied Developmental Science* 7, no. 3 (2003), 165–171.

28. Ibid.

29. C. J. Boyatzis, D. C. Dollahite, and L. D. Marks, "The Family as a Context for Religious and Spiritual Development in Children and Youth," in Roehlkepartain et al. (eds.), *The Handbook of Spiritual Development in Childhood and Adolescence*, 297–309.

30. Ibid.

31. M. Cox, *The Book of New Family Traditions: How to Create Great Rituals for Holidays and Everyday* (Philadelphia: Running Press, 2003).

32. Boyatzis, Dollahite, and Marks, "The Family as a Context for Religious and Spiritual Development in Children and Youth."

33. Ibid.

34. D. R. Brown and L. E. Gary, "Religious Socialization and Educational Attainment among African Americans: An Empirical Assessment," *Journal of Negro Education* 60, no. 3 (1991): 411–426.

35. E. Crawford, M. Wright, and A. Masten, "Resilience and Spirituality in Youth," in Roehlkepartain et al. (eds.), *The Handbook of Spiritual Development in Childhood and Adolescence*, pp. 355–370.

36. W. Silverman and A. M. La Greca, "Children Experiencing Disasters: Definitions, Reactions, and Predictors of Outcomes," in A. M. La Greca et al. (eds.), *Helping Children Cope with Disasters and Terrorism* (Washington, D.C.: American Psychological Association, 2002), pp. 11–33.

37. M. Cole and S. R. Cole, *The Development of Children*, 3rd ed. (New York: W. H. Freeman, 1996), pp. 260–289.

38. S. Batchelor, *Buddhism without Beliefs* (New York: Riverhead Books, 1997).

39. Mahoney, Pendleton, and Ihrke, "Religious Coping by Children and Adolescents."

40. K. D. Schuck and B. J. Liddle, "Religious Conflicts Experienced by Lesbian, Gay, and Bisexual Individuals," *Journal of Gay and Lesbian Psychotherapy* 5, no. 2 (2001): 63–82.

41. W. L. Haight, *African-American children at Church: A Sociocultural Perspective* (New York: Cambridge University Press, 2002). The term "African American Church" is not meant to imply that all predominantly African American Churches share the same beliefs. The term refers to religious organizations that provide spiritual guidance and support predominantly African American congregation. Haight studies the First Baptist Church in her research.

42. Ibid.

43. Ibid.

44. Hart, "Spiritual Experiences and Capacities of Children and Youth."

45. Ibid., see p. 164.

46. Hart, *The Secret Spiritual World of Children.*

47. Noddings, *Happiness and Education.*

48. Hart, "Spiritual Experiences and Capacities of Children and Youth," see pp. 167–168.

49. Museum of Modern Art, *Masterworks of Modern from The Museum of Modern Art* (New York: Scalavision/ibooks, 2005).

50. Ibid.

51. P. Catalfo, *Raising Spiritual Children in a Material World* (New York: Berkley Books, 1997).

52. Hart, *The Secret Spiritual World of Children.*

CHAPTER 8

1. J. P. Toomey, "Sherman's Lagoon," *San Jose Mercury News*, March 19, 2006, comics section.

2. J. A. Brown, "Media Literacy and Critical Television Viewing in Education," in D. G. Singer and J. L. Singer (eds.), *Handbook of Children and the Media*, (Thousand Oaks, CA: Sage Publications, Inc., 2001), 681–697.

3. Ibid.

4. R. Quin and B. McMahon, "Monitoring Standards in Media Studies: Problems and Strategies," *Australian Journal of Education* 37, no. 2 (1993), 182–197.

5. Brown, "Media Literacy and Critical Television Viewing in Education."

6. See www.childrennow.org.

7. American Psychological Association: www.apa.org; American Academy of Pediatrics: www.aap.org.

8. See www.tvturnoff.org.

9. B. Bartindale, "District May Go for Junk-Food Jugular," *San Jose Mercury News,* March 9, 2006.

10. K. Hill-Scott, "Industry Standards and Practices," in Singer and Singer (eds.), *Handbook of Children and the Media,* 605–620.

11. D. Kunkel and B. Wilcox, "Children and Media Policy," in ibid, 589–604.

12. See conference report, "Digital Television, Sharpening the Focus on Children," www.childrennow.org/issues/media/media_dtv.html. Digital television is new technology that allows broadcast and cable stations to offer more channels and better image and sound quality.

13. See www.simplelivingamerica.org.

14. M. Craig-Lees and C. Hill, "Understanding Voluntary Simplifiers," *Psychology and Marketing* 19, no. 2 (2002), 187–210.

15. A. Etzioni, "Voluntary Simplicity: Characterization, Select Psychological Implications, and Societal Consequences," *Journal of Economic Psychology* 19 (1998), 619–643.

16. M. E. Huneke, "The Face of the Un-consumer: An Empirical Examination of the Practice of Voluntary Simplicity in the United States," *Psychology and Marketing* 22, no. 7 (2005), 527–550.

17. www.simplelivingamerica.org.

18. Huneke, "The Face of the Un-consumer."

19. H. Hodson, "Why Choosing Motherhood Is in Fashion," *Harper's Bazaar Magazine* (March 2006).

20. Huneke, "The Face of the Un-consumer."

21. Craig-Lees and Hill, "Understanding Voluntary Simplifiers."

22. Huneke, "The Face of the Un-consumer."

23. R. V. Kozinets and J. M.Handelman, "Adversaries of Consumption: Consumer Movements, Activism, and Ideology," *Journal of Consumer Research* 31 (2004), 691–704.

24. P. H. Ray and S. R. Anderson, *The Cultural Creatives: How 50 Million People Are Changing the World* (New York: Three Rivers Press, (2000).

25. Ibid.

26. *Oprah Winfrey Show,* "The Secret Lives of Teenage Girls," originally aired April 15, 2006.

INDEX